DIRKSEN OF ILLINOIS

DIRKSEN OF ILLINOIS

Senatorial Statesman

Edward L. Schapsmeier
and
Frederick H. Schapsmeier

UNIVERSITY OF ILLINOIS PRESS
Urbana and Chicago

This book is printed on acid-free paper.

Library of Congress Cataloging in Publication Data

Schapsmeier, Edward L.
  Dirksen of Illinois.

  Bibliography: p.
  Includes index.
  1. Dirksen, Everett McKinley. 2. Legislators—United
States—Biography. 3. United States. Congress. Senate—
Biography. 4. United States—Politics and government—
1945- . 5. United States. Congress. Senate—Minority
leader—History—20th century. I. Schapsmeier,
Frederick H. II. Title.
E748.D557S33 1984   328.73′092′4 [B]   83-21578
ISBN 0-252-01100-7 (alk. paper)

To Mary with love

Contents

Foreword

THE FIRST TIME I met Everett Dirksen, I was standing with my wife and him on the top of the old Adams Hotel in downtown Phoenix on a cold night in November with a full moon shining down.

Everett had just very abruptly said to me, "Young man, why don't you run for the United States Senate?" And, there I was still shaking from the cold. I was, at that time, a city councilman of Phoenix and to think of running for such a prestigious spot as the Senate was something that had never entered my mind. In fact, it really didn't enter it at that moment, but he kept pounding and finally I said, "Well, I'll think about it." Then, by golly, I did it, and that was my introduction to Dirksen-style politics.

Writing a foreword for a book on Everett Dirksen is not easy. It's not easy because he became for me a father-confessor type who was a real man whom I enjoyed working with and listening to. It wasn't only the fact that he had a wonderful voice or spoke with great clarity and intelligence. Every time you heard the man, you remembered the great courage, and this is what he lived with.

As with any politician, it would be an easy task to take his public record, cut and paste it together, and call it a biography. But, Everett Dirksen was a man of many human qualities that a purely public-record approach cannot begin to fathom. If there was one thing that stands out in my mind as one of these qualities, it would have to be his ability to "disagree without being disagreeable." Indeed, there were many times when this approach to his senatorial duties probably got him a lot further than he could have hoped for reasonably.

While he was a member of the House, he was told that he was losing his sight and would go blind. Leaving the Congress, he went back to his home in Illinois and there he took up the teachings of God. So strongly did he follow those teachings that his eyesight began to get better and then the danger completely left. Because of this, his life became a living example to me of what faith in the Almighty can give to a person.

Whatever this book is, it cannot be just about Everett alone. Everything that Everett ever did, Louella did with him and she stood behind him through thick and thin. And, if there was ever a case of a man being what he was because of the woman behind him, you could put Louella and Everett together and there was the example. She was a sweet, kind, and understanding woman who made everybody who knew her, love her. This devotion was reflected throughout their entire lives together.

I never will forget the night, sitting in my apartment alone with Everett, just before the 1964 convention in San Francisco. When he read what he wanted to say about me when introducing me — I had asked him to introduce me to the convention — he did it in a way that caused tears to come to my eyes, and they reappeared the same way during the convention.

Regardless how many years God allows me to live, there will always be, way up at the top of my memory list, the name of Dirksen. He deserves my eternal thanks for everything that he did for me.

You who are about to read this book are privileged to be able to enter into the life of one of the greatest men that we have ever produced in this country. You're going to finish the book being all the better for having read it.

Barry M. Goldwater

Preface

WHEN EVERETT DIRKSEN arrived in Washington late in 1932 as a member-elect of the House of Representatives, he had to ask directions to the Capitol building. By 1969, at the time of his death, Senate Minority Leader Dirksen had long been one of Washington's most recognizable and colorful figures. To millions of his countrymen, Dirksen symbolized the Senate of the United States, epitomized the virtue of loyal and principled opposition, and embodied the fading standards and values of rural America. Senator Dirksen's extensive vocabulary, combined with his inimitable oratorical style, was a key ingredient in his success as a legislative leader. As the authors of this book explain, "With his oratory, he could ensnarl an adversary in a web of words or build a golden bridge of rhetoric to permit an opponent to cross over to his side of the issue."

To tell adequately the story of a senator whose public career spanned the entire middle third of the twentieth century is an enterprise of staggering proportions. While modern transportation and communication facilities have tended to erode the research value of a senator's written correspondence, the volume of that correspondence has expanded dramatically, in part as a result of the growth of congressional staffs and the proliferation of legislative issues. When Everett Dirksen died, he left behind 1.2 million pages of personal papers and office files as well as scores of sound- and videotapes and hundreds of photographs. This documentary legacy now fills more than 1,000 feet of shelving space at the Dirksen Congressional Leadership Research Center in Pekin, Illinois.

When the major portion of the Dirksen collection was opened to research use, Edward and Frederick Schapsmeier were among the first to probe its enormous bulk. In addition to mining the Dirksen collection, the Schapsmeiers studied the papers of Dirksen's colleagues, and the presidents with whom he served, in libraries across the nation. The result of their careful and exhaustive research is contained in this well-written volume, the first scholarly biography of Everett Dirksen. The Schapsmeiers have lived up to the promise of their subtitle by analyzing, from Dirksen's perspective, the techniques and frustrations of minority leadership. They have captured the essence of a senator who, in their words, was "vigorous but not vindictive, courageous but not cantankerous, clever but not cruel."

At the time of Senator Dirksen's death, Senate Majority Leader Mike Mansfield observed that the former minority leader would be "remembered with affection, with respect, and with esteem." The Schapsmeiers' book will awaken and enrich the memories of those who knew Senator Dirksen and will enlighten future generations as to the life and times of this most remarkable American statesman.

Richard A. Baker
Senate Historian

Acknowledgments

WE WISH TO EXPRESS our gratitude to the Everett Mc-
Kinley Dirksen Congressional Leadership Research Center at
Pekin, Illinois, for a research grant and to Dr. Frank H. Mack-
aman, its executive director, and his staff for their excellent assistance. Our thanks are extended likewise to the archivists of the
following presidential libraries: Herbert C. Hoover, Franklin D.
Roosevelt, Harry S. Truman, Dwight D. Eisenhower, John F.
Kennedy, and Lyndon B. Johnson. We are also grateful for the
help rendered by the Illinois State Historical Society at Springfield
and the Wisconsin State Historical Society at Madison. We are
likewise indebted to Richard H. Immerman, associate director,
Presidency Studies Program of the Department of Politics at
Princeton University, and to Robert L. Peabody of the Department of Political Science at Johns Hopkins University for reading
the manuscript and offering constructive suggestions. Finally our
appreciation is extended to Alberta Carr for her diligence in
proofreading and typing.

Edward L. Schapsmeier
Bloomington, Illinois

Frederick H. Schapsmeier
Oshkosh, Wisconsin

Abbreviations

The following abbreviations are used throughout the notes and are here listed for the reader's convenience.

AE   Arthur Ehrlicher
AES   Adlai E. Stevenson
AI   Author's Interview
C   Clippings
CF   Central File
CHS   Chicago Historical Society
COF   Chicago Office File
CVB   Carl Von Boeckman
DDE   Dwight D. Eisenhower
DDEL   Dwight D. Eisenhower Library
DPH   Dirksen for President Headquarters
EMD   Everett McKinley Dirksen
EMDC   Everett McKinley Dirksen Center
FDR   Franklin D. Roosevelt
FDRL   Franklin D. Roosevelt Library
FJ   Frank Jibbens
FJF   Frank J. Fonsino
GGC   Glee Gomien Collection
HCH   Herbert C. Hoover
HCHL   Herbert C. Hoover Library
HER   Harold E. Rainville
HST   Harry S. Truman
HSTL   Harry S. Truman Library
IF   Information File
ISHS   Illinois State Historical Society
JFK   John F. Kennedy

JFKL   John F. Kennedy Library
LBJ   Lyndon B. Johnson
LBJL   Lyndon B. Johnson Library
LC   Library of Congress
LD   Louella Dirksen
LF   Legislative File
LFO   Lawrence F. O'Brien
MC   Memorabilia Collection
MJ   Margaret Juchems
OF   Official File
OHI   Oral History Interview
PHD   Paul H. Douglas
PHDP   Paul H. Douglas Papers
PPP   Post-Presidential Papers (Herbert C. Hoover)
PRNC   Proceedings of the Republican National Convention
PWF   Public Works File
RC   Russell Campbell
RCLF   Republican Congressional Leadership File
REWP   Robert E. Wood Papers
RP   Roy Preston
R&R   Remarks and Releases
SWL   Scott W. Lucas
SWLP   Scott W. Lucas Papers
TRD   Thomas Reed Dirksen
WJD   William D. Jansen
WP   Working Papers

DIRKSEN OF ILLINOIS

1

The Formative Years: Growing Up in the Heartland of America

NESTLED ALONG the banks of the Illinois River lies a small town with the unusual name of Pekin. Located in central Illinois, Pekin is surrounded by some of the Prairie State's most fertile farmland. It is the seat of rural Tazewell County and constitutes part of what Illinois residents refer to as being "downstate." The latter embraces that portion of the state below Chicago and metropolitan Cook County.

Despite being a port town, Pekin was in many ways the epitome of a small midwestern community. Relatively modest in size and sedate in tone, its townspeople mingled easily with the surrounding rural population. On Saturday nights Pekinites chatted with farmers milling about the courthouse square and on Sundays worshipped with them in the town's many churches. There were common bonds uniting town residents and country folk. They were white, Anglo-Saxon, and predominantly Protestant. Common acceptance of the Protestant work ethic made self-reliance, hard work, and frugality virtues to be commended. Pekinites were generally old-fashioned, staunchly patriotic, and strong believers in law and order. Other than to keep the public peace, most were of the opinion that the agrarian credo of Thomas Jefferson about the least government being the best was correct. Traditionally Pekin's populace was politically conservative, economically self-sustaining, and socially provincial in outlook. Situated in the heart of Illinois, Pekin became a politically conservative stronghold and a bastion of isolationism.

Near the turn of the century the north side of Pekin acquired the appellation of "Beantown."[1] This name came from the large number of bean patches cultivated by the residents of this particular area of town, heavily populated by German immigrants and semirural in nature. Beantown, or "Bohnchefiddle"[2] in the Low German vernacular of its inhabitants, was dotted with white frame houses, each adjacent to a sizeable garden. Those living in this locale were of a lower economic status than others in Pekin, yet the neat appearance of the homes belied this fact. Beantown may have been the so-called poor end of town, but in no way was it a slum or a run-down section of Pekin.

It was into this particular political, social, and economic milieu that Everett McKinley Dirksen would be born and raised. His parents, Johann and Antje, were both German immigrants. Johann Frederick Dirksen, Everett's father, had left Ostfriesland in northern Germany to come to the United States in 1866. Although he had little formal education, Johann Dirksen was reflective by nature and possessed a scholarly disposition. His Vandyke beard made him look like a studious character out of a Dickens novel. Dirksen was a devout churchgoer and, in fact, helped build Pekin's Second Reformed Church in 1874. He had an artistic bent and earned his living as a design painter at the Pekin Wagon Works.

Antje Conrady Dirksen, Everett's mother, also had come from the Ostfriesland region of Germany. She emigrated to America in 1873 with her brothers to take up farming on the Scully lands[3] in Hartsburgh, Illinois. In a short while she moved to Pekin and within a year married an Ostfrieslander named Bernhardt Ailts. He died in 1892 leaving her with two sons, John and Henry. The widowed Mrs. Ailts met Johann Dirksen at a church service, and, after finding out they were both from the same part of the old country, she allowed the fifty-one year old widower to court her. Johann and Antje were married on October 15, 1892.[4]

The Dirksen's first child was born on November 16, 1895. He was promptly named Benjamin Harrison after the twenty-third president of the United States. Another pair of boys, twins, were born on January 4, 1896. Johann's ardent fealty to the Republican party was again reflected when he named his sons Everett McKinley and Thomas Reed. William McKinley was elected president in 1896 and Thomas "Czar" Reed was then Speaker of the U.S. House of Representatives. Johann Dirksen did not live long enough to have any marked influence on Everett's life. In 1901, at fifty-nine years of age, Johann suffered a stroke and remained an invalid until his death in 1905. Again a widow, this time with five boys, three from Dirksen and two from her previous marriage, Antje's life was destined to be one of prolonged toil and deprivation.

From her late husband's meager estate, Antje Dirksen bought a one-and-one-half acre plot of land, upon which stood an old farmhouse, at the far end of Beantown. On this acreage the Dirksens kept cows, chickens, a horse, and occasionally a pig. The boys peddled milk from the cows to customers across town. Young Everett walked many miles, carrying two buckets of milk astride a broom handle over his shoulder, making deliveries to their biggest customer—the Central House Hotel. Every spring the Dirksen boys cultivated a huge garden which supplied most of their own food needs and provided additional vegetables to be sold door-to-door all summer. Everett's boyhood was filled with the back-breaking stoop-labor involved in weeding by hand and picking bugs from fragile plants. Much like a country boy, he learned to get up early to do chores before going to school and to stay with his tasks until all the work was completed for the day. This demanding regimen had a lasting influence on him. He habitually rose early and later in life automatically pulled a weed whenever he saw one in someone's flower garden. Despite the grueling work related to growing their own food during these hard years, gardening became a lifelong passion with Dirksen. He loved the touch of the soil and the taste of fresh vegetables— a fondness inculcated in him while helping his mother and brothers survive in Beantown.[5]

Mrs. Dirksen rode herd on her five boys with a stern hand, yet tempered this strict Calvinist discipline with kindness and motherly wit. Her drive and ability to do hard work served both as an example to her sons and provided the wherewithal to obtain the bare necessities for her brood. Her constant admonition to the boys was to "do your work good or don't do it at all."[6] Although Everett and Thomas received hand-me-downs from their older brothers, their clothes were always clean and neatly patched. The mother was aware that all work and no play was not good, so she managed at least once a month to find a nickel for each so that they might go to a movie. More often the Dirksen boys found their entertainment under the street light at Twelfth and Charlotte where the "Beantown Gang"[7] met nightly. Here they played "Ducks on the stump," tag, or hide-and-seek. Promptly at nine o'clock calls from parents broke up the gathering and all went home after an evening of childish fun and frolic.

From childhood, Everett was his mother's favorite son. Since he was smaller than his twin brother, Thomas, Mrs. Dirksen called Everett "the little one." In her Low German dialect this phrase sounded like "luttin." Subsequently Everett's brothers and play-mates dubbed him "Lute."[8] Being a religious woman, Mrs. Dirksen envisioned Lute becoming a preacher. Nightly she read the Bible to Lute and his brothers and taught them to call upon God in prayer.

Early in youth Lute displayed certain characteristics that were different from either his twin brother or his half-brothers. Young Lute developed a proclivity for reading and a love of learning. Unlike his brothers, who did little reading for pleasure, Lute had his nose in a book whenever time permitted. Young Dirksen often retold what he had read to his buddies in the Beantown Gang and on occasion delighted them with made-up stories drawn from his fertile imagination. Words fascinated him. This was so because he equated a large vocabulary with being well educated. This penchant for enlarging his personal lexicon continually prompted him to dig into the dictionary to find big words to substitute for little ones.[9]

In the early 1900s it was not the custom for children of lower class status to complete the eighth grade. When Tom, Lute's twin brother, announced one day, "Ma, I got a job,"[10] Mrs. Dirksen permitted him to quit school at the sixth-grade level, but when Lute indicated he wanted to continue school, and even attend high school, she gave her approval. Her fond hope was that he would become a minister of the gospel, and for a time it seemed highly probable Lute would ultimately be a man of the cloth. His demeanor was exemplary, and it was obvious he tried to implement Christian principles in daily life.

During his teen years Everett Dirksen's leadership qualities came to the fore as a youth leader in the Second Reformed Church. Everett, still known as Lute by Beantowners but called Ev by others, started his duties at church by pumping the hand organ. He then joined the choir and subsequently became the perpetual president of the Young People's Christian Endeavor. It still seemed highly possible at this stage in his life that he would fulfill his mother's hope by becoming a clergyman.

At Pekin High School Ev became an excellent student. He was a gangling six-footer with tousled brown hair, blue eyes, and an infectious grin. Usually going without socks and wearing shoes with cardboard insoles, Ev was glad just to be in school. He excelled scholastically, particularly in chemistry and mathematics. Now aspirations entered his mind that one day he would become a chemical engineer. An avid reader, Ev started keeping a notebook in which he wrote one new word each day to incorporate into his already large vocabulary. He made use of his growing lexicon as a member of the debate team where his prowess as an impromptu speaker was readily evident to all. To increase his forensic skills, Ev practiced giving speeches in the barn to imaginary audiences, or he would put a coat on a broomstick and conduct a mock debate with his scarecrow-like opponent. Brother Tom recalled his mother's frequent comment on Ev's barn oratory when she would say, "Just listen to him out there."[11]

During his senior year in high school Ev entered a national oratorical contest. Dirksen did so well that he got to the finals held in Lexington, Kentucky. Although eventually losing out, he proved to himself that his speaking talent was far above average. More important to him in terms of self-improvement was his contact with William Jennings Bryan. The Great Commoner, who was then secretary of state in the administration of Woodrow Wilson, addressed the finalists at a closing banquet. The Nebraskan, a three-time Democratic presidential nominee, treated his young audience to a typical Bryan Chautauqua performance.

At the close of the speech, Ev went up to this veteran political orator and point-blank asked him what technique he employed to hold the attention of such a large crowd. Bryan told his young admirer the trick was to always "talk to the last row and everybody else will hear you."[12] This bit of information was filed away in Ev's memory to be employed when he would one day face many large audiences.

Despite having to do his early morning chores, since he was now stuck with them entirely because his brothers worked at full-time jobs, Ev managed not only to make good grades in high school but to participate in extracurricular activities. He was a member of the *Deutsche Verein,* a literary club promoting the reading and speaking of the German language; treasurer of the Philomathean Society; and business manager of *The Pekinian,* the high school yearbook. In sports Ev played center on the varsity football team, although weighing only 144 pounds, and was a miler in track. As vice-president of his senior class in 1913, Ev was selected salutatorian in recognition of his scholastic endeavors. At the graduation ceremony he treated the graduating class, faculty, and parents to a truly grandiloquent speech. The would-be Demosthenes of Beantown utilized for the first time a technique he learned while singing in his church's choir: he made use of his diaphram to project his voice. This gave his voice an unusual mellifluous quality. It was as if his vocal cords were those of an organ and words came out as well-modulated tones. Years later no one remembered the content of Ev's graduation oratory, but they recalled well the emotional impact of its delivery.[13]

In *The Pekinian* of 1913 was this caption under Ev's photograph: "Dirk, the man of many words, is that type of fellow with whom one must be intimately acquainted before he is fully appreciated. He merits the high regard in which he is held and is one of the ablest fellows of the class. He has all those sterling qualities that win the friendship of those with whom he is thrown in contact, and is truly a man's man."[14] It was also comically indicated that the "gentleman from Bohnchefiddle" was afflicted with "BIGWORDITUS."[15]

At age seventeen Everett Dirksen was the only member of his family to have a high school diploma. He was studious, industrious, responsible, and quite religious. Ev had inherited his father's intellect, but it was his mother's personal and moral influence which imparted to him a strong religious faith, indefatigable drive, and dogged determination. She set an example for him with her stoic demeanor, capacity for work, and acceptance of God's providential design. Mrs. Dirksen preached constantly of the need to perform one's duties diligently and not to complain about life's aches and pains. Everett both loved and admired his mother. Later in life he always referred to her as that "saintly soul."[16] As an adult, reflecting on the formative years spent in Pekin, Dirksen asserted: "Character has a chance. Everything by way of human attribute has a chance for better anchoring, better formulation, in a small town, better than the hurly-burly of a metropolitan center." Summing up succinctly his feeling about being raised in a small town, he said simply, "Life is pristine, it's simple."[17] Ev forever remained a Pekinite in heart and spirit. "All the major decisions of my life have been made here," he once mused about Pekin. "This is my native city, where the family taproot goes deep, and it will ever be."[18]

Immediately after graduation Dirksen pondered his future. He gave some consideration to taking up teaching as a profession. At nearby Normal was Illinois State Normal University (now Illinois State University), the state's leading teacher-training institution. Also in his deliberations was the study of law at the University of Illinois at Urbana-Champaign. The Lincoln lore in and around Pekin had made a deep impression on Ev. It did not elude him that the humble rail-splitter rose up from hardship and poverty by becoming a highly successful lawyer. Dirksen was also aware that the practice of law opened doors to the world of politics. As a serious student of history, he understood the close affinity between law, politics, and oratorical ability. What to do?

There was another possible profession that competed in Ev's thinking relative to a life career. This was acting. Ev's love of the theater was ignited during his junior year in high school when he got a role in the class play, a three-act comedy called "The Colonel's Maid."[19] The bright lights, applause, and popular acclaim received for his performance made it appear to young Ev that the life of an actor might be exhilarating. This feeling was reinforced after he joined a local Pekin group named the Eugene Minstrels. In a period when black-faced minstrel shows were not considered racist or derogatory to Negroes (of which Pekin had none), these types of performances were as common in small towns as was vaudeville in larger cities. Ev's ability to sing and tell stories made him the hit of the Eugene Minstrels but produced little more than pocket money when expenses were deducted. Nonetheless, this experience strengthened in him the desire to pursue a life on the stage.[20]

During this decision-making time, while living in the family home in Beantown and saving his money with the same frugality displayed by his mother, Everett built up a nice nest egg in one year. Using some of his savings, Ev decided to take a trip to Minneapolis to visit one of his half brothers. While sightseeing there Ev happened to tour the campus of the University of Minnesota. This renewed in him the desire to go to college, so he wrote his mother informing her of his wish to enroll as a student at the University of Minnesota. His ultimate goal was to become a lawyer. The elderly Mrs. Dirksen not only approved heartily but promised additional financial support by giving him a share of her meager lifetime savings. She was proud of her son's aspiration to be a lawyer. For one born and raised in Germany, where higher education was linked to rank and privilege, Antje Dirksen gave thanks to God that her son was given an opportunity to raise his station in life.

Those who attended state universities in 1914 were generally from fairly well-to-do families. Few high school graduates, compared to today's standards, could even contemplate going to a college or university. Those who did usually could afford to join fraternities or sororities, participate in social functions, and partake of the rah-rah activities associated with sports or extracurricular events. Not so with Everett Dirksen, who went to classes in the daytime but worked at night. His job at the Minneapolis *Tribune,* handling classified ads, went from 6:00 P.M. until midnight; he would then rise at 5:30 in the morning to do his homework, go to classes, and again repeat his nightly tasks at the *Tribune* office. This type of schedule permitted no time for socializing or college-type antics. Women were attractive to him, but he had no social grace, no time, and no money for dating coeds. College was to him a serious business and he let nothing interfere with his studies.[21]

The summer after his freshman year, Ev did not join with most fellow classmates in enjoying a vacation or taking a trip home; instead, he got a job as a salesman for the Home Remedy Book Company. He spent the entire summer on the road in the rural areas of Minnesota and the Dakotas selling books to farmers. In today's parlance, these do-it-yourself manuals informed farmers how to treat their livestock for a myriad of diseases. Among other jobs, he worked for a shipping firm and also sold magazine subscriptions door-to-door. While not inundated by commissions, Ev made enough money from these various ventures to acquire the necessary funds for fall tuition. Quite significantly he discovered that he could meet many types of people, and talking with them was truly an enjoyable experience.

Back on campus, Ev decided to join the Reserve Officers Training Corps (ROTC) in 1916 for the simple reason the uniform appealed to him. Because of his tight financial situation, he possessed a rather limited and drab wardrobe. Being in the ROTC meant free clothing, and in a fancy uniform he was indistinguishable from other male college students. Although World War I started in Europe while he was a freshman, Ev never considered the possibility of making the army a career. Unknown to him, international events would place him on the battlefields of Europe within several years.

During his sophomore year at the University of Minnesota, Everett Dirksen became involved in politics for the first time in his life. He belonged to a student political organization akin to today's Young Republicans. Ev caught the attention of fellow club members with his oratorical ability and was soon in demand at campus rallies as a speaker. He would also challenge campus Democrats to debate the issues and in so doing gained a solid reputation as being a formidable student spokesperson for the GOP. It was not long until he was asked by local Republicans to speak at off-campus political gatherings. An engagement of this type brought him into contact with the first member of Congress he ever met personally, Representative Ernest Lundeen (R-Minn.), who was up for reelection in 1916. Lundeen was considered fairly liberal on domestic issues and a rabid isolationist relative to foreign affairs. Ev campaigned not only for Lundeen but also for Governor Charles Evans Hughes of New York, the GOP presidential nominee in 1916 who lost an extraordinarily close election to incumbent Woodrow Wilson. Involvement in these political campaigns was fascinating to Dirksen. He loved the crowds, the excitement, and the feeling of being an important part of the political process. His first taste of politics increased his appetite for it and might have led to early and increased participation had it not been for America's entry into World War I.[22]

In 1917, when Everett was a junior in college, the United States became an official participant in the war raging in Europe. With millions of others, Ev had to register for Selective Service, although he hoped he would be able to finish school before being drafted. Being in ROTC made it seem likely he would not be called up until after attaining his bachelor's degree. German-Americans in central Illinois, as elsewhere in the country, were undergoing persecution. Super-patriots demanded the German language be dropped from high school curriculums and that sauerkraut henceforth be called "liberty cabbage." In Pekin it was well known that Mrs. Dirksen kept a picture of Kaiser Wilhelm on the wall. It was one of the few possessions that she had brought from Germany. Anti-German sentiment was so strong that a band of Pekinites came to her house in Beantown and demanded its immediate removal. It was further intimated that if her boys did not fight for the United States it would be an indication of their disloyalty. Veiled threats were made that if the Dirksens did not join the battle against the so-called hated Hun, the torch might be put to her house.[23]

Mrs. Dirksen was terrified. She informed Everett of what had taken place. Ev was well aware that similar happenings were occurring against German-Americans in Minnesota. Under these circumstances Ev decided to join the army right away. His twin brother, Tom, had been given an exemption because he was married. His older brother, Ben, had been drafted but was released because of a physical disability. Thus it fell to Ev to clear the family name of any taint of pro-German sympathy. By voluntarily entering the service, he felt it would dispel any vigilante-type vandalism that might result in physical harm to his beloved mother.

After enlisting in the army in 1917 Everett Dirksen was sent to Battle Creek, Michigan, for basic training. Because of his prior experience in ROTC, Ev rose quickly from private to corporal and then to sergeant. In January of 1918 he was sent to France and was assigned to an artillery battery. While in the field he was commissioned a second lieutenant. During the battle at St. Mihiel, Lieutenant Dirksen was attached to the 19th Balloon Company of the 328th Artillery.[24] He had the frightening experience of manning an observation balloon at a height of over 3,000 feet while German fighter planes were trying to shoot it down. Displaying bravery while under fire, Ev never flinched from his duty. He relied on prayer and accepted God's judgment as to whether he would emerge alive and unscathed. Relative to his wartime experience and his trust in God, Dirksen once reminisced, "When I was on the Western front fifty years ago, I picked up a khaki-covered Bible in Paris . . . that became the favorite of all books."[25]

Following the signing of the armistice on November 11, 1918, Lieutenant Dirksen did not return immediately to the United States; instead, he accepted an assignment in the censor's office of the Army of Occupation. He was specifically chosen because of his fluency in the use of the German language. In staying overseas he took advantage of the opportunity to see most of the countries on the European continent and to travel to England and Ireland. For a small-town boy who had never been out of the Midwest, it was an educational and horizon-broadening experience. While on duty in Germany Everett met a young German woman for whom he developed a great infatuation. He would have married her had it not been for his mother's disapproval.[26] Mrs. Dirksen counseled against it on the basis it would hurt any future political career. She recalled Ev's excitement in 1916 when he wrote her about his participation in a political campaign. At that time he also indicated keen interest in entering politics as a life's career. Mrs. Dirksen worried that anti-German sentiment might make a foreign bride a liability, not realizing this type of hysteria was but a wartime phenomenon.

In October of 1919 Lieutenant Dirksen was honorably discharged from the army. When the train pulled into the Pekin depot, Ev was met by his mother, brothers, and a crowd of Beantown well-wishers. He was made to feel like a war hero. Once back home, Ev did not really know what he wanted to do. Leaving Pekin to go back to the University of Minnesota seemed out of the question. The years in the army made him want to remain among members of his family and those he knew as friends. Also, his aged mother was getting feeble and needed his help. Ev decided he would live in the old house in Beantown and assume full support of her. This he did until she died in 1923.[27]

The years from 1919 to 1926 were for Everett Dirksen a period of indecision and drifting from one job or venture to another. Ev worked for a time at a grocery store owned by his brothers, but this did not suit him. Then, with savings accrued from his years in the service, he formed a partnership with Hubert Ropp, a high school friend, to form a company to manufacture electric washing machines. While such an appliance soon became very popular, it was still quite novel in the 1920s. Their venture failed basically because Ev's partner did not want to spend money on advertising, and this would have been the only way to make homemakers aware of the advantages of this new machine. In any case, Dirksen's first attempt at being a businessman failed.[28]

Again out of a job, Ev once more joined his brothers, this time in the bakery business. They had started the bakery in the mid-twenties and now Ev added his savings and joined them as a partner. The business soon expanded to where they were baking a railroad boxcar-load of flour each month. It was Ev's slogan that was used on the letterhead of the company called the Dirksen Brothers Bakers. It read: "If It's Made of Dough, We Make It."[29] Rising very early in the morning, Everett helped prepare the bakery goods and in the afternoon made deliveries to retail grocers. Their best seller was bread sold under the brand name of "Red Stripe."[30] Other delicacies included pies and German-type rolls. With a flourishing bakery business Ev made enough money to tidy up the Beantown home, buy a used Maxwell automobile, and increase his bank savings. Living so frugally, Dirksen always seemed a bit unkempt, since he wore clothes long after others would have discarded them.

The death of Antje Dirksen on December 7, 1923, created a void in Everett's life. His immigrant mother had been a positive force in his life. On her deathbed she extracted two promises from her favorite son. First, that he "look after" his brothers to make sure "they're gonna get along all right." Second, that he would not ever make a professional career out of "stage acting."[31] Mrs. Dirksen was of the old school and was firmly of the belief that the theater was not quite proper for decent folk. Ev acceded to his mother's wishes and agreed solemnly to take care of his brothers and to forswear becoming a Thespian as a life's career. This did not mean he would give up his theatrical activity in amateur productions, which continued until his entry into politics in 1926.

Dirksen's interest in the theater originally stemmed from his first role in the junior class play while in high school. After returning from France in 1919 he renewed this interest in community playhouse activities and in writing. Until he promised his mother he would not become a professional actor, he seriously considered both the theater and writing. He had a flair for drama and as an author-actor did many performances and penned numerous literary works. From 1919 to 1926 he wrote some one hundred works, including plays, short stories, and poems.[32] Only one such endeavor, a play called *Chinese Love,* was sold. It brought $300 from a Chicago publisher. It was a sentimental melodrama by today's standards and was seldom, if ever, produced outside of Pekin.

Being a member of the Pekin Players was important to Dirksen's future. First, through this association he met Louella Carver, his bride-to-be. Second, while acting, he developed communication skills that would later prove useful in politics. Regarding the latter, the ability to memorize scripts and to perform before live audiences greatly enhanced Ev's proficiency as a public speaker. He could memorize a written speech and make it sound impromptu. Likewise, Ev learned much about inflection, timing, and voice projection.

During this time when Dirksen was flirting with an acting career he was also in great demand as a speaker. This was primarily because of his affiliation with the American Legion. Urged to join this newly formed veteran's organization by Scott W. Lucas, a country lawyer from Havana, Illinois, and later a U.S. senator whom Dirksen would challenge in 1950, Everett soon became the local district commander. In this role he was called upon to make dedications, talk at school commencements, and give patriotic speeches on such occasions as the Fourth of July. It was evident in the successful manner of his delivery that as a platform speaker he was becoming very accomplished. His voice, gestures, and delivery incorporated many techniques utilized by actors. In this realm of political speechmaking he would become a peerless master.

After meeting Louella Carver at a play practice, Everett Dirksen was attracted to her immediately. The only child of Alfred and Lillie Carver, Louella worked as a bookkeeper at a department store in Peoria and participated in amateur productions purely for the fun of it. She had attended normal college at what now is Illinois State University. She had not been able to complete the college training necessary for a teacher's certificate because of the death of her father which forced her to quit school and get a job.

When Ev decided to call upon Louella, he was so shy it took him several walks around the block to get up the courage to knock on her door. The two liked each other immediately, although his courtship was hardly a script for a movie. Since he could not dance, the couple spent their evenings together singing around the piano, consuming malts at the local soda fountain, or merely strolling around the town square. Ev fell deeply in love with Louella and she reciprocated. At thirty years of age, and while working for a construction company that did not have a bright future, Ev decided to get married. On Christmas Eve in 1926 he proposed by asking Louella, "Would you like a ring or a radio?"[33] Somewhat startled, Louella had the presence of mind to indicate a preference for the ring. This acceptance initiated a one-year engagement. On Christmas Day Ev gave his future wife both an engagement ring and a radio. The latter was a crystal set, a new-fangled gadget just put on the market. On subsequent days when they were together, each would sit with a pair of earphones listening to programs coming from such seemingly far-away places as Chicago and St. Louis.

It was on Christmas Eve in 1927 when Everett and Louella became man and wife. It was what Ev later in jest called a "Scotch wedding." They were married at the bride's home in a simple ceremony with Tom, Ev's twin, serving as best man. Following the wedding ceremony refreshments of homemade cake and ice cream were served to the few relatives and guests who were present at the reception.

The Dirksen marriage was a model of happiness and mutual love. In describing its success many years later Ev revealed that at the outset of their married life they agreed that "voices must not be lifted in anger and especially not at breakfast, lunch, or dinner." Furthermore, he went on, "We developed a complete understanding that if anyone was moved by anger and wanted to raise his voice above the normal conversational level, he or she was to leave the table and come back, according to their conscience, when they cooled off."[34]

Following his marriage Ev ceased any further participation with the community playhouse but instead increased his activity in the American Legion. This, he felt, was more worthwhile since it contributed to contacts that helped his bakery business. Ev had joined the legion in 1922. By 1924 he was commander for Taze-well County and in 1926 was elected commander of the legion's sixteenth district, encompassing the same territory as the Six-teenth Congressional District. Known as the "baker boy with the golden voice,"[35] he had established a considerable reputation as an effective speaker and one who could talk on almost any subject—and do so intelligently. Patriotic speeches were his forte with Abraham Lincoln his favorite subject. Typical of one of these patriotic renditions was a speech entitled, "Our Buddy, George Washington." Washington was portrayed as a general who supported his men no matter what happened.[36]

While serving as post historian Dirksen won a state essay contest and, in turn, was appointed chairman of the State Committee Post Activities. Because of Ev's leadership qualities and his prow-ess on the platform, some of Dirksen's legion comrades began to encourage him to enter politics. This urging soon prompted him to seek a municipal post in his first formal quest for political office.[37]

In 1926 Ev decided to throw his hat into the ring by filing for the primary election in pursuit of one of the four positions on the city council. In all there were forty-four candidates competing for these four nonpartisan positions. Dirksen led the field in the primary and also finished first in the final election. He drew 2,715 votes.[38] Second place finisher Oscar J. Hill was more than 200 votes behind Ev. In this particular election, the highest vote-getter automatically became commissioner of accounts and finance. At age thirty-one Dirksen became finance commissioner at a salary of $75 a month.[39]

It was not long before Ev was dubbed the "young Turk from Beantown."[40] Dirksen boldly promoted such issues as paving streets, gaining municipal control over the local water works, enacting zoning ordinances, revising city codes, and constructing a new bridge over the Illinois River.[41] The council chamber usually had but few spectators. When Dirksen came on the council large numbers began to attend just to hear Ev give one of his fact-laden, eloquent speeches. "It was standing room only," Tom Dirksen recalled. "All hell couldn't stop him," his twin remembered, once Everett had made up his mind on an issue.[42]

The year 1929 started in an auspicious way for the Dirksens. On February 10 they were blessed with the birth of a baby girl. Given the name of Danice Joy, thereafter to be called Joy, it was to be their one and only child. Later in that same year came the fall of the stock market, soon to be followed by the Great Depression. The subsequent economic belt-tightening on the part of Pekinites reflected itself in loss of business at the Dirksen bakery. Likewise, as finance commissioner, Dirksen was acutely aware of the difficulty faced by townspeople in paying their taxes. Ev became even more cognizant of the magnitude of the Depression when he was appointed to a local committee as an adjunct to the Illinois Committee on Unemployment. By 1930 Ev was definitely of the opinion that the federal government had to do more to alleviate the dire economic conditions over which the states, local communities, and individual citizens had no control.

More and more Everett Dirksen took keen interest in the national scene. He followed closely what was going on in Congress, especially as it related to anti-Depression measures. He became increasingly dismayed at the actions of the local Republican congressman, William Edgar Hull. The latter held the seat of the Sixteenth Congressional District which encompassed Tazewell and five other counties. Representative Hull, who was a millionaire, held fast to the laissez-faire dictum that government should not interfere in the economy. Hull consistently voted for cuts in the federal budget and overall retrenchment rather than for funds to render assistance to victims of the Depression or for expansion of governmental services. Mulling it over in his mind, Dirksen came to the conclusion he could do more for the people in his district than the seemingly insensitive incumbent.[43]

When Everett Dirksen filed for the Republican primary as a challenger to Representative Hull, few outside of Pekin and the American Legion even knew who he was. Ev started with no campaign organization, no funds, and no party endorsement. The Sixteenth Congressional District was made up of the following counties: Bureau, Marshall, Peoria, Putnam, Stark, and Tazewell. Ev decided to concentrate his campaign efforts in Tazewell, with Pekin as the county seat, and Peoria, which contained the city of Peoria. The latter was the most populous metropolitan area in the district, and it was Hull's place of residence.

The strategy used by the thirty-four-year-old Dirksen was to stress his sixty-four-year-old opponent's age and to attack Hull's voting record. Ev denounced the incumbent's apparent lack of concern for the economic distress of his constituents. In particular, Dirksen scored with voters in Pekin and Peoria by attacking Hull's support of Prohibition. Both communities had major distilleries that were virtually destroyed by Prohibition.

In this 1930 political campaign, the only one Everett Dirksen ever lost, the odds for victory were overwhelmingly slim at the outset. Hull had newspaper support, controlled the district's GOP machinery, and possessed unlimited money to finance his bid for renomination. In an attempt to denigrate Ev in terms of age and experience, Hull dubbed Dirksen "that baker boy from Pekin."[44] Realizing that Dirksen continued to gain momentum, some of

Hull's supporters resorted to a tactic of dirty politics during the final days of the campaign. Circulars were distributed claiming that Dirksen was a member of the Ku Klux Klan (KKK). This angered Ev, and hurt him at the polls, but it was too late to refute this unfounded smear.

After making his final delivery of bakery goods on April 8, 1930, Dirksen wearily came home to wait with Louella to see what the outcome of the primary election would be. The final vote tally gave Hull 28,127 to 26,612 for Dirksen. Ev lost by a mere 1,515 votes out of a total of 54,739 votes cast. Ev won Tazewell County by some 1,250 votes and Peoria by almost 2,000. Dirksen lost by very small margins in such rural counties as Marshall, Putnam, and Stark, and by over 2,000 in Bureau County.

Friends and foes alike considered Dirksen's performance truly amazing. The Peoria *Star,* which had supported Hull, commented editorially: "The district has never experienced anything just like him. Without newspaper support, with the business interests of the district arrayed against him, he waged one of the most astonishing campaigns this district has ever witnessed. That he came so close to victory is a tribute to his ability as an orator, his good nature, and his unbounded energy. He has arrived."[45]

Everett Dirksen had not only arrived on the political scene in the Sixteenth Congressional District, but he planned to stay as a permanent fixture. When a reporter from the Pekin *Times* asked Ev about his plans for the future, Dirksen replied jauntily that "another campaign is just beginning."[46] In his first attempt, he had made a whirlwind campaign in a six-county area that was about 120 miles in length. In so doing he lost thirty pounds and was totally exhausted. Trying to canvass for votes in such a short time while continuing to work at the bakery made for a killing pace. Now he would have two years to crisscross the district in a more thorough and leisurely manner.

From 1930 to 1932 Dirksen drove his old Maxwell to every town, village, and hamlet in the Sixteenth Congressional District. He would, as his twin brother put it, "wiggle into any meeting."[47] Ev spoke at countless Farm Bureau affairs, women's organizations, service clubs, conventions, churches, lodges, schools, county fairs, and anywhere voters might get to know him. It was no wonder he was dubbed the "talkin'est man in Tazewell County."

During the course of Dirksen's campaign to win the Republican primary election, the most important issue to emerge related to the Great Depression. The prolonged nature of the economic collapse had caused increased unemployment, yet Hull continually opposed federal public works, relief, or any type of government assistance to hard-pressed individuals out of a job. Dirksen called this stand unjustified and repeatedly attacked Hull for it.

Coming down the homestretch of his campaign, Dirksen displayed great skill in the political art of attracting votes. He parried Hull's reproachful aspersions to his youth and humble status by deftly appealing to veterans and those of similar economic standing. "I was not too young to fight for my country," Ev declared with patriotic fervor, "not too young to face the bullets."[48] Admitting his bakery business was faltering and that he was in debt, Dirksen elicited the sympathy of others in the same plight. If one had to be a millionaire to be a member of Congress, Ev averred, then "God pity this country."[49] He reminded audiences that Abraham Lincoln came from humble origins, had failed in business, and was $700 in debt when he was elected to Congress. This type of appeal effectively thwarted the attempt by Hull to portray Dirksen as a poor baker boy lacking the ability to sit in Congress.

Dirksen sensed the tide was with him in the waning days of the campaign. On April 12, 1932, when the GOP primary votes were counted, Ev polled 22,184 to 20,577 for Congressman Hull. Dirksen's margin of triumph was 1,627. It must be noted he captured Bureau County with a plurality of 522 votes, having lost it by over 2,000 in 1930. Almost unnoticed at the jubilant scene in the Dirksen home was the fact that the Democrats in their primary had nominated E. S. Carr to be their candidate for Congress in the Sixteenth District.[50] Under normal circumstances winning the Republican primary would have been tantamount to election, but not in the Depression year of 1932. Heading the GOP ticket in the fall would be President Herbert C. Hoover. This did not augur well at a time when terms such as "Hoover

Depression" and "Hooverville" were part of the political lexicon used mockingly by the Democrats.

NOTES

1. Louella Dirksen with Norma Lee Browning, *The Honorable Mr. Marigold, My Life with Everett Dirksen* (Garden City: Doubleday, 1972), p. 35, hereafter cited as LD, *Mr. Marigold.*
2. Ibid.
3. For an account of the Irishman Willliam Scully see Paul James Weaver, "William Scully and the Scully Estates of Logan County, Illinois" (Master's thesis, Illinois State University, 1964).
4. Very little is known about Johann's early life except that he was married previously and had children by that marriage. See the oral history interview with Thomas Reed Dirksen, July 23, 1976, as quoted from the study, "The Early Life and Career of Everett McKinley Dirksen, 1896-1932: Using Oral History as Source Material," in Frank J. Fonsino, "Oral History as a Research and Teaching Tool" (Ph.D. dissertation, Illinois State University, 1979). Since Professor Fonsino conducted this oral history interview, the above citation will hereafter be cited as OHI-TRD-FJF. All other oral history or personal interviews quoted from this study will also have the author's initials as part of the citation.
5. Author's interview with Louella Dirksen, October 8, 1970, hereafter cited as AI-LD.
6. Oral history interview with Carl Von Boeckman, July 29, 1976, FJF, hereafter cited as OHI-CVB-FJF.
7. Interview with Margaret Juchems, July 29, 1976, FJF, hereafter cited as MJ-FJF.
8. Interview with Thomas Reed Dirksen, July 23, 1976, FJF, hereafter cited as TRD-FJF; oral history interview with Arthur Ehrlicher, July 22, 1976, FJF, hereafter cited as OHI-AE-FJF.
9. OHI-TRD-FJF.
10. Quoted in Milton Viorst, "Portrait of a Man Reading," *Book World* (Mar. 3, 1968), reprint in Glee Gomien Collection, Everett McKinley Dirksen Congressional Leadership Research Center, hereafter cited as GGC-EMDC.
11. TRD-FJF.
12. "Everett Dirksen's Washington," documentary and interview by Howard K. Smith (ABC-TV), Jan. 22, 1968, script in Remarks and Releases, 1941-69, EMDC, hereafter cited as R&R-EMDC.

13. *The Pekinian* (1913); AI-LD.
14. AI-LD.
15. AI-LD.
16. "Senator Dirksen Interviewed," Sept. 15, 1966, WRC-TV (NBC), Washington, D. C., transcript in R&R-EMDC.
17. Ibid.
18. *Pekin Sesquicentennial* (Pekin: Pekin Chamber of Commerce, 1974), p. 180.
19. AI-LD.
20. OHI-AE-FJF; oral history interview with Roy Preston, July 26, 1976, FJF, hereafter cited as OHI-RP-FJF; oral history interview with Russell Campbell, July 27, 1976, FJF, hereafter cited as OHI-RC-FJF.
21. Reprint of *Current Biography* (1941) in Information File, EMDC, hereafter cited as IF-EMDC.
22. AI-LD; LD, *Mr. Marigold,* pp. 37-38.
23. Oral history interview with Frank Jibbins, Aug. 7, 1976, by Frank J. Fonsino, hereafter cited as OHI-FJ-FJF.
24. "Biographical Data," n.d., IF-EMDC; OHI-TRD-FJF; OHI-FJ-FJF.
25. Viorst, "Portrait of a Man Reading," GGC-EMDC.
26. MJ-FJF.
27. AI-LD.
28. "Biographical Data," IF-EMDC; OHI-TRD-FJF.
29. LD, *Mr. Marigold,* p. 48.
30. AI-LD.
31. Oral history interview with Louella C. Dirksen, Sept. 6, 1976, FJF.
32. AI-LD.
33. LD, *Mr. Marigold,* p. 43.
34. Ibid., p. 44.
35. AI-LD.
36. Pekin *Daily Times,* Feb. 23, 1928, p. 1.
37. Interview with Frank Jibbens by Frank Fonsino, Aug. 7, 1976; OHI-RP-FJF; Pekin *Daily Times,* Oct. 29, 1928.
38. Pekin *Daily Times,* Apr. 20, 1927, p. 1.
39. Pekin City Clerk, *Minutes of Meeting,* City Council of Pekin, Illinois, May 2, 1927, hereafter cited as *Minutes of City Council.*
40. Pekin *Daily Times,* Feb. 2, 1928, p. 3.
41. *Minutes of City Council,* Sept. 7, 1927; Apr. 4, 1928; Feb. 16, 1928; July 5, 1928; June 25, 1930. See also Pekin *Daily Times,* June

30, 1927; Oct. 20, 1927; Sept. 8, 1927; Oct. 13, 1927; Feb. 3, 1928; July 19, 1928; May 23, 1929; Nov. 29, 1930.
42. OHI-TRD-FJF.
43. AI-LD. See also her later remembrances in the Chicago *Tribune,* Dec. 4, 1967, p. 11.
44. LD, *Mr. Marigold,* p. 61.
45. Peoria *Star,* Apr. 9, 1930, reprint in IF-EMDC.
46. Pekin *Daily Times,* Apr. 10, 1930, p. 1.
47. OHI-TRD-FJF.
48. Pekin *Daily Times,* Mar. 7, 1932, p. 1.
49. Ibid.
50. Pekin *Daily Times,* Apr. 13, 14, 15, 1932.

2

Apprenticeship in Congress: The Years in the House of Representatives

POLITICALLY, 1932 was obviously a bad year to be running as a Republican candidate no matter what the office. To avoid certain defeat by identifying himself with President Hoover, Ev carefully planned his strategy for the 1932 campaign against the Democratic nominee in the Sixteenth Congressional District. Taking a pragmatic, nonpartisan approach, which involved a certain amount of expediency, Dirksen explained the game plan he used in this manner: "I first . . . assured the voters that our problems were economic and appealed to citizenship rather than partisanship. . . . This seemed eminently acceptable to Republicans who intended to vote for Roosevelt and to Democrats who intended to vote for me."[1]

As a campaigner Everett Dirksen was indefatigable. He shook literally thousands of hands, gave hundreds of speeches, and made appearances in every section of the Sixteenth Congressional District. Louella, when not at his side, would make campaign placards or distribute homemade handouts door to door. From the meager financial contributions he was able to solicit, Ev bought some advertising in newspapers and purchased radio time in Pekin and Peoria. The climax of his campaign came on election eve when a parade was organized to "give a rip snortin' windup to a great campaign."[2] Made up of legion buddies, high school classmates, local friends, and a pick-up band, the parade snake-danced past Dirksen's home on Buena Vista Street, wound around town, and terminated at the courthouse square where Ev gave his final speech.

Sitting by the radio on election night, Ev and Louella were astounded by the landslide proportions of Franklin D. Roosevelt's win over Herbert Hoover. Since local returns were given later than national results, Ev's mother-in-law, Mrs. Carver, was sure the Democratic tidal wave would inundate Everett as it did most Republicans in Illinois. But when the vote tally from the Sixteenth Congressional District began coming in, Dirksen led from the beginning. By the early hours of the morning, the count had progressed to the point where it was certain Ev had won by at least 20,000 votes over his Democratic opponent. A Chicago reporter phoned Ev to get an update on the vote. The connection was poor, and when Ev mentioned the figure 20,000, it was mistakenly thought to be the amount Dirksen was behind. Ev corrected him by saying, "You understand, don't you that mine is different. . . . Mine is a twenty thousand Republican lead!"[3] Ev laughed heartily when he later repeated this story to friends.

The exact amount of Ev's plurality was 23,147. He thus defeated Carr, the Democrat, by a vote of 67,949 to 44,802 and carried his district by over 1,000 more than did FDR. It was obvious that Ev's "almost Machiavellian strategy,"[4] as one newspaper put it, plus his effectiveness as a campaigner, drew the necessary votes from Democrats and pro-Roosevelt supporters to win a surprising victory. The baker from Pekin had defied the odds and won. He was one of only four Republicans in the twenty-seven congressional districts of Illinois to survive the Democratic avalanche.

As a member of the minority party, a position in which Dirksen would perpetually find himself, he had to decide exactly what his role should be. As part of the loyal opposition should he blindly oppose FDR's proposed New Deal program? Should he always go along with his own party despite his own personal feelings? He pondered over these questions and arrived at a well-thought-out decision. Ev reasoned that the "function of the minority party is, after all, in the salutary influence which it can exercise in resolutely opposing things which are fundamentally wrong and supporting those measures which are right." Thus at the very outset of his national career he understood the importance of compromise and working within the context of political circumstances. "This is a time for the exemplification of citizenship and Americanism rather than partisanship," commented Dirksen, "else how can we make any hopeful degree of progress out of this cataclysm?"[5] Ev summarized the life-long stance he was about to assume by maintaining that those in political life "can best serve their constituencies when they serve their country best."

So eager was Everett Dirksen to learn how Congress operated that he went to Washington, D.C., quite some time before his term officially started to observe the lame duck session. His heart beat faster at the first sight of "the Hill." The white dome of the Capitol seemed so majestic to him that he truly felt proud to be a part of all that was around him. After hiring an assistant, Wendel Cable, he quickly set about the task of learning the ropes. To begin with he would sit in the galleries when the House of Representatives was in session to acquire a working knowledge of its parliamentary procedure. Then he would sit as a spectator in committee meetings to see how they were conducted. He would also roam through the corridors to seek out important members of the House and introduce himself. Of the 148 freshman members of the House of Representatives who were sworn in on March 4, 1933, Dirksen was one of the best prepared for the hectic legislative business that lay ahead.

Although Bertrand H. Snell of New York was the Republican minority leader, Dirksen did not seek to cultivate his friendship since he was an older man whose old-fashioned views seemed outmoded. Instead Ev decided to develop a close acquaintance with Joseph Martin of Massachusetts, the assistant to the minority leader. He was a younger man, was more flexible, and was deemed by Dirksen to be a rising star within the ranks of the GOP. Ev's assessment was correct. Martin's voting record was closer to Dirksen's than was that of Snell, and in 1939 Martin became minority leader.[6]

At the outset of the 73rd Congress Dirksen was audacious enough to request such top-flight committee assignments as Appropriations, Interstate and Foreign Commerce, and Ways and

Means. What he received was membership on three relatively unimportant committees, District of Columbia, Immigration and Naturalization, and Territories. As he accrued seniority and status in the House, Ev would eventually gain such key committee assignments as Appropriations, Banking and Currency, and the Special Committee on Reorganization of the Executive Branch. Other special committees on which he served included those investigating crime in the District of Columbia and in the real estate bondholder business.[7] No matter on which committee he served, Ev was always diligent and did his homework. In fact, when he dropped his membership on the District of Columbia Committee to accept a choicer spot, residents of the District actually petitioned the House to retain Dirksen. People living in Washington regarded Ev as their champion and did not want him to leave the committee. Normally membership on the Appropriations Committee, one of the most important in the House, meant dropping off of the lesser committees. In this case the House made an exception and permitted Dirksen to remain as a member of the District of Columbia Committee.

The legislative work accomplished during the first Hundred Days of the New Deal was indeed monumental. Dirksen rose regularly at 5:30 a.m. and retired about midnight. He studied legislation thoroughly, attended his committee meetings, and was seldom absent from a roll call. Residing alone in the Mayflower Hotel, he usually walked to the Capitol. It would not be until Ev was reelected to a third term in 1938 that Louella would move to Washington, D.C. By this time her husband had completed his law degree by studying with a practicing attorney and was a member of the bar in both the District of Columbia and Illinois. They rented a small apartment on Rhode Island Avenue which they retained throughout Everett's tenure in the House. Their modest way of life reflected the small-town upbringing of both.

Most freshman congressmen remain relatively quiet and stay in the background. As backbenchers, so to speak, they follow the recommendations of committees and take direction from party leaders. Not so with Everett Dirksen. From the outset he was vocal and independent in his voting. Two weeks after entering the House, Ev gave his first speech. It was dotted with jokes and anecdotes, immediately marking him as a popular personality; his reputation as a speechmaker was established early. What was not noticed for a time was how well Dirksen had mastered the rules of the House and the fact that he studied thoroughly all pieces of legislation. Every evening he could be seen carrying a bulging briefcase. He did his homework until midnight and then rose with the sun to continue poring over complicated bills. To better understand the content of legislative proposals, he read widely to collect background information. What Dirksen soon discovered was that many measures were poorly drawn or vague in areas where they should have been specific. Supporters of certain bills all too frequently did not have their facts correct. Ev was a stickler for detail and a glutton for work. Within two years Dirksen's stature was such that he was appointed to the Republican National Congressional Committee. It was obvious from the outset Ev was a man on the move.

The one thing in the House which Ev detested most was the Democrats' use of the gag rule to cut off debate. He once wrote his wife, "We know in advance that the old gag rule and the steamroller will flatten us out plenty from time to time but anyway, we'll fight them the best we know how."[8] Since the majority party controlled what legislation would be enacted, Dirksen came to the realization that any influence on the content of pending bills would have to be via the amendatory process. He soon became an expert at proposing amendments. His penchant for compromise was incorporated into skillfully worded amendments geared to draw support from Democrats. In this manner he made his mark trying to modify legislation which normally he would oppose.

From the very beginning of his political career Dirksen displayed this pragmatic flexibility. As a practitioner of politics, theory did not interest him very much. He was a conservative by nature but always took cognizance of reality. As a small businessman and one who worked hard for everything he had ever received, Ev defended the free enterprise system but not in dogmatic terms. He was conservative in outlook but never took a doctrinaire stance. Ev did not attempt to codify his beliefs or bind himself to a predetermined set of rigid tenets; rather, his outlook was guided by a set of broad and competing norms in which flexibility and compromise permitted modification to suit the needs of the time. To those who would criticize him for inconsistency or even expediency, Everett would answer in this vein: "I have often thought that the only people who do not change their minds are sleeping peacefully in some cemetery or in an institution involuntarily—and have lost the capacity of changing their minds. So I hope the time will never come when I can't adjust to new circumstances and new conditions, because it is an accelerated world."[9]

The pattern of Dirksen's political behavior was one of personal interaction with events. He did not automatically vote the party line but used his independent judgment as to the merit of any given piece of legislation. All politicians must respond in some way to the will of their respective constituencies. So did Dirksen, but if he felt the temporary wishes of the people were not in their long-range best interests, he would vote his own mind and risk the political consequences. Being a Republican in the 1930s meant that he had to maintain lines of communication with important Democrats in order to have some influence on the course of legislation. Also incumbent upon him was the need to maintain a modicum of contact between the two major factions within the GOP. These intraparty considerations frequently forced Ev to seek the middle road. As a moderate centrist he could formulate compromise. Being ambitious and wanting to move up to a position of leadership within his party, Ev likewise could not ignore which faction controlled party policy. In Congress the conservative-isolationist wing generally prevailed, but on the national level where presidential candidates were chosen the liberal-internationalist faction tended to control party machinery. All of these complex factors created a tricky maze for Dirksen to traverse on his way toward achieving political advancement.

Dirksen's success in mastering the political skill of compromise was attested to by George E. Reedy, Lyndon Johnson's legislative aide and press secretary. He compared Dirksen to Speaker Sam Rayburn by stating: "They were technicians who could calculate to a millimeter the precise point at which a compromise could be struck which would maintain political solidarity even though it might leave everyone vaguely dissatisfied. It was a form of power brokerage ideally adapted to a system in which political parties are primarily coalitions rather than ideological groupings."[10]

Aside from adhering to party policy and the machinations which take place as politicians maneuver for political advantage, success or failure often hinges on intangibles not readily evident to the less than keen observer. Everett Dirksen possessed a personality that made him stand out among his peers from the first day he entered the House. He was a serious yet friendly man who met people with ease. His openness, sense of humor, and flair for the dramatic made him appealing. Even his appearance made him look different from others. A bushy shock of hair added a distinctive quality to the contours of his countenance and his rumpled clothes gave him a homespun quality. Ev's voice also got immediate notice. Politicians live by uttering words and Dirksen's unique manner of speaking as well as his unusual vocabulary were of enormous advantage. In 1934 Ev was besieged with requests from fellow Republicans up for reelection to come into their districts and give a speech. This, in turn, indebted many to Ev and enhanced his role as an emerging leader. Visibility is everything in politics. Dirksen had it from the very beginning.

The voting record amassed by Representative Dirksen during the pre-war days of the Roosevelt administration was such that one newspaper later labeled him a "GOP New Dealer and humanitarian."[11] While his innate individualism and experience as a small businessman made him suspicious of big government regulation per se, or federal competition with private enterprise, Dirksen was a realist in terms of reacting to the dire wants of his constituents. He agreed with the necessity for some federal intervention in the economy to stimulate recovery and to provide jobs for the unemployed and relief to the indigent. His rationale was simple enough. In this economic emergency the temporarily increased role of government was justified as being necessary for the general welfare. Overriding any personally held ideological objections in favor of assuring practical assistance to those in need, he therefore voted for the following New Deal measures: Banking Act, Federal Emergency Relief Act, Agricultural Adjustment Act (AAA), National Industrial Recovery Act (NIRA), Gold Reserve Act, Social Security Act, Fair Labor Standards (Wages and Hours) Act, United States Housing Act, Soil Conservation and Domestic Allotment Act, and for creation of the Civilian Conservation Corps. When the U.S. Supreme Court declared both the AAA and NIRA unconstitutional, Dirksen denounced the "Nine Old Men" by declaring, "The mind is no match for the heart in persuasiveness; constitutionality is no match for compassion."[12]

New Deal legislation opposed by Representative Dirksen, because he viewed it purely as government meddling, included the following: Economy Act of 1933, lowering salaries of government employees and reducing veterans' benefits; Tennessee Valley Act, setting up the TVA; Securities and Exchange Commission, establishing the SEC; Public Utilities Holding Act, outlawing utility holding companies; National Labor Relations (Wagner) Act, creating the NLRB and legalizing collective bargaining; and the reciprocal Trade Agreements Act, reducing substantially the high rates of the Hawley-Smoot Tariff. The nay votes cast by Dirksen on these pieces of legislation, which were enacted anyway, gave evidence of his antipathy toward public power, the collective power of labor unions, and government regulation of business, as well as his loyalty to the traditional Republican resistance to low tariffs.

Although a member of the loyal opposition, Dirksen realized pragmatically that administration-sponsored legislation aimed both at ending the Depression and rendering help to its economic victims was worthy of support. What angered him was the evidence of poor administration and the deliberate politicization of federal programs. Too often politically appointed bureaucrats acted in an overtly partisan manner in implementing governmental work relief projects that were supposed to be nonpolitical. In addition, Dirksen became so disenchanted with the Works Progress Administration (WPA) for its dispensation of jobs as political patronage that he voted to reduce the $4 billion price tag attached to the Relief Act of 1935. Ev wrote his wife he would "probably catch cain"[13] from his constituents for doing so, but he felt the WPA bureaucracy was mismanaging its affairs so grievously as to border on the scandalous. Likewise, reports had reached him that in Chicago the Cook County Democratic organization (Kelly-Nash machine) made use of relief and public works as political patronage. By 1936 Dirksen had come to the conclusion that the number and size of the alphabetical agencies of the New Deal should be reduced drastically to prevent them from virtually buying votes in the upcoming presidential election.

Because domestic issues relating to the Depression overrode those of foreign policy, during the years from 1933 to 1936 Representative Dirksen found little to criticize in Roosevelt's conduct of international relations. But from 1937 until a period about three months before Pearl Harbor, Dirksen openly began opposing the president. This was caused by Dirksen's observation that, as time went on, FDR's foreign policy became so blatantly interventionist that it eventually evolved into an undeclared war against Nazi Germany. The only exception prior to September 18, 1941, when Ev suddenly reversed his position, was a vote for the Naval Expansion Act of 1938. Dirksen's isolationism did not stem from disillusionment over Woodrow Wilson's failure to make the world safe for democracy, as was the case with many idealistic Americans. Ev, however, came from a pro-German ethnic background that never considered World War I to be a noble crusade at all. Instead, Dirksen put forward the argument that Robert Lansing, Wilson's secretary of state, had from the start "shaped our national policy in the direction of the Allies."[14] People in the rural, small-town areas of the Midwest reflected a strong feeling that the United States should not again get involved in another foreign war.[15]

Downstate Illinoisans were also avid readers of Colonel Robert R. McCormick's Chicago *Tribune*. It was without doubt the leading isolationist newspaper in the nation.[16] It should be stated here that while Everett Dirksen shared, at times, the foreign policy views of McCormick, he was never the colonel's protégé or puppet. Ev never solicited or received advice (let alone orders) from either McCormick or the *Tribune*'s political editor, Walter Trohan. Allegations were frequently made that Dirksen was McCormick's man, but actually he was totally independent.

In 1935 Dirksen joined with the overwhelming majority of his party to vote for the Neutrality Act. This was an attempt to legislate neutrality by imposing an arms embargo upon the United States relative to any belligerents involved in a war. President Roosevelt signed the measure on August 31 and on October 3 Benito Mussolini ordered Italian legions into hapless Ethiopia. Even though Dirksen did not like the fascist government in Italy and did not sanction its obvious aggression, he simply wanted noninvolvement on the part of the United States. When President Roosevelt sought discretionary embargo powers, Ev opposed the move. Because its mandatory embargo provisions were not strong enough to suit him, Dirksen, in fact, was one of the 27 in the House who voted against the 1936 extension of the Neutrality Act (with 353 voting for it). The logic of Ev's isolationist position at this time was that strict neutrality meant just that. He did not want the United States to maneuver its policy to favor one side or another, lest this inevitably drag America into the horrors of another overseas war.[17] He pleaded against accidental involvement due to a nonneutral stance because "mothers, wives, and sisters, and other God-fearing women in my district . . . shudder at the very thought of war."[18]

In January of 1938 FDR asked Congress to bolster the nation's defense. An administration-sponsored measure, the Vinson Naval Expansion bill, sought to upgrade and increase the size of the U.S. Navy. Since 1937 Dirksen had been a member of the powerful House Committee on Appropriations and as such was deeply involved in the struggle for naval appropriations. As only one of eighty-nine Republicans pitted against the numerically superior Democrats, Ev scrutinized every dollar requested by the administration. Not only did the president ask for more money for the navy, but he also asked for additional funds to expand the air corps. Dirksen agonized over his decision and finally rationalized that appropriations for defense were justified. He thus voted for the naval expansion bill, but opposed expenditures for the development of offensive weapons. Ev helped kill the authorization of $5 million to fortify Guam on the basis that it was a waste of money to attempt to make a fortress of this tiny island.[19]

During the heated debates over military and naval appropriations, Dirksen wrote his wife: "Don't be surprised if within three or four months, we may be asked to sanction a course of block-ading Japan. . . . So, get ready the wreaths when that time comes."[20] Apprehensive of the future in 1938, with the talk of war resounding throughout the halls of Congress, Ev suggested to Louella that they buy a farm and get away from it all. While in a depressed mood he wrote: "I don't like this war business that is going on and don't like the thought of the regimentation and dictatorship that goes with it. I shall feel infinitely better when we get a bit of land with a snuggly little house on it and be able to say—Come what may, here we shall till the Good Earth and raise food and provender."[21]

After the fall of France in 1940 Dirksen became even more worried that the United States would get entangled in a European war. He expressed his deep concern to Louella: "I entertain a sense of dread as I hear members . . . say that soon we shall be in war. It's a bit of irony! To have served in one war and perhaps be called to vote on another, twenty-three years later. Let us hope and pray that it will not be."[22] In a vain attempt to prevent FDR from promoting intervention, Dirksen voted against selective service in 1940 and against its renewal in 1941. In the latter instance the extension passed the House by only one vote. He also voted against Lend-Lease, to no avail, which Speaker Sam Rayburn (D-Tex.) had cleverly numbered HR 1776.

Then, on September 18, 1941, Everett Dirksen made a dramatic volte-face. Speaking from the well in front of the Speaker's desk, Ev reacted to the reality of a Europe overrun by Nazi Germany and publicly repudiated his isolationist position. He then voiced his support for FDR's interventionist policy. "That policy is now known to all the world," declared Dirksen. "To disavow or oppose that policy now could only weaken the president's position, impair our prestige, and imperil the nation."[23] His former isolationist colleagues were shocked. What prompted this change in position? Much had taken place the previous month to influence Ev's thinking in a profound manner.

The United States had assumed the stance of a belligerent nation because of the following actions initiated by FDR: enacting the destroyer deal (trading fifty overaged U.S. war ships for 99-year leases on British air and naval bases in the Americas); authorizing some $7 billion in war matériel to Great Britain via Lend-Lease; sending U.S. troops to occupy Greenland and Iceland; ordering the U.S. Navy to patrol the Atlantic Ocean halfway to Britain; issuing the "shoot on sight" order after the U.S. destroyer *Greer* was attacked by a German submarine; freezing German and Italian assets in the United States; sponsoring a Selective Service (draft) Act, which was passed; and with British Prime Minister Winston Churchill signing the Atlantic Charter indicating a virtual alliance had been concluded.

In his own mind, Dirksen had come to the conclusion the United States was in fact already at war. Now the time had come to rally around the flag and support the president. In time of war, Ev reasoned, it was imperative that the nation have only one spokesperson and not a chorus of dissonant voices. As a patriot and rational member of Congress, Dirksen felt compelled to end the debate over whether we were to get into the war. For all intents and purposes that decision had been made. The time had come to cease fomenting dissension in order to assure final victory over Hitler in the long and hard struggle to come.

Much like Arthur Vandenberg of Michigan in the Senate, Dirksen became a leader in the House seeking to convert GOP isolationists to internationalism. In this sense he ran counter to the Republican leadership in the House. It was, however, more in tune with the internationalism espoused by Wendell Willkie in 1940 and that of Governor Thomas E. Dewey of New York in 1944.

Differences of opinion relative to domestic or foreign policy issues with his Republican colleagues did not deter Dirksen from serving his party loyally at election time. As chairman of the Republican National Congressional Committee, a post held from 1938 to 1946, he was called upon to give hundreds of speeches for GOP candidates all over the country. Ev could afford to do this because his own district was so secure he did not have to do extensive campaigning for reelection every two years. Touring the country for other Republicans made him popular with House colleagues and gave him national exposure. When Ev had been an isolationist, he nevertheless campaigned for internationalists. Likewise, after his conversion to internationalism he nonetheless campaigned for isolationists. Similarly, he worked for the election of both liberals and conservatives within his party. This endeared him to all camps and caused his name to be mentioned prominently in 1941 for the chairmanship of the Republican National Committee, a position that ultimately was retained by Joseph Martin. It was Dirksen's contention that the Republican party possessed a political umbrella large enough to cover all viewpoints. Ev respected the conscientious beliefs of fellow Republicans and he expected them to respect his. Politically speaking, Ev was on cordial terms with all factions in the GOP and this served to enhance his growing role as a leader in the House.

Understanding the mechanics of politics, Dirksen sought to promote internationalism within the Republican party, but in such a manner as not to alienate those whose proclivity for isolationism was still strong. In preparing for the midterm elections of 1942, Everett joined with Representative J. William Ditter (R-Pa.) to draft a statement on foreign policy upon which all Republicans could run. This document, which was ultimately signed by 115 GOP members of Congress, declared that "the United States has an obligation and responsibility to work with other nations to bring about a world understanding and cooperative spirit which will have as its supreme objective the continued maintenance of peace." Former isolationists were mollified by the qualifications that "in so doing we must not endanger our own independence, weaken our American way of life, or our system of government."[24] Likewise, when the Fulbright Resolution, sponsored by J. William Fulbright (D-Ark.), to commit the United States to membership in a postwar international organization was before the House, Dirksen toned it down sufficiently to get former isolationists to vote for it. It passed 360 to 29.

Everett Dirksen was not only active in restructuring his party's position on foreign policy, but he also sought to implement congressional reforms to make the monitoring of federal programs more effective. In 1943 Dirksen received favorable national publicity when *Fortune* magazine featured him in an article entitled, "Congressman: A Case Study."[25] Describing Ev as being "well above the congressional average in ability and industry," the story related in detail all of the many activities of a typical Dirksen seventeen-hour day as a member of Congress. Considerable attention was given to Ev's plan for congressional reform. During the New Deal many so-called alphabetical agencies had come into existence. Much of this governmental expansion was supported by Dirksen, but what troubled him was the inability of Congress to supervise properly this huge bureaucracy. To solve this problem he proposed the use by congressional committees of expert staffs to check up on federal agencies. Ev explained their need as follows: "There is nothing so discouraging as an Appropriations subcommittee hearing, with the members on one side of the table and the agency heads and their experts lined up on the other. They have all the facts at their fingertips, but all they need to tell us is what they want us to know. We have no way of checking up on them."[26]

The opportunity to implement his plan came in 1945 when on February 19 Congress set up a bipartisan committee to reorganize itself. Dirksen was made a member of this special, twelve-man joint committee of the House and Senate. He teamed with Representative Mike Monroney (D-Okla.), who was vice-chairman of the special committee, and others to cosponsor a bill that became the Legislative Reorganization Act of 1946. Ev played a major role in its enactment. It not only provided for a staff of experts for each congressional committee but sought to reduce the overall number of committees. In the Senate thirty-three permanent committees were reduced to fifteen and in the House forty-eight were cut to nineteen. The measure also sought to simplify committee structure, eliminate the creation of select committees, clarify duties, prevent jurisdictional disputes, and regulate lobbying. In addition it raised salaries and provided for a system of retirement pay for members of Congress.[27]

In the midst of this activity, the presidential bug suddenly struck Everett Dirksen. He had risen steadily in stature in the House and had been one of forty-nine Republicans constituting the Postwar Advisory Council which met at Mackinac, Michigan, to draft the Mackinac Charter. It called for a reorientation of the GOP. It recommended the abandoning of isolationism and the embracing of an internationalistic point of view. In 1940 Wendell Willkie had considered Ev for the post of Republican national chairman. Louella Dirksen had long since jettisoned her small-town provincialism. She was active in the Congressional Club, a bipartisan group of political wives, and was well adapted to the social life associated with being the wife of a leading congressman.[28] Ev, too, had broadened his organizational affiliation, having joined, in addition to the American Legion, the Veterans of Foreign Wars, Eagles, Elks, Moose, Masons, and Shriners.

In preparing for this premature but sincere bid for the GOP presidential nomination, Everett Dirksen hired Harold E. Rainville, an advertising man, as his campaign manager and set up headquarters in Chicago. Ev had Rainville approach Republican Governor Dwight H. Green to see if Dirksen might be made the favorite son of the Illinois delegation.[29] Governor Green seemed to be agreeable, but as it turned out he had vice-presidential ambitions himself and never really promoted Dirksen's candidacy. Everett took the initiative and went to see Colonel Robert McCormick, the first time he had ever met him personally, to inform the publisher of the Chicago *Tribune* of his presidential aspirations. The colonel listened politely but made no commitment about newspaper support and gave no encouragement.[30]

The strategy Dirksen planned to use to launch his presidential campaign was to draw up a statement that purported to be a draft. Working with Representative Leslie Arends (R-Ill.), a close friend and colleague, a committee of congressional sponsors was set up. Arends headed it. He then circulated the Draft Dirksen for President petition among the GOP members of the House. Thirty-six Republicans signed it, representing thirteen states. Most of the signatories, however, were from the Midwestern states of Illinois, Iowa, Kansas, Missouri, Nebraska, and South Dakota. Following this supposedly spontaneous call for Ev's candidacy, Dirksen summoned a news conference on December 2, 1943. The press release given to reporters gathered at the Mayflower Hotel read in part, "Acceding to the request of his associates in Congress, Representative Everett M. Dirksen, Pekin, Illinois, today announced his candidacy for the Republican nomination for President of the United States."[31]

Ev gave his first speech as a presidential aspirant at the national convention of the American Farm Bureau Federation (AFBF) in

Washington, D.C. In it Dirksen praised the traditional independence and self-reliance of the rural sector. "To permit or
encourage the complete domination of agriculture by a central
government," Ev charged, "is to confess a distrust or a lack of
faith in the capacity and willingness of farmers to do a reasonable
thing."[32] Dirksen had voted for the Agriculture Adjustment Act
in 1933, but during the war Congress had attached the Steagall
Amendment to the AAA. This amendment, sponsored by Representative Henry B. Steagall (D-Ala.), eliminated low, flexible
price supports in favor of high, rigid parity payments. Also, the
number of agricultural commodities covered was greatly expanded to include nonbasics and perishables. It was to be in force
until two years after the official termination of the war. Dirksen
had voted against the Steagall Amendment since it greatly increased federal management of agriculture far beyond the original
AAA. Ev told his AFBF audience: "The very essence of a sound
agriculture, in war or peace, is a free farmer whose hope of reward
for long and arduous toil lies in an adequate price in an open
market. This is the climate of freedom and incentive to which
his own efforts will be the measure of his prosperity."[33]

Everett Dirksen was a tough campaigner and could articulate
in hard-hitting terms the GOP criticisms of the Roosevelt administration. In a press release Ev hit at FDR's attempt to pack the
Supreme Court and thus "impair the power and jurisdiction of
the judiciary." Roosevelt was also condemned for excessive "con-
centration of power in the executive branch of the government"
and "moral obtuseness," and for fostering the "doctrine of collectivism." Other aspects of the New Deal that came under fire
by Dirksen were the "enormous debt," "shameful use of relief
funds . . . to debauch free elections," "coddling of radicals,"
"management of public opinion" by bureaucrats, a "staggering
public civil payroll of nearly 3,000,000 persons," and the "habit
of taking objectionable personnel from agencies liquidated by
Congress and transferring them to other agencies that their bold
radicalism might continue to ferment in government."[34]

In the early days of the New Deal Everett Dirksen had feared
the collectivist ideas of brain truster Rexford G. Tugwell, who
for a time served in the Roosevelt administration as assistant

secretary of agriculture. By 1944 Representative Dirksen's concern focused on Vice-President Henry Wallace's call for a revival of the New Deal in the upcoming, postwar era. Among Wallace's proposals were recommendations for intensive planning by the federal government regarding public works to ensure full employment, enactment of more welfare measures, extension of the TVA prototype to other river valley authorities, and expansion of the ever normal granary concept (embodied in the Agriculture Adjustment Act of 1938) on an international scale. Dirksen interpreted these proposals as constituting further steps in the direction of creating a welfare state, which might lead eventually to the evolution of an outright socialist economy. This prospect was repugnant to him.

In a speech carried nationally over the radio, he insisted, "Collectivism in which the individual is considered as but a part of the mass or group is but another name for totalitarianism." This may have been a bit of verbal overkill, but he believed it. Ev posed the question: "Will the American system of living, which rests upon the morals of individualism, become the victim of a pious collectivism and will freedom be just a word or a way of life?" Dirksen was not a reactionary who wished to repeal outright the New Deal. He did, however, want the expansion of federal power checked so that personal incentive and the freedom to make economic decisions would remain an important aspect of the American way of life. Seeing America as the world's defender of democracy and free enterprise, Dirksen declared: "To abandon even a small part of the freedom we have known, and which accounts for the greatness and leadership of this land, is to abandon the greatest spiritual advantage in civilization. . . . Without freedom there can be no full healing at home. Without freedom there can be no strength to bring succor to a confused world. One of our greatest attributes is our power of example to bewildered people everywhere."[35]

Early in 1944 three governors were the leading contenders for the GOP presidential nomination: Thomas E. Dewey of New York, John W. Bricker of Ohio, and Harold E. Stassen of Minnesota. To strengthen his weak position, Everett Dirksen sought to forge a Midwest-West alliance with Governor Earl Warren of

California. Warren was promised the vice-presidency in return for his support of Ev for top spot on the ticket. When the Californian refused to enter into this arrangement, Dirksen knew Governor Dewey was unbeatable. Ev had canvassed for delegates in thirty states but had no firm commitments. Realizing that the New Yorker was the front-runner, Ev switched his attention to the vice-presidency. He believed his progressive voting record on domestic issues and internationalistic stance on foreign policy made him politically compatible with Dewey, and his being from Illinois would give the ticket a geographic balance.

To promote Dirksen's vice-presidential aspirations, Ev's close friend, Representative Dewey Short (R-Mo.), wrote a letter to the editors of *Life* magazine. Henry Luce, the publisher of *Life,* had been supporting Dewey so this channel of communication seemed a good way of getting the New York governor's attention. Extolling Ev's virtues as a midwesterner, Short declared: "There is a friendly aura about the Midwest. That aura clings to 'Ev' Dirksen, as we so affectionately call him. Like the Midwest, he is robust, cheerful, friendly, and his colleagues will take off their shirts for him. We are for a congressman . . . on the national ticket."[36]

When the 1944 Republican National Convention met in Chicago on June 26, Governor Dewey had the nomination sewn up when Bricker and Stassen withdrew even before the start of the first roll call. After being selected unanimously for the presidency, Dewey picked Governor Bricker as his vice-presidential running mate. Ironically, in connection with Dirksen's hopes for the vice-presidential nod, Dewey was not interested in political compatibility but wanted someone to placate the conservative-isolationist wing of the Republican party. As a professional politician in the best sense of the word, Dirksen understood Dewey's decision and accepted it gracefully. Ev personally liked the young New York governor and campaigned for him at every opportunity. In a national radio speech given for the GOP ticket Dirksen alluded to Dewey's youthful vigor in contrast to FDR's age and ill health by stating: "Well, times have greatly changed. Mr. Roosevelt has greatly changed. The long years in office have taken their tragic toll." Dirksen was truly disappointed when the Dewey-Bricker duo was defeated by the Democratic ticket of Roosevelt and Truman.

As usual, Dirksen spent very little time campaigning in his own district. By now he was a political fixture in the Sixteenth Congressional District of Illinois. He never had a challenger in the Republican primary and at no time did a Democratic opponent pose any real threat at the polls. Dirksen's orientation was so national he paid little attention to state politics and did nothing in the way of building a political base for himself in the capital of Springfield. He created no political fiefdom. This hurt Ev in 1944, as it did in other presidential elections, because he could not get the nod as the Prairie State's favorite son. Ev's independence from the state GOP relieved him of involvement in party problems and patronage concerns, but it handicapped him in connection with opportunities of becoming a presidential or vice-presidential candidate.

When Everett Dirksen had announced that he was going to seek the 1944 GOP presidential nomination, the Republican party in Illinois gave his candidacy little real support. None came in terms of monetary assistance. Most of Dirksen's financial support came from a group of Pekinites who raised a campaign fund for him. Because of the abortive nature of Ev's endeavor, a portion of the money thus collected was never spent. Some $4,000 lay idle. Following Dirksen's reelection to Congress those in charge of the fund suggested Ev use the money to finance a world tour. The idea was that it would be educational and enlightening, thereby contributing to his ability to deal with world problems as an increasingly important member of the House of Representatives. The proposition appealed to Dirksen. He accepted the generous offer of his friends.

In February of 1945 Congressman Dirksen embarked on a four-month inspection trip that took him to Europe, Africa, the Middle East, and Asia. Ev was given the opportunity to meet world leaders, assess war damage, evaluate Lend-Lease aid, appraise the work of the United Nations Relief and Rehabilitation Administration (UNRRA), investigate U.S. overseas programs, talk with U.S. ambassadors, and visit with American soldiers.[37]

Traveling by himself, Dirksen witnessed firsthand the ugly ruins of war. The dire economic condition of war-torn countries was in evidence everywhere. All of Europe lay in desolation. It constituted a dangerous power vacuum. Ev became acutely aware that the Soviet Union posed a serious threat to the survival of countries in both Eastern and Western Europe as truly independent nation-states. He witnessed the activities of communist parties which were taking advantage of the economic chaos to undermine existing governments. From Augsburg in Germany Ev wrote somberly to his wife: "As I contemplate the destruction of these great cities—the utter destruction of bridges, railroads, homes, business buildings and what not, I have a feeling that European civilization is done. The whole condition is now ideal for the engulfment by . . . communism."[38] What Dirksen saw frightened him. "Freedom is being mocked and leached away in certain places," he wrote again to Louella. "I see the vigorous propagation of certain ideologies which imperil the very thing for which young Yanks have died."[39] After an exhausting journey totaling thousands of miles of travel, Ev was glad to return to the United States.

While Dirksen was making his private journey abroad, he was shocked by the news of President Roosevelt's death. He was genuinely surprised when the new president, Harry S. Truman, requested a report from Ev on what he had seen and heard on his trip. On June 4, 1945, Dirksen sent the president a confidential memorandum containing both his observations and recommendations. Ev praised the military occupation forces and stated that their "achievements have been superb." Regarding "civilian functions," he indicated that most U.S. personnel serving overseas were "capable and diligent" but "lacked proficiency in foreign language." UNRRA's relief operations were criticized as being "generally disappointing." The suggestion was then made regarding UNRRA that "a searching inquiry should be instituted from top to bottom." Concerning Lend-Lease, Ev strongly recommended it "be made a weapon of freedom." Although the Cold War technically was not yet in existence, and that descriptive phrase not yet in use, Dirksen wanted U.S. relief and economic assistance used to forestall the formation of what later became the Soviet satellites or Iron Curtain countries. In counseling Truman, Ev exhorted, "If continued, Lend-Lease . . . should be judiciously used on a quid pro quo basis as an instrument for the establishment of real freedom in those areas where freedom does not in fact exist."[40] He wanted Truman to get tough with the Russians and make the United States the champion of the Free World.

Because Dirksen viewed communism as a menace to the Free World, he requested materials from the Library of Congress relating to communism. From this research he supervised the preparation of a 141-page booklet entitled *Communism in Action* (1946). Published as a government document, it became somewhat of a best seller. In 1947 the House authorized the printing of an additional 500,000 copies.[41] His fear of communism was reinforced that same year when he was part of a congressional junket making an inspection tour of occupied Germany. It saddened him to see East Germany forcibly being made into a communist state. His concern now was to save West Germany, France, and Italy, as well as Greece and Turkey, from being taken over by the communists. Upon returning to the United States Dirksen prepared a speech he titled "Aid to Europe is the Price of United States Freedom." In it he warned, "The Soviet Union is feverishly preparing for military war." Among his anticommunist rhetoric were such ringing rubrics as: "The Red spider spins his web"; "Communism is a conspiracy against freedom"; and "To abandon Europe now is to abandon freedom not only for them but for ourselves."[42]

In the fall of 1945 Representative Clare Booth Luce (R-Conn.) made a proposal that the United States not only supply food and medicine to war-torn Europe, but that reconstruction of the continent be fostered by massive U.S. economic aid. Needing someone with the technical expertise to draft a bill and knowing that Dirksen agreed with her, she consulted with Everett on her plan for rebuilding Europe's industrial capacity. The resulting Luce-Dirksen bill, calling for economic assistance to Europe, was dropped in the legislative hopper in January of 1946. This precursor of the Marshall Plan was not enacted and no large-scale help was directed to Europe until passage of the Economic Cooperation Act on April 3, 1948.[43]

The Republicans won control of Congress in the midterm elections of 1946. Whn Joseph Martin was elevated to Speaker of the House by his GOP colleagues, it left the position of House majority leader vacant. Dirksen made a bid for the job but lost out to Representative Charles Halleck (R-Ind.). Ev was smart enough to withdraw before the balloting began. Since his party was in the majority, it meant Dirksen became chairman of the Committee on the District of Columbia as well as head of the agriculture subcommittee of the Appropriations Committee.

From 1945 to 1948 Everett Dirksen gave valuable support to President Truman in the realm of foreign policy. Truman, in turn, courted Ev even as he did Senator Arthur M. Vandenberg (R-Mich.). In the House Dirksen did as much as Vandenberg in the Senate to forge a bipartisan foreign policy in the early years of the Cold War. It was Ev who bucked Republican isolationists in order to help bring about U.S. membership in the United Nations. In 1945 Dirksen also gave vigorous support to the implementation of the Bretton Woods Agreement, which established the International Bank for Reconstruction and the International Monetary Fund. He fought for additional appropriations for UN-RRA, U.S. participation in the United Nations Educational, Scientific, and Cultural Organization (UNESCO), and for funds to carry out the Foreign Information and Educational Program, which set up the Voice of America.

In 1946, however, Ev opposed a fifty-year loan of $3,750,000,000 at 2 percent interest to Great Britain, along with a generous settlement of its Lend-Lease obligations, for two reasons. First, the new Labor government of Clement Attlee that had been installed recently announced its intention of nationalizing British industry. Second, Dirksen was incensed over British policy in Palestine, which sought to thwart the formation of Israel by Jewish refugees. On another issue, though, he did fight hard for $400 million in aid for Greece and Turkey in 1947. In 1948, his assistance was likewise invaluable in the enactment of the Economic Cooperation Act. The latter authorized the expenditures of $6.1 billion to carry out the Marshall Plan and provided additional military aid to Greece and Turkey as well as assistance to Nationalist China. In the heated debates surrounding the approval of foreign aid programs, Dirksen warned his GOP colleagues that Congress "must not be niggardly" if Europe was to be saved from communism. When Republican isolationists bitterly denounced the Marshall Plan as unnecessary U.S. involvement and a waste of huge sums of money, Ev countered by arguing, "If we fail in the first year of the European Recovery program, we fail for good."[44]

While rendering much-needed support for almost all of Truman's foreign policy, Dirksen was more selective when it came to domestic issues. He voted for such key administration measures as the Employment Act of 1946, extension of selective service, the Federal Employee Loyalty Act that set up the Loyalty Review Board, the Atomic Energy Act, and a one-year extension of the Reciprocal Trade Agreements Act, to which Ev was instrumental in securing an amendment giving the Tariff Commission the right to set quotas when U.S. industry was unduly hurt from an excess of imports. Dirksen was also a strong supporter of civil rights legislation. He voted for the anti-poll tax bills of 1945 and 1947 and for the antidiscrimination amendment to the Federal School Aid bill sponsored by Representative Adam Clayton Powell (D-N.Y.). Ev was for the Veteran Emergency Housing Act, a $100 million federally funded cancer research program, the creation of a select committee on small business, Hawaiian statehood, a constitutional amendment to limit the presidency to two terms, and the Presidential Succession Act. On the other hand, deficit spending by the Truman administration concerned Dirksen very much; he voted repeatedly to cut Truman's domestic budget and opposed those measures which required undue heavy spending.

In 1945, although it was agreed to by a vote of 208 to 186, Dirksen opposed making the House Committee on Un-American Activities (HUAC) a permanent committee since he felt there were too many committees already. When charges were made that communists and their fellow travelers were active in the United States, however, he voted many times to uphold its contempt citations against uncooperative witnesses, including those against Gerhard Eisler, Corliss Lamont, and Albert Maltz. Ev was for an investigation of the magazine *Amerasia* and voted for passage of the Mundt-Nixon bill or Subversive Activities Control

Act of 1948, requiring registration of communist organizations.[45] The logic that motivated Dirksen was simplistic but straightforward. Why spend billions to stop communism abroad only to permit it to undermine American freedoms at home? It bothered him that alleged communists in the United States freely used constitutional prerogatives to defend their right of free speech, while in communist-controlled nations this very freedom was totally abridged. His apprehension grew relative to this problem when the Alger Hiss case came to the foreground. Revelations of wartime espionage, Soviet spy rings, and security leaks reinforced his fears that communist subversion in the United States might actually undermine the U.S. government.

At this time, but unknown to his colleagues, Everett Dirksen labored under a severe handicap. On Memorial Day in 1946 Dirksen complained to Louella that his eyesight had suddenly become blurred. During the next several weeks he tried to rest his eyes, but the press of daily work made it impossible to do so. He could not, in his words, "get the cobwebs out of my eyes."[46] While on a congressional junket to Europe in 1947, Ev went to eye specialists in Vienna and Paris. One diagnosed his problem as an eye inflammation of the type that frequently led to blindness, and the other said it was a serious malignancy. Subsequent visits to the Mayo Clinic and then to the Wilmer Clinic at Johns Hopkins University seemed to confirm the fact that Dirksen had cancer of the retina, or in medical terms suffered from an infliction known as *chorioretinitis.* It was ascertained the malignant growth had started in the right eye and was spreading rapidly to the left one.

The results of the final tests reached Everett on Christmas Eve, 1947, in Pekin where he and his wife were celebrating their eighteenth wedding anniversary. Part of the bad news was the doctor's recommendation for an immediate operation to remove the right eye. This enucleation was advised to prevent the cancer from spreading, thus greatly reducing the possibility of a slow and painful death. Ev spent much time during the holiday season in meditation and prayer seeking divine guidance in making his decision.[47] It was revealed many years later by the Reverend Archibald J. Carey, Jr., a minister of the African Methodist Church, that Dirksen had made a pledge to God. In presenting a $1,000 contribution to Reverend Carey in 1951 Dirksen, then a senator, told the surprised clergyman: "I promised God if ever I could recover my sight and continue my work in gainful employment, I would give a substantial portion of my income to help others."[48]

When Congress reconvened after the New Year recess Ev contacted the surgeon at Johns Hopkins. Dirksen recalled vividly the exact moment he informed the doctor that no operation would take place. "I remember telling the surgeon . . ." he reminisced at a later date, "I had consulted another doctor and came to the conclusion that I would not permit the removal of my eye. He said, 'What doctor?' Oh, I said a very big Doctor, He lives upstairs."[49]

Along with having decided against any surgery Dirksen also made up his mind he would not seek reelection in 1948. With the future status of his health in doubt he felt it would be impossible to continue his career in Congress; nevertheless, because important foreign policy legislation was before the House, Ev did decide to finish out his term despite the handicap of near blindness. In preparing speeches, he would have his secretary, Mrs. Glee Gomien, take dictation. At home that evening Louella would read the text aloud until Ev memorized it. Having been an actor, albeit an amateur, Dirksen possessed the ability to memorize dialogue. It was relatively easy for him to have total recall of lengthy speeches. Ev performed so well he could even elaborate on a memorized text. Often the entire speech sounded impromptu. When Dirksen privately informed Joseph Martin, the Republican Speaker, and John McCormack, the Democratic minority whip, of his intent to retire from the House, both attempted to talk him out of it. The latter, unusual as it may seem, counseled him instead to take a long period of rest and then run again from his Sixteenth Congressional District.[50]

Despite second thoughts, prompted by his great love of the House, Dirksen stuck to his decision not to file for reelection. He believed that with a period of prolonged and total repose, and with the help of God, his malady might be healed. "You can believe me that the decision not to seek renomination for Congress was not an easy one and was dictated only by consideration for my family and my physical welfare," he wrote to Harold E. Rainville back in Illinois. "I am confident that with an adequate amount of rest this condition can be overcome. I consider it as an interlude in my public career and expect to render many more years of service as soon as I have regained my energy."[51] The folks back in Pekin were shocked to hear that their hometown favorite would not again represent them in Congress. Prayers were spoken in local churches on Dirksen's behalf, and many people sent letters to Ev saying they were praying for his recovery.[52]

The Washington press reacted kindly to Dirksen after he announced his intention of not running for reelection. The Washington *Post* editorialized:

> By dint of hard work, native intelligence, and a commendable flexibility of mind, Mr. Dirksen has become one of the most powerful and highly esteemed leaders in the House of Representatives. In large measure he has achieved the happy feat of looking forward without losing touch with current realities. And his dynamic personality, his skill in debate, and his habit of informing himself on every major public issue have given his influence a contagious quality.[53]

The Washington *Evening Star* also tossed kudos to Dirksen when it observed: "An able, hard-working member of Congress since he first came to Washington, Mr. Dirksen has steadily risen in the esteem and respect of his colleagues and has become an outstanding member of the House. . . . For while he made himself a great asset to the majority, he was never a narrow partisan and always constructive in committee and debate."[54]

With sadness in his heart, Everett Dirksen made plans for his departure from Washington, D.C. He rented a small cottage in Bay Republic, Maryland, near Chesapeake Bay, where he planned to live for awhile in seclusion with Louella. He would be away from all legislative cares or problems confronting the nation. The little beach house was accessible only via a dirt road and it had no phone.[55]

Before leaving the capital city, Ev stopped at the White House to say farewell to President Truman. He, too, tried to talk Dirksen out of retiring. In the House fellow Republicans and Democrats across the aisle paid tribute to Ev. Former Speaker Sam Rayburn (D-Tex.) declared, "If they are going to send Republicans to the House, let them send Republicans of the Everett Dirksen kind."[56] After many handshakes, and a few sips of bourbon and water with intimate colleagues, Dirksen took his leave. Deep down in his heart Ev did not feel his exodus would be permanent. Divine providence, he believed, had not ordained his adieu be a lasting one. Politics had become his whole life. He loved it with a passion. In the House he had risen rapidly and was considered by political observers to be right behind Sam Rayburn and Joseph Martin in power and prestige. The speakership might one day have been his. Dirksen soon would return to Congress. It would not be to the House; rather, it would be the Senate. In the upper chamber Dirksen was destined to find a legislative forum that would ultimately allow him to attain the top leadership position within his own party and become a nationally known political figure.

NOTES

1. Everett M. Dirksen, "Mr. Dirksen Goes to Congress," *New Outlook* (Mar., 1933), reprint in IF-EMDC.

2. Pekin *Daily Times,* Nov. 7, 1932, p. 1.

3. Ibid., Nov. 9, 1932, p. 1.

4. Peoria *Star,* Mar. 12, 1933, reprint in GGC-EMDC.

5. EMD, "Mr. Dirksen Goes to Congress," IF-EMDC.

6. Joseph Martin as told to Robert J. Donovan, *Joe Martin, My First Fifty Years in Politics* (New York: McGraw-Hill, 1960), pp. 73-83.

7. *Current Biography* (1941), reprint in IF-EMDC.

8. LD, *Mr. Marigold,* p. 85

9. Everett M. Dirksen and Herbert V. Prochnow, *Quotation Finder* (New York: Harper and Row, 1971), p. 19.

10. George E. Reedy, *The Presidency in Flux* (New York: Columbia University Press, 1973), p. 126.

11. "Lucas vs. Dirksen," St. Louis *Post Dispatch,* Oct. 22, 1950, copy in Clippings-EMDC, hereafter cited as C-EMDC.

12. Annette Culler Penny, *Dirksen: The Golden Voice of the Senate* (Washington, D.C.: Acropolis Books, 1968), p. 36.

13. EMD to LD, Jan. 23, 1935, *Mr. Marigold,* p. 87.

14. Manfred Jonas, *Isolationism in America, 1935-1941* (Ithaca, N.Y.: Cornell University Press, 1966), p. 138.

15. David B. Danbom, *The Resisted Revolution, Urban America and the Industrialization of Agriculture, 1900-1930* (Ames: Iowa State University Press, 1979), pp. 99-100.

16. See Chapter 5 of Jerome E. Edwards, *The Foreign Policy of Col. McCormick's Tribune, 1920-1941* (Reno: University of Nevada Press, 1971).

17. For an excellent overview of the isolationist mentality of the 1930s see Selig Adler, *The Isolationist Impulse, Its Twentieth Century Reaction* (New York: Collier Books, 1961); for a comprehensive analysis of FDR's internationalist-isolationist position see Robert Dallek, *Franklin D. Roosevelt and American Foreign Policy, 1932-1945* (New York: Oxford University Press, 1979).

18. Neil McNeil, *Dirksen: Portrait of a Public Man* (New York: World Publishing, 1970), pp. 65-66.

19. Of his vote, Dirksen said in a letter to H. Davis Rockford, May 12, 1961, "Prior to World War II there was before the House the question of fortifying Guam. . . . In the interest of economy many of us resisted the move and I can say from experience that that mistaken issue was raised in at least three different elections thereafter."

20. EMD to LD, Jan. 10, 1938, *Mr. Marigold*, p. 92.

21. EMD to LD, n.d. (circa Mar., 1938), *Mr. Marigold*, p. 93.

22. EMD to LD, n.d. (circa Dec., 1940), *Mr. Marigold*, p. 99.

23. McNeil, *Dirksen*, p. 68.

24. Robert A. Divine, *Second Chance: The Triumph of Internationalism in America During World War II* (New York: Atheneum, 1967), p. 71.

25. *Fortune* (Apr., 1943), reprint in IF-EMDC.

26. Ibid.

27. George B. Galloway, *History of the House of Representatives* (New York: Thomas Y. Crowell, 1976), pp. 60-61.

28. AI-LD.

29. Unpublished memoir of Harold E. Rainville, Dec., 24, 1969, Chicago Office File, EMDC, hereafter cited as Rainville Memoir, COF-EMDC. See also author's interview with Harold E. Rainville, Oct. 8, 1970, hereafter cited as AI-HER.

30. AI-HER.

31. Press Release, Dec. 2, 1943, R&R-EMDC.

32. Address to the National Convention of the American Farm Bureau Federation, Washington, D.C., Dec. 7, 1942, R&R-EMDC.

33. Ibid.

34. Press Release from Dirksen for President Headquarters, hereafter cited as DPH, Chicago, n.d. (circa Jan., 1944), R&R-EMDC.

35. Address by EMD over NBC Radio, June 20, 1944, script in R&R-EMDC.

36. Dewey Short to "Letters to the Editors," *Life* (June 19, 1944), reprint in IF-EMDC.

37. He left Montreal by plane on February 21 and was gone for ninety days. His itinerary included England, France, Italy, Germany, Austria, Greece, Turkey, Iran, Iraq, Syria, Lebanon, Palestine, Egypt, Ceylon, and India.

38. EMD to LD, May 12, 1945, *Mr. Marigold*, p. 112

39. EMD to LD, May 8, 1945 (from Paris), *Mr. Marigold*, p. 111.

40. "Confidential Memorandum to the President," June 4, 1945, Official File, Harry S. Truman Library, hereafter cited as OF-HSTL. In a reply from HST to EMD, dated June 13, 1945, the president called it a "thoughtful memorandum" and commented, "I find it extremely interesting and some of the recommendations very helpful."

41. EMD, "Red Fascism: Freedom Is in Jeopardy," *Vital Speeches* (Apr. 1947), reprint in IF-EMDC.

42. EMD, "Aid to Europe Is the Price of United States Freedom," Nov. 18, 1947, text of speech in R&R-EMDC.

43. Stephen Shadegg, *Clare Booth Luce, A Biography* (New York: Simon and Schuster, 1970), pp. 212-13.

44. McNeil, *Dirksen,* p. 80.

45. Voting Record of EMD, IF-EMDC.

46. Beverly Smith, "The Fur Is Going to Fly in Illinois," *Saturday Evening Post* (Aug. 26, 1950), reprint in IF-EMDC.

47. AI-LD.

48. Archibald J. Carey, Jr. to Harold E. Rainville, Feb. 13, 1970, COF-EMDC. That same year Dirksen gave one-third of his salary to religious groups including his own Presbyterian church, a Roman Catholic church, and a Jewish temple.

49. Interview of EMD by Joseph F. McCaffrey, WMAL-ABC, Feb. 7, 1965, script in R&R-EMDC.

50. AI-LD.

51. EMD to HER, Jan. 10, 1948, COF-EMDC.

52. AI-LD.

53. Washington *Post,* Jan. 5, 1948.

54. Washington *Evening Star,* Jan. 5, 1948.

55. Rainville Memoir, COF-EMDC.

56. Alfred Steinberg, *Sam Rayburn: A Biography* (New York: Hawthorn Books, 1975), p. 264.

3

Dirksen Returns to Congress: The 1950 Senatorial Campaign

WHEN THE 81ST CONGRESS convened in January of 1949 Everett M. Dirksen no longer represented the Sixteenth Congressional District of Illinois in the House of Representatives. During the primaries in the spring of 1948 he had spent much time fishing and gardening at his Chesapeake Bay hideaway. In the evenings Louella would read to him or they would sing songs to the accompaniment of old records. This total relaxation, interspersed with religious meditation, went on for several months. One night, when his wife was reading to him, Ev told her excitedly he could see the print. Miraculously, it seemed to him, his sight was restored. Whatever the merits of his rest cure, plus taking massive doses of vitamins, his eyesight had returned to near normal by fall. Thereafter the sight in his right eye was 20/20 and in his left 20/40. The left eye was damaged by scar tissue, a macula, so it had only peripheral vision. Once having regained his eyesight to a point where he could read, Dirksen became impatient. Following the remission of his eye cancer, Ev wanted to take part in the 1948 political campaign even though he himself was not a candidate for any office.[1]

When Dirksen inquired of Governor Thomas E. Dewey of New York, again the GOP presidential candidate, how he could help, Ev was asked to lend a hand by helping Governor Earl Warren of California. Dirksen went to California to assist Warren, the Republican vice-presidential nominee, but soon left the Golden State to stump by himself. Ev was of the opinion that Warren's

53

speeches were not hard-hitting enough.[2] When the public opinion polls indicated Dewey was far ahead of President Truman, the New York governor also began to speak in meaningless platitudes. This bothered Dirksen, who believed it was always best to conduct an exciting campaign to ensure that the interest and enthusiasm of the electorate would be sustained until election day. It did not surprise Ev when, on the second Tuesday in November, President Harry S. Truman won reelection in what is considered as one of the major upsets in American history. Truman stunned pollsters and political pundits alike by his come-from-behind victory over Dewey.

Dirksen was much distressed by what took place in his home state of Illinois. Not only did Truman win the electoral vote, but two Republican incumbents went down to defeat. They were Senator C. Wayland Brooks and Governor Dwight H. Green. Brooks was beaten by Professor Paul H. Douglas of the University of Chicago and Green by Adlai E. Stevenson II. To make matters worse in Dirksen's opinion, Scott W. Lucas, the senior senator from Illinois, became Democratic majority leader in 1949. The Democrats were thus solidly entrenched in Illinois as well as in the White House and Congress.

Following the fall elections in 1948 the Dirksens returned to Pekin to take up residence in the Carver home. After deciding to practice law for a living, Ev accepted an invitation to become a member of the Peoria law firm of Davis, Morgan, and Witherell. Before he could really get started in his new career as a lawyer, Everett was besieged by leading Illinois Republicans to return to active politics.[3] GOP leaders virtually begged Dirksen to lead them out of the political wilderness in which they found themselves by seeking either the governorship of Illinois or a seat in the U.S. Senate. Ev cared little for state office, but the prospect of a Senate seat, which appealed to him, seemed out of the question. It would be Scott Lucas who would be up for reelection in 1950. To tackle a majority leader, who was also a popular Senator and an old legion friend, seemed somewhat ludicrous. Other factors made it seem very unwise to challenge Lucas. The latter was also a down-state man and had won reelection in 1944 by a plurality of over 214,000 votes. Sensing that Ev really wanted to return to Congress, Louella and Joy, the Dirksens' daughter, promised that they would help him campaign if he wanted to try for a seat in the U.S. Senate.

In addition to Dirksen's own inner desire to return to politics on the national level, and the pressure applied by members of his own party, he was deeply disturbed by the legislative direction of the Truman administration. The Fair Deal, which to Ev meant another step toward achieving a total welfare society, included such controversial proposals as national health insurance and the Brannan plan to subsidize agriculture. The former was considered by Dirksen to be an undesirable form of socialized medicine and the latter a costly scheme devised by Agriculture Secretary Charles F. Brannan to place farming under the complete management of the federal government. Ev also began to have doubts about the advisability of renewing carte blanche the Reciprocal Trade Agreements Act, since some Illinois businessmen were complaining about unfair foreign competition. Complaints were also being made about the rapidly rising rate of inflation. By the end of February, 1949, the cost of food had risen 20 percent in just one year. Unemployment, too, had risen to over 4 million. In the face of such economic conditions Dirksen believed government spending should be reduced substantially and the unfettered free enterprise system should be given an opportunity to provide new jobs and more goods at lower prices. He considered Truman's budget request of $41,858,000,000 as being unreasonably high. It would merely add fuel to the inflationary spiral without getting the nation out of the recession it seemed to be in.

Ev was furthermore uneasy about the Point Four Program proposed by Truman to enlarge the scope of foreign aid to include U.S. assistance to the underdeveloped nations of the world. Dirksen had helped get the Marshall Plan through Congress, but he did not envision it or any other type of expanded foreign aid as a permanent fixture. During his last year in Congress Ev had proposed that Marshall Plan aid be progressively phased out and in its place American dollars be invested abroad. He saw free enterprise both as the antidote to communism and a means of bolstering the economy of lesser-developed countries while at the same time not making them permanently dependent upon the United States.[4]

Although it was not until September 18, 1949, that Everett Dirksen formally announced his candidacy for the U.S. Senate, he had made up his mind to do so by April of that year. A week before making his formal announcement Ev went to the twenty-fourth floor of the Tribune Tower in Chicago to inform Colonel McCormick of his decision to run for the U.S. Senate. The ex-congressman had hoped to secure McCormick's unreserved endorsement, since the colonel's newspaper was widely read in Illinois. "There was no deal,"[5] declared Dirksen when later queried about it by a reporter. What Ev did not tell the reporter was that the colonel had attached a condition for *Tribune* support, but it was turned down. McCormick indicated for his "newspaper help" there are "certain things you could do for us in Washington. . . ." Dirksen promptly answered, "When I am elected, if there is anything I can do for you in Washington, I would be very glad to do so. . . But not for a price." In reaction to this peremptory reply the colonel terminated the meeting with a brusque, "Good day."[6]

The political contest between Everett Dirksen and Scott W. Lucas[7] for the latter's Senate seat was an unusual one from the outset. Both men were longtime friends, having met frequently because of their mutual affiliation with the American Legion. It was Lucas, in fact, who had persuaded Ev to join. Both men lived in small, downstate river towns, Dirksen in Pekin and Lucas in Havana. Both lived in a rural environment, came from poor homes, and worked their way through college. Both started their careers in the House, Ev in 1933 and Scott in 1935. Each was considered a moderate within his respective party and each was regarded as an excellent speaker. Both gave general support to most New Deal measures, both voted for the Neutrality Act, and both opposed FDR's court-packing scheme. Dirksen and Lucas rose quickly to positions of leadership, each tending to work harmoniously with the various wings of his respective party, Ev with the liberal-internationalist and conservative-isolationist divisions in the GOP and Lucas with the liberal-northern and the conservative-southern factions. As majority leader in the Senate,

Scott Lucas frequently found himself mediating between the liberal New Dealers and the conservative Democrats. Ironically, this placating of the left and right was the identical role Dirksen would have to play in the Senate when he rose to a position of leadership in the Republican party. Ev once described this political plight to one of his Illinois constituents as follows:

> There are times when the middle road is the proper course to pursue and especially so in view of the extreme thinking with which one must contend both left and right. I am afraid some of my friends forget that my job as party leader is to bring about a maximum area of agreement between the extremes in the party. Has it ever occurred to you how far apart Senator [Barry] Goldwater on the one hand and Senator [Jacob] Javits on the other really are, yet both are voting Republicans in the Senate.[8]

Wearing two hats, one as the senior senator from Illinois and the other as the Democrat majority leader, Scott Lucas likewise found himself in a quandary on more than one occasion. Lucas voted for the Taft-Hartley Act in 1948 but upon becoming majority leader in 1949 had to lead the fight for its repeal. His differences with Harry S. Truman surfaced again when he voted to override the president's veto of the Internal Security Act of 1950. Two key programs of the Fair Deal, which Lucas was supposed to guide through the Senate, were national health insurance and the Brannan plan. Lucas opposed both. In a lukewarm fashion he shepherded through the Agriculture Act of 1949 but without the inclusion of Agriculture Secretary Charles Brannan's proposals, and through inaction shelved health insurance, which he regarded as socialized medicine. Scott Lucas also wanted to cut the Truman budget but had to remain silent on that issue. Likewise, he was not keen on Truman's intervention in Korea, yet he had to defend it 100 percent as the Senate spokesman for the administration.

Everett Dirksen and Scott Lucas both had their problems in establishing their political posture for the 1950 senatorial election. Dirksen finally received the support of the Chicago *Tribune* and because of it had to deny repeatedly that he was Colonel McCormick's political puppet. Lucas was an administration spokesman and because of his role simply could not disassociate himself from controversial Fair Deal measures or disavow certain mistakes in foreign policy. Dirksen had united GOP support, but Republicans had been routed in 1948 and held no important state positions. Lucas had Senator Paul H. Douglas and Governor Adlai E. Stevenson to help him but would be victimized by a scandal involving the Cook County Democratic organization. Dirksen was backed by business, the medical profession, and the Illinois Agricultural Association (state Farm Bureau), while being opposed by organized labor. Lucas was given tremendous backing by both the American Federation of Labor (AFL) and the Congress of Industrial Organization (CIO) but received only lukewarm support from black leaders since Truman's civil rights program was hamstrung by southern Democrats.

To prepare for his election battle in 1950, Lucas had his staff research Dirksen's voting record. The result was a two-volume document cleverly titled: "The Diary of a Chameleon: Being the 'Record' of Everett McKinley Dirksen in the Congress of the United States (1933-1948)." Its final assessment was:

> *He has literally stood for nothing.* One can employ the statements of Dirksen to sustain and support the most extremely liberal legislation on the one hand and at the same time the most reactionary legislation on the other.
> It should be stated that one cannot review intensively the legislative record of Everett Dirksen . . . without coming to the very definite conclusion that he is a man of the greatest insincerity and hypocrisy. He has been alternately a rabid isolationist and an ardent internationalist.[9]

Under different circumstances Lucas and Dirksen could have found a large area of agreement, but pitted against one another in a political campaign, much like Lincoln and Douglas in 1858, their differences were grossly exaggerated. Both also would be guilty of obfuscation, hyperbolical aggrandizement, and self-serving statements. In this rock-'em, sock-'em campaign both candidates were not above allowing verbal blandishments to sink to the level of political cant and exaggerated rhetoric. The adversary nature of a one-on-one campaign, pitting a challenger against an incumbent, increased the tendency to take cheap shots for partisan advantage rather than foster rational debate.

Everett Dirksen not only had the advantage of starting his campaign much earlier than his opponent, but as the challenger he was in the position to play the role of critic. It was Ev's overall strategy to make Lucas a symbolic surrogate for the entire Truman administration. Therefore Dirksen campaigned against the Fair Deal and Truman's foreign policy as if Lucas, as majority leader, were responsible for all of it. In fact, at times, Dirksen made the 1950 election a referendum on the past performance of the Democrats from the New Deal onward.

On a tactical level Ev used the ploy of challenging Lucas to debate him face to face. This is something incumbents do not like to do, since it only gives exposure to their lesser-known challengers. Lucas refused to do so although once Senator Paul Douglas stood in for the majority leader as a substitute debater. They debated the merits of the Marshall Plan and the effectiveness, or ineffectiveness from Ev's point of view, of the foreign policy forged by the Democrats during and since the conclusion of World War II. Douglas, too, had difficulty in making the charge stick that Dirksen's movement from isolationist to internationalist and then back to isolationist was evidence of inconsistency. Douglas himself had formerly been a pacifist and an isolationist. It was not until 1935, when Benito Mussolini announced Italy's invasion of Ethiopia that Douglas renounced his pacifism to become an interventionist. The erstwhile University of Chicago professor of economics also had been a socialist who was once highly critical of the New Deal. Thus charges of who was consistent or not, or who waffled on the issues, had little merit. All of the principals—Dirksen, Lucas, and Douglas—had past records that indicated both equivocating and making major shifts in position on key issues.

From Dirksen's vantage point the most important issues in the 1950 campaign were the Korean War, communism, creeping socialism, and corruption. From the moment the U.S. became involved in Korea, Ev focused his attention on it. In a speech at the Republican State Convention in Peoria in the fall of 1950, Ev excoriated President Truman and Secretary of State Dean

Acheson for their "bungling and blundering which they would like us to bury in nonpartisan silence." Dirksen blamed Acheson, whom he called a "veritable genius for error," for letting it be known publicly that South Korea was outside of the U.S. defense perimeter. This mistake, Ev claimed, encouraged the invasion by the North Koreans. "We must put the responsibility where it belongs," Dirksen demanded. "Anything less than this would be a moral disservice to the holy young dead who are already coming back in wooden boxes from Korea."[10]

Once having established the political fact that the Democrats were responsible for the Korean tragedy, Dirksen broadened his assault to include the blunders of FDR's foreign policy. To his partisan GOP audience he claimed, "But we appeased Stalin at Yalta by selling Poland and China into his hands whereby communism could thrust itself deep into Europe and expand its domain in Asia by adding 450 million people in China." Ev pointed out to a nodding and excited crowd that since 1945 the United States had spent nearly $90 billion for military purposes which now seemed wasted. The Truman administration had likewise formulated the North Atlantic Treaty Organization (NATO). "For months, the Senator from Havana has been declaiming that peace is the issue," stated Ev. "For months, he has been asserting that the Marshall Plan is cheaper than war—that it is a bargain," Dirksen reminded fellow Republicans. "For months," repeated Ev, "Lucas has extolled the virtues of the Atlantic Pact as a guarantee of peace." Linking Lucas to Korea, Ev emphasized that the incumbent's "endless declamations of what he has done for peace . . . are now lost in the noise of gunfire from Korea."[11]

Dirksen then broadened the thrust of his campaign salvos to denounce the Democrats for their "long and steady sitdown strike against action on Reds and Pinks on the home front." Ev contended, "Has it ever occurred to you that had it not been for the Republicans in Congress Alger Hiss [convicted for perjury] would still be occupying a high position in the State Department?" Dirksen's dragonnade against the Truman administration included mention of the Brannan plan, socialized medicine, an unbalanced budget, high taxes, inflation, bureaucratic corruption, and "failure to re-appraise the foreign aid programs in the light of our capacity to bear these burdens. . . ."[12] Obviously, in any campaign and of whatever party, the outs generally blame the ins for everything bad while the ins take credit for everything good. In this instance Ev, as the challenger, had the upper hand. Lucas was put on the defensive and never could mount an offensive. When Lucas did disavow support for socialized medicine and the Brannan plan, Dirksen could counter with the charge: "Men like Lucas can throw their convictions overboard with all the ease of the man on the flying trapeze for the sake of political victory."[13]

The temper and tone of the 1950 campaign were reflected in newspaper coverage. Dirksen always seemed to be on the offensive as indicated by these captions: "Korea War Bred by Democratic Errors—Dirksen" (Chicago *Tribune,* July 11); "Dirksen Says Scott Lucas Coddles Reds" (Herrin *Journal,* September 14); "Dirksen Hits 'Creeping Socialism' " (Chicago *Sun-Times,* September 26); "Dirksen Calls Democratic Plan Backdoor Socialism" (Clinton *Journal,* September 30); and "Dirksen Campaign Geared to Top Speed" (Chicago *Daily News,* September 28).

In contrast, the press captions covering Lucas reflect a defensive attitude and thus influenced public opinion negatively. Examples are: "Scott Lucas Still Refuses to Debate Everett Dirksen" (Dixon *Telegraph,* October 9); "Lucas Ignores Dirksen Request to Hold Debate" (Watseka *Times,* October 12); "Polish Sellout Denied by Lucas" (Peoria *Journal,* October 16); "Lucas Defends Yalta Pact" (Marion *Republic,* October 16); and "Lucas Counters GOP Charges of Bungling" (Quincy *Herald-Whig,* October 25).

In politics the capricious and unanticipated happenings can and do alter the best laid plans of even the most seasoned campaigner. Two events occurred, unexpected intangibles, which greatly influenced the outcome of the campaign. The first took place on October 23 when Lucas was felled by a virus condition that took him out of the campaign until November 6. Fighting off laryngitis, Senator Lucas made his last feeble appeal for votes on a statewide radio hookup. In this broadcast Lucas described the Marshall Plan, NATO, and the Korean War as "bold steps to block the ruthless forces of communism." He boasted that the "facts show that all the decisive blows against communism in this country have been struck under Democratic leadership." The majority leader likewise praised the Truman administration for "more than sixty-two million jobs, the highest incomes in history, and the highest level of farm prosperity."[14]

The second event to hamper Lucas's election effort was far more significant in its repercussion. A veritable bombshell was exploded by the Chicago *Sun-Times,* a liberal and usually Democratic newspaper, on November 2, just five days before election day. An investigative reporter, Ray Brennan, purloined secret testimony given before Senator Estes Kefauver's Special Committee to Investigate Organized Crime in Interstate Commerce. Lucas had specifically asked the Tennessee Democrat not to bring his crime committee to Chicago before election day. Kefauver felt it imperative that his committee go immediately to Chicago when two men, Bill Drury and Marvin Baas, both of whom were investigating organized crime in Cook County, were murdered within twenty-four hours of each other.

Secret testimony was taken from Daniel Gilbert, a captain in the Chicago police force, who was also the Democratic candidate for sheriff of Cook County. This testimony, which was not supposed to be released until after the election, came out prematurely when reporter Brennan posed as a member of Kefauver's committee and got hold of the official transcript.[15] It revealed that Gilbert, dubbed the "richest cop in the world," confessed to financial assets of $360,000. He blithely attributed his wealth to good fortune in gambling. Concerning Gilbert's gambling, Rudolph Halley, chief counsel for the Kefauver Committee, posed the question, "This gambling you do—that is not legal gambling, is it?" Incredible as it may seem, Gilbert answered, "Well, no. No, it is not legal. No."[16] Also depreciatory was the fact that previously, while working for eighteen years as the chief investigator for the state's attorney general, Gilbert's work had never culminated in the conviction of an important gangster. He had been slated for sheriff by Colonel Jacob Arvey, chairman of the Cook County Democratic organization, against the advice of both Lucas and Douglas, but the Democratic party boss, for reasons known only to himself, insisted upon doing so. The exposé was devastating in and of itself, but coupled with earlier disclosures of organized gambling in Mason County (including Havana), it cast an aura of guilt by association upon Lucas. These revelations resulted from raids conducted by the state police. Governor Adlai E. Stevenson wrote apologetically to Lucas, "I am distressed if the state police anti-gambling raid in Logan and Mason Counties caused you any embarrassment . . . . I personally knew nothing about the raid and am sorry it was scheduled for such an awkward time."[17]

Lucas might have weathered the adverse publicity surrounding local gambling, but the Gilbert performance before the Kefauver committee was too much. Page after page of secret testimony made Gilbert out to be insensitive to the proper decorum and behavior expected of a law enforcement officer. On November 7, 1950, many Republicans won offices in Cook County because of the Gilbert affair. Gilbert, by the way, lost his bid for sheriff by over 300,000 votes.

Everett Dirksen, meanwhile, returned to Pekin to wrap up his marathon campaign. His canvass for votes had required great physical stamina on his part. He and his family had lived on the road for so long it was nice just to have a home-cooked meal for a change. On election eve Ev joined in a torchlight parade that wound around the main streets of his home town. With red flares lighting up his yard, making visible a sign reading "Walk In," hosts of friends dropped in to wish Ev success in his bid for the Senate.[18] Dirksen was confident of victory. He had the right feeling. Rising early on November 7, looking fresh and alert, he was ready to vote when the polls opened. With him were Louella and Joy; for the latter, who had just reached twenty-one, it was the first time she ever voted. All three were excited as they waited for the election returns to come in on the radio.

The normal voting pattern in Illinois is for Republicans to amass a large downstate vote and Democrats to win big in Cook County. In 1950 the Democratic machine, led by Jake Arvey, ground to a halt because the Gilbert scandal had caused many Chicagoans to deviate from their normal voting habit. As a result, Dirksen drew many unexpected votes from Cook County and, with his large total in downstate Illinois, won over Lucas by a

plurality of over 290,000. The exact vote was 1,951,984 for Dirksen and 1,657,630 for Lucas. Republicans were jubilant. Not only
had they upset Truman's majority leader, but they won many
unexpected national and state offices all across the country. Two
other notable Republican senatorial victors in addition to Dirksen
were Representative Richard M. Nixon of California, who won
over Democrat Helen Gahagan Douglas, and Robert A. Taft, who
won reelection to the Senate from Ohio. When the Ohioan tele-
phoned his congratulations to Dirksen on election night, Ev
quipped, "I guess we broke their backs this time."[19] The next day
Dirksen was elated to receive a telegram from former President
Herbert C. Hoover, who praised Ev for his victory with the com-
pliment, "That was magnificent!"[20] Still euphoric over his triumph,
Dirksen wrote Hoover, "I honestly believe we accomplished something for America on election day."[21]

Being the conqueror of the majority leader of the Democrats
immediately catapulted Everett M. Dirksen into the public limelight. With this newly won celebrity status Ev was besieged with
requests for speaking engagements from Republican groups all
around the nation. Guy G. Gabrielson, Republican national
chairman, promptly scheduled a cross-country speaking tour for
Dirksen. In Springfield, the capital of Illinois, GOP Sangamon
County Chairman Conrad Noll started a "Dirksen for President
Club."[22] For one so recently retired from the House, and seemingly
having terminated his involvement in politics, Dirksen's political
future now looked extraordinarily bright. Before embarking to
Washington, D.C., to start his career as a senator, Ev, with Louella
and Joy, took a well-deserved vacation in Miami, Florida. It was
the first break Ev had taken since his enforced idleness in 1948.
Dirksen would rest only briefly before once again plunging into
the maelstrom of national politics.

NOTES

1. AI-LD.
2. Unpublished memoir of Harold E. Rainville, Dec. 24, 1969, Chi-

cago Office File, EMDC, hereafter cited as Rainville Memoir, COF-EMDC.

3. "Draft Dirksen, G.O.P. Urges," Decatur *Herald and Review,* Feb. 19, 1949; and "Illinois Republicans Favor Dirksen to Lead Party in '50," *Illinois National Republican,* Apr. 25, 1950, C-EMDC.

4. EMD, "Working Our Dollars Abroad," *Atlantic* (Feb., 1948), reprint in IF-EMDC.

5. "Scott Lucas and Everett Dirksen in Hot Fight in Illinois Over Senate Seat—Outcome in Doubt," *St. Louis Post-Dispatch,* Oct. 22, 1950, copy in C-EMDC.

6. LD, *Mr. Marigold,* p. 139.

7. A more complete summary of Lucas's political career is contained in the authors' "Scott W. Lucas of Havana: His Rise and Fall as Majority Leader in the United States Senate," *Journal of the Illinois State Historical Society,* 70 (Nov., 1977), pp. 302-20.

8. EMD to Agnes T. MacMeekin, Mar. 2, 1962, GGC-EMDC.

9. "The Diary of a Chameleon: Being the 'Record' of Everett McKinley Dirksen in the Congress of the United States (1933-1948)," pp. 6-7, Papers of Scott W. Lucas, Illinois State Historical Society, Springfield, hereafter cited as SWLP-ISHS.

10. EMD, Address to Republican State Convention, Peoria, Ill., Aug. 11, 1950, text in R&R-EMDC.

11. Ibid.

12. Ibid.

13. Press Release, Charleston, Ill., Oct. 11, 1950, text in R&R-EMDC.

14. Script of statewide radio broadcast, Nov. 6, 1950, SWLP-ISHS.

15. Joseph Bruce Gorman, *Kefauver: A Political Biography* (New York: Oxford University Press, 1971), pp. 82-83.

16. Len O'Connor, *Clout: Mayor Daley and His City* (Chicago: Henry Regnery, 1975), p. 72.

17. AES to SWL, Oct. 12, 1950, SWLP-ISHS.

18. Pekin *Times,* Nov. 8, 1950, in C-EMDC.

19. Ibid.

20. Telegram, HCH to EMD, Nov. 8, 1950, Post-Presidential Papers, Herbert C. Hoover Library, hereafter cited as PPP-HCHL.

21. EMD to HCH, Nov. 17, 1950, PPP-HCHL.

22. Pekin *Times,* Aug. 15, 1950; *Illinois State Journal,* Aug. 16, 1950, in C-EMDC.

4

The Junior Senator from Illinois:
An Ally of Taft and McCarthy

EVERETT M. DIRKSEN was a man with a mission when he went to Washington to assume his post on January 3, 1951, as the junior senator from Illinois. It was his deep conviction that the Fair Deal of Harry Truman was taking the nation inexorably down the road of welfare statism. Economic freedom was being stifled, he felt, by a myriad of new government controls and regulations administered by the heavy hand of a growing bureaucracy. The time had come not only to check this trend but to roll it back to prewar levels. Senator Dirksen was equally fearful of the repercussions of the new global programs of foreign aid and military commitments initiated by the Truman administration. Instead of peace, he wondered, would this policy lead inevitably to involvement in World War III? Ev was likewise angered by the fact that American soldiers were dying in Korea while supposed allies, who had been recipients of U.S. aid, did little or nothing to help. It also aroused his ire to see American GIs sacrifice their lives on a foreign battlefield to defend freedom and self-determination while at home alleged communists and their left-wing sympathizers spoke out against the war.

In his zeal to save the country from its communist enemies at home and abroad, Senator Dirksen acted conscientiously in terms of how he viewed their threat on the domestic scene and in world affairs. Courage and conscience, however, do not always make for clear perception and wise action. Ev felt compelled to speak out, to sound the cry of alarm for all to hear, and to fight increasingly and uncompromisingly for the good of the nation as he personally perceived it. Dirksen was deeply convinced that the truth must be told about the dangers of communism if the American people were to react positively in defense of their freedoms to ensure the country's survival as a bastion of democracy. What Ev did not realize, but would learn in time, was that anticommunist zealotry can run roughshod over constitutional rights. What Dirksen failed to take into consideration was the idea expressed by the theologian Hans Küng, "The neglect of truthfulness leads to hypocrisy, but the exaggeration of truthfulness leads to destructive fanaticism."[1] In short, the anticommunist crusade of the Cold War era sometimes degenerated into irrational hysteria.

The day after becoming the junior senator from Illinois, Everett Dirksen celebrated his fifty-fifth birthday. Representative Harold Velde, Ev's Republican successor in the Illinois Sixteenth Congressional District, threw a party in Dirksen's honor. This was to become an annual event and over the years it became a status symbol in socially conscious Washington to be invited to Ev's birthday party. On this, the first of these celebrated parties, the occasion became more of a GOP victory celebration than a birthday party. Present, in addition to family and former colleagues from the House, were Senate Minority Leader Kenneth S. Wherry of Nebraska, Robert A. Taft of Ohio, and Joseph R. McCarthy of Wisconsin. Dirksen regarded Taft as the real GOP leader in the Senate. He admired Taft (who chaired the Senate Republican Policy Committee) and would become his loyal political ally as well as his close friend and confidant. Ev likewise admired McCarthy for his tough anticommunist attitude, although he did not always agree with his tactics. As to Wherry, Dirksen liked him as an individual because he was such a congenial person.

Some former House members who were influential in the lower chamber, upon shifting to the upper chamber, found themselves unable to adjust to the markedly different setting of the Senate. This was not so with Everett Dirksen. The Senate was a forum ideally suited to his style. It was an exclusive club with a relatively small membership. The more intimate nature of the upper chamber and the unlimited time for debate allowed Ev to give sway to his proclivity for speechmaking. Initially he took undue advantage of this prerogative to ventilate his views at great length as if he were a spokesman for verities that would not be heard unless uttered by him. Early speeches also tended to be either overly filled with fierce fulminations or overburdened with pompous platitudes. It took awhile for Ev to discipline himself and curb his loquacity. In time he became a superb Senate debater who deftly used the spoken word to prod and persuade reluctant colleagues.

From the time Dirksen entered the upper chamber, he was courted by top GOP senators as well as by leading southern Democrats. Robert A. Taft of Ohio had his eye on the Republican presidential nomination for 1952. As one representing the Old Guard-isolationist wing of the GOP, the Ohioan wanted Ev as his political ally. Michigan's Arthur M. Vandenberg, leader of the Republican internationalists and an architect of America's bipartisan foreign policy, strove to win Dirksen over to his side. The Democrats only controlled the Senate by a margin of two, which meant that a voting coalition of Taft Republicans and conservative southern Democrats was highly effective in blocking much of Truman's Fair Deal program. Because Democratic Majority Leader Ernest McFarland of Arizona (who would be defeated two years later by Barry Goldwater) was a weak leader, the power wielded by the veteran Richard Russell of Georgia was enormous. The Georgian went out of his way to extend the hand of friendship to Everett Dirksen and thus strengthen the ties of southern Democrats with midwestern Republicans.

The competition among GOP factions for Dirksen's support worked to his advantage. Senator Taft maneuvered to have Ev named chairman of the Republican Senatorial Campaign Committee in 1951. This was an unusual assignment for a freshman senator. No doubt Taft was looking toward the following year when he would seek the GOP presidential nomination. Dirksen did support Taft's candidacy in 1952 and, in the following year, when the Ohioan was Senate majority leader, Ev was rewarded with three important committee assignments—Appropriations, Judiciary, and Government Operations. The latter committee was chaired by Joseph McCarthy of Wisconsin. McCarthy had already pandered to Ev's ambitions in 1951 when the Wisconsinite played a leading role in getting Dirksen on the Rules Committee. This maneuver, made possible when Kenneth Wherry died, was aimed surreptitiously at getting Dirksen the chairmanship of the Rules Subcommittee on Elections.

McCarthy's game plan, which in due time worked, was to give Dirksen the post held by Margaret Chase Smith of Maine. Her "Declaration of Conscience," which was critical of McCarthy's tactics, angered the Wisconsinite no end. He laid secret plans to push her off the subcommittee. This plan came to fruition after her subcommittee conducted an investigation into the celebrated defeat of Senator Millard Tydings (D-Md.). Her findings, embodied in the Smith report, claimed that a photograph, widely circulated during the election campaign, showing Tydings standing next to Earl Browder, a longtime head of the Communist party, was a deliberately doctored picture. Use of such a phony photostat was deemed "false, malicious, devoid of simple decency and common honesty." The report furthermore stated that this tactic was a "shocking abuse of the spirit and intent of the First Amendment to the Constitution."[2] Although Dirksen did not condone misrepresentation of this kind, he did benefit by McCarthy's power move. With Wherry dead, H. Styles Bridges of New Hampshire became minority leader. Bridges was an indifferent leader who paid deference to Taft and McCarthy. Dirksen's power and influence in the Senate increased, therefore, in direct proportion to the closeness of his political alliance with the powerful duo of Taft and McCarthy.

When the Dirksens returned to Washington, D.C., in 1951, they did not resume living in the Mayflower Hotel but leased a modest flat at the Berkshire Apartments on Massachusetts Avenue. Ev was not above walking to the Capitol, but more frequently took the bus. Their daughter, Joy, lived with them until her marriage on December 22, 1951, to Howard H. Baker, Jr., a lawyer from Huntsville, Tennessee, and the son of Representative Howard Baker (R-Tenn.). In 1966 Howard Baker, Jr., would win election to the U.S. Senate and serve under his father-in-law, who was then minority leader. Senator Baker would himself become minority leader in 1977, a presidential candidate in 1980, and majority leader in 1981.

In the Senate Everett Dirksen was as energetic in fulfilling his duties as he had been in the House of Representatives. He devoted much time and effort to meeting the responsibilities delegated to him by virtue of his chairmanship of the Republican Senatorial Campaign Committee. As a kind of political luminary within his own party for having defeated Scott Lucas, he was in great demand as a speaker and fund raiser. In many ways he was a more formidable representative and spokesman for the Taft wing of the GOP than Taft himself. The Ohioan engendered deep respect among his loyal followers as a man of high principle and one who was a fearless advocate of old-time Republicanism, but Taft's austere demeanor and colorless platform style were negative factors in terms of crowd appeal. "Mr. Republican," as Taft was called, was blessed with a sharp mind and personal charm but lacked the ability to sway audiences or project any public charisma. In contrast to Robert Taft, or Joseph McCarthy for that matter, Senator Dirksen could charm audiences. Ev was a raconteur from whose lips a bon mot came effortlessly.

Soon after becoming a senator, Dirksen was asked to appear on a television program called the "American Forum of the Air" to debate the senior senator from Illinois, Paul Douglas. Ev accepted, of course, and discovered TV was a wonderful new medium for him. The mellow tones of his voice, his craggy features, and the flamboyant style of his delivery were intensified for the viewer by seeing and hearing him simultaneously.

In 1951, liberal Democrats were charging that Senator Dirksen was an ultrareactionary, an isolationist, a member of the Old Guard in the GOP, and a mouthpiece for big business. Rejecting these allegations, Ev regarded himself as a "moderationist"[3] in both foreign and domestic policy. He was not calling for repeal of the New Deal nor was he advocating total withdrawal from international commitments. He was, in fact, a typical Cold War warrior in his anticommunist stance and, like many liberals at the time, was a globalist. Ev was insisting upon containing communism abroad and strengthening the free enterprise system at home. Whether right or wrong he did believe capitalism was so intertwined with democracy in American history that the death of the former would lead inevitably to the doom of the latter. To Dirksen economic liberty and personal freedom were a tandem set of tenets indispensable to a free society.

To a graduating class at DePaul University in Chicago, Ev asserted, "Freedom is the flaming moral issue of our times." He explained: "Today more than ever, freedom is being challenged from within. It is challenged by the moral cripples who would destroy it; by those who would socialize America in the image of the Old World; by those who have completely twisted the very meaning of the word 'freedom'; and by those bogus philosophers who look upon man as a means and not as an end. . . . Without it, there can be no lasting peace. . . . It is doubtful that the Christian Destiny can be fulfilled without freedom." The Illinois senator concluded his remarks with the asservation: "Long ago Tacitus observed that 'Genius died by the same blow that ended public liberty.'"[4]

To implement his philosophy Dirksen took the initiative in the Senate to introduce legislation or, in some cases, to make use of the amendatory process to mold bills more to his liking. He was one of the first members of Congress to react to the drug problem. In 1951 Ev introduced S. 1702 to extend provisions of the federal criminal code to "persons convicted of violating certain narcotic laws."[5] It would have provided for prison terms of from two to five years for importers and sellers, and the death sentence for those selling drugs to minors. As a war veteran Dirksen wanted military personnel in Korea to be eligible for the so-called G.I. Bill. His S. 1720 would "extend to persons in the active service of the Armed Forces on or after June 27, 1950, certain benefits provided by law for veterans of World War II."[6] In order to strengthen Truman's loyalty program, Ev dropped S. 1849 in the Senate hopper. It would "authorize the release of the personnel files of federal officers and employees to congressional committees."[7] S. 1971, another Dirksen proposal, would "establish a Commission on the Public Debt"[8] empowered to investigate and make recommendations relating to fiscal policies and management of the national debt. Of these bills only the extension of the G.I. Bill to Korean War veterans passed because it was also an administration measure.

On March 6, 1951, Senator Dirksen introduced a Senate resolution calling for an expression of sentiment on the part of the members of the upper chamber in support of a "Free Ireland."[9] Ever since visiting Ireland as a soldier following World War I, Ev had taken a liking to the Irish. He felt Britain should allow Ireland to unite and not keep part of it as a satellite. When John F. Kennedy entered the Senate in 1953 he and Dirksen periodically cosponsored a similar resolution. Ev sincerely subscribed to the principle of self-determination, but his resolution had no effect on British public opinion. It did serve, however, to please the Irish-Americans in Boston and Chicago. In this sense it was good politics to twist the British lion's tail even though it contributed little toward settling the Irish question.

When President Harry Truman relieved General Douglas MacArthur from his command in Korea in 1951, Everett Dirksen defended the deposed general. In a speech to a convention of Missouri Republicans, Ev decried the fact that "the drift is toward the 38th parallel [the boundary between North and South Korea] precisely where we started fourteen months ago, except that since then 80,000 young Americans are inscribed on the casualty list. The slogan seems to be 'anything but victory.' "[10] At another time Dirksen demanded "elimination of the Yalu River [the boundary between North Korea and the People's Republic of China] insanity that permits communist forces to maintain sanctuary behind that border."[11] Previous to this occasion Dirksen declared, "If America wants to prevent a third world war, we must liquidate politically the men who have a penchant for war."[12] This theme had been used before in a Senate speech when Ev asked, "Which is the War Party?" His voice was tinged with sarcasm as he spoke: "So the Democratic Party is the party of peace. There is the naked record in 1917. There is the record in 1941. There is the record in 1950. Peace?"[13]

Because Ev's mail on the Truman-MacArthur episode (over 100,000 pieces) was 90 percent in favor of the general, Dirksen was on safe political ground in criticizing the president. However, when Truman sought to contain the war and keep it limited, Ev criticized that also. Obviously Dirksen was exploiting Truman's conduct of the war, some by legitimate criticism, and some by expediency. This was possible since it was not clear to the public just what constituted U.S. policy. Was it liberation of North Korea or merely defense of South Korea?

When the Mutual Security bill came before the Senate in 1951, Dirksen led a major fight to reduce appropriations for foreign aid. He introduced an amendment calling for a modest cut of $500 million from the proposed figure of $7,535,750,000 requested by the Truman administration. Eventually Ev succeeded in getting a reduction of only $250 million.

In the ensuing debate Dirksen took the floor on August 31 to give a lengthy and much-publicized speech. His opening argument was that a specific schedule should be set to phase out the Marshall Plan, now called the European Recovery Program (ERP), lest it become "more or less perpetual." Legislatively establishing some definitive end to a program is now called a "Sunset Law." He then posed the question about the large communist vote in France's last election: "So, I begin to wonder, in an hour of trial and challenge, are they going to be in our corner, or whether five million people who have solemnly indicated by marking a ballot that their sentiments are on the Red side are probably going to sabotage what we intend to do over there. Is that the favor, is that the reward of the billions of dollars we have already spent in France?" Dirksen then asked, "When we look at Britain, what do we find?" He gave the answer: "An anti-American peace crusade is under way there at the present time. Frankly, I think the American people are becoming a little sick and tired of doling out money to keep a lavish, paternalistic, socialistic system going for people who are unwilling to make the sacrifice which we have a right to expect them to make."[14]

Getting his second wind, Dirksen continued his verbal assault on the foreign aid program. Voicing concern about the solvency of the United States and its ability to spend billions annually, Ev declared, "It seems to me that 'give-away' has become a mania. It is astonishing what a strange passion has grown up in the country that a checkbook is a cure for every problem, foreign and domestic."[15]

Senator Dirksen concluded his presentation in favor of reducing appropriations for the Marshall Plan by comparing the amount of the gross national income spent by the United States for military defense and that expended by recipients of aid from the European Recovery Program. The U.S. was spending at a 20 percent level whereas the highest for any ERP country was 9.3 percent, with most being far below that figure. "Is it quite fair?" Dirksen queried. He reasoned: "I think the time has come when there must be a more tangible and persuasive manifestation of will and spirit on the part of those who have been the recipient of American largess. Until that time, I think, among other things, that we have a responsibility to think also about the self-preservation of America and to think about the inordinate burden which is being pressed upon our compassionate and humble people."[16]

Because of Dirksen's prominence in leading the economy fight against the Truman administration, there were those in Republican circles who wanted to tout Ev as a candidate in the race for the 1952 GOP presidential nomination. In a poll of 3,000 Republicans, taken in June of 1951, which included the delegates and alternates of the last two GOP national nominating conventions, the serial rankings for president were Taft, MacArthur, Eisenhower, and Dirksen. For the vice-presidency the order was Taft, Dirksen, MacArthur, and Eisenhower.[17] In a secret poll of Republican House members in the fall of 1951 the choice for president ran as follows: Taft—71; Eisenhower—54; MacArthur—14; Dirksen—13; and Governor Earl Warren of California—5.[18] Back in Illinois, key Republicans were pushing hard for Ev's candidacy as the head of the national ticket. Conrad Noll, GOP Sangamon County chairman, sponsored a Springfield rally at which the Dirksen for President Club was founded.[19] In October of 1951 the Republican Central Committee of Illinois overwhelmingly endorsed Dirksen as its state's favorite son.[20]

All of these efforts to promote Dirksen for the presidency were for naught. Ev had long before committed himself heart and soul to the candidacy of Senator Robert A. Taft of Ohio—the Mr. Republican of his times. Ev made his preference known publicly on September 11, 1951, on a "Meet the Press" television program.

When reporter May Craig asked him whether he would support Taft or Ike for the GOP presidential nomination, Dirksen answered without hesitation, "Bob Taft." Ev was then asked to explain his choice. He replied, "I'm for him because first of all he is a colleague, secondly he is a friend, and third we sort of speak the same language when it comes to the fundamental things."[21] This was a magnanimous decision for a politically ambitious man such as Dirksen because it was an opportune time for him to seek the Republican presidential nomination. Furthermore, it virtually ruled out any hopes for the vice-presidency. Taft and Dirksen represented the same wing of the GOP, and the states of Illinois and Ohio were too close geographically for a balanced ticket. On November 19 Dirksen was named head of Taft's campaign in Illinois, and in December Ev opened the headquarters for the Illinois Robert Taft for President Committee at Chicago. Dirksen's aide, Harold E. Rainville, was designated executive secretary of the committee.[22] Ev's efforts on behalf of Taft paid off in January of 1952. He was named to the Senate Rules Committee even though he already held an assignment on Banking and Currency.

One of the disadvantages Senator Taft had to overcome in seeking the presidential nomination was the fact that he had taken public stands on the extremely controversial issues of the day. On the other hand, no one knew precisely where General Dwight D. Eisenhower stood on any issue. In order to force Eisenhower to speak up, Dirksen sent a telegram to Senator Henry Cabot Lodge, Jr. (R-Mass.), a leading promoter of Eisenhower's candidacy, with the following message: "The Republican voters of this country are entitled to know whether the candidate, who only a few months ago couldn't say whether he was a Democrat or a Republican, is now an advocate of Republican or Democratic national policies. . . . Certainly we are entitled to know from your candidate himself where he stands on just eight national issues. . . ." Enumerated were the following [with authors' brackets to indicate Taft's position]: Taft-Hartley Act [against repeal], federal Fair Employment Practices Commission [reluctant to expand its power], Social Security benefits [against raising], military spending [maintain at present level], taxes [lower], foreign aid [reduce], Brannan plan for agriculture [opposed], and national health insurance [disapproved of it as being the equivalent of socialized medicine]. Dirksen concluded the telegram, which he made public, with the assertion, "Senator Taft's positions on all national issues are well known."[23]

The fight for the 1952 GOP presidential nomination soon narrowed down to a bitter contest between Taft and Eisenhower. The Midwest was Taft's stronghold and his supporters within the Republican party came primarily from Congress. The Ohioan represented the conservative-isolationist wing of the GOP which had not been able to name a presidential candidate since the days of Herbert Hoover. Eisenhower was being championed by Senator Lodge and Governor Thomas E. Dewey of New York. The latter two were key spokespersons for the eastern-liberal-internationalist faction of the party. Ike's supporters advanced the argument that their man was a famous war hero who could win the general election whereas Taft was a colorless politician doomed to defeat because he could attract no Democratic votes.

Dirksen tried to counter this negative image attached to Taft by stressing his great personal virtues. When introducing Senator Taft to a convention of District of Columbia Republicans, for instance, Ev reasoned: "He did not come by the title of Mr. Republican by accident. It is a deserved honor. . . . He has the moral courage to disdain the easy and expedient course. He dares to differ even when politics might dictate otherwise. He is not only Mr. Republican but also Mr. Integrity." Bringing it out in the open and thereby hoping to quash it, Dirksen took issue with the charge that Taft was a sure loser. "The subtle rumor has gone forth that he is probably our most capable candidate but that he cannot win," noted Ev. "The answer is that he has been winning under a constant baptism of fire."[24]

When the Republican National Convention convened in Chicago on July 8, the Taft forces claimed to have more than the 604 delegates needed to win. Senator Dirksen, who headed the 60 delegates from Illinois (of whom all but 1 were strongly pledged to Taft), knew the Ohioan had no more than a little over 500. Ev, nevertheless, felt confident Taft would take the nomination. Dirksen and a throng of Taftites were at Midway Airport to meet their favorite candidate. A chant immediately went up from the crowd, "Taft for me, Taft for you, Taft will win in fifty-two."[25]

At the convention hall, however, things did not look good for Taft. Senator Lodge and other pro-Eisenhower leaders planned to contest sixty-eight seats from the delegations of Georgia, Louisiana, and Texas on the basis they were not selected fairly. Southern delegates were often handpicked by state party leaders on the basis of their own personal preference and not on which presidential candidate was more popular. Pro-Eisenhower forces considered this an unfair procedure and planned to conduct a floor fight to contest the seating of these three delegations. Senator John Bricker of Ohio, a Taft man, sought to get the upper hand by making a motion for the convention to adopt the same rules used to govern the proceedings of the 1948 convention. Adoption of this motion would have meant that the contested delegates, who had been approved by the Republican National Committee, would be allowed to participate and vote on convention business even before they had been certified by the Credentials Committee and accepted by the convention.

The strategy of the Eisenhower forces was to have Governor Arthur B. Langlie of Washington propose a "Fair Play Amendment."[26] It would deprive the sixty-eight contested delegates of the right to vote or participate in convention business unless they had received approval of more than 80 percent of the 106-member national committee. Representative Clarence Brown of Ohio, a loyal Taft supporter, rose to offer an amendment to the Fair Play Amendment. Brown's amendment would have exempted seven of Louisiana's delegates from any rules revision of the convention because the legality of their selection was not being disputed. It was hoped by Taftites that a vote on this less controversial (and more defensible) issue would give them an early convention victory. The Brown amendment, to the surprise of the Taft camp, went down to defeat, 658 to 548. The convention then went on to adopt the Fair Play Amendment by a voice vote. Robert Taft had suffered a stunning defeat on the first day of the convention.

On the following day the Credentials Committee, controlled by pro-Taft people, voted 31 to 20 to approve seating the contested pro-Taft Georgia delegation. Senator Lodge and Governor Dewey, as planned, took the matter to the convention floor. Their cohort, Governor Sherman Adams of New Hampshire, moved that the recommendation of the Credentials Committee be set aside so that the pro-Eisenhower Georgia delegation could be seated. What it meant was, whose delegates were to be approved? Those of Eisenhower or those of Taft? A vote on this motion was crucial since it would determine whether the forces of Taft or those of Eisenhower controlled the convention. Obviously, such a decision would indicate clearly which of the two would be nominated for the presidency even before a formal vote was taken. Amid these floor fights, Dirksen had striven to keep his own Illinois delegation in line for Taft. On the Brown amendment the Illinois delegation voted 58 to 2 for it in a losing cause. Senator Taft now called upon Dirksen to take the podium and present the case for the majority report of the Credentials Committee. Ev had already prepared his speech for nominating Taft but dutifully responded to this emergency call by quickly improvising a new speech.

The thousands of delegates, alternates, and visitors in the galleries quieted down as Everett Dirksen stood motionless at the podium. Millions watching and listening on television were somewhat in awe that Ev actually got the mass of humanity quiet before beginning his address. In his breathy, baritone voice Dirksen began to speak: "And so, in the time available to me let us reason for a moment with a sense of responsibility that is becoming to the trustees of the Republican Party who are assembled in this Convention tonight." He reminded them, "We have a habit of winning conventions and losing elections in the last twenty years."

Sitting in the front row at the head of his New York delegation was Governor Thomas E. Dewey. With a confident smile, he watched and listened to Dirksen trying to use all his oratorical skill and political wile to persuade the delegates to defeat the Adams motion. It would be the only way to save Bob Taft. Dewey knew it and Dirksen knew it. Carried away by the emotion of the moment and frequently ad-libbing comments to his hastily prepared text, Ev's voice reached a crescendo. He looked down at Governor Dewey, pointing his finger at him, and spoke words that would reverberate for months to come. "To my friends from

New York: when my friend, Tom Dewey, was the candidate in 1944 and 1948 I tried to be one of his best campaigners, and you ask him whether or not I didn't go into eighteen states one year, and twenty-three states the next. Reexamine your hearts before you take this action in support of the Minority Report, because we followed you before and you took us down the path of defeat."[27] The convention exploded with a mixture of applause and boos. Excited cries of support for the statement clashed with thunderous catcalls of disapproval.

Everett Dirksen was utterly surprised by the hostile reaction of the pro-Eisenhower delegates to his remarks aimed at Dewey. The pandemonium continued out of control as Taft and Ike followers taunted each other. Finally Ev was constrained to plead: "Will the delegates please take their seats? This is no place for Republicans to be booing any other Republican." A rippling of applause greeted his last remark. "Fellow delegates," Dirksen asserted, "I assure you that I didn't mean to precipitate a controversy."[28] He really did not.

In a letter to a friend a few days later Dirksen sheepishly explained: "I hope my remarks to the Convention did not convey the impression that I was making a personal attack on Governor Dewey or any other person. I thought I was simply expressing a fact and making a plea for what I esteemed to be the welfare and the victory chances of our party in November."[29]

Ev was astonished by the crowd reaction to his "you took us down the path of defeat" remark, but once the words were uttered they could not be recalled. It had inadvertently added another element to the bitterness between the warring Taft and Eisenhower camps and made Dirksen persona non grata to Dewey and many eastern Republicans. Oddly enough, on live TV it was an exciting drama. This speech made Ev the star of the convention even though it was in a losing cause. He was instantly a national celebrity. Typical of the acclaim he received was a congratulatory letter telling him, "You were the one who emerged from the convention as the leader of our kind of Republicans."[30] It was from ex-President Herbert C. Hoover. The Adams motion to accept the minority report, which seated the pro-Eisenhower Georgia delegates, won by a vote of 607 to 531. Despite a gallant try, it was a despondent Dirksen who hastily conferred with Taft on how certain defeat could be averted.

Dirksen was enough of a pro to realize that the momentum was now with the Eisenhower camp, yet he would remain steadfast in his loyalty to Taft right up to the bitter end. Ev had kept the Illinois delegation in line when it voted 59 to 1 to reject the seating of Eisenhower's delegates from Georgia. It was Dirksen's duty now to make the Taft nomination speech. Then he would see to it the Ohioan received the 59 votes due him from Illinois. Before mounting the podium again, Ev had been besieged by reporters and television interviewers. Most wanted to hear if there would be more verbal fireworks. The strategy embodied in Ev's nominating speech was simple enough. He would seek to counter the allegation that Taft could not win and then to contrast his candidate's political qualifications with those of the inexperienced Eisenhower. To be stressed also was the moral right of Mr. Republican to be the GOP presidential nominee. Mingled amid these appeals would be the usual partisan attack upon the Democrats.

Following Dirksen's nomination of Robert A. Taft, bedlam broke out as the cheers were followed by a prolonged and noisy demonstration. But on that July 11, when the speeches were over and the demonstrations concluded, the first roll call created the real excitement. Illinois voted 59 for Taft and 1 for Eisenhower. When the roll call was finished, the tally stood 595 for Eisenhower and 500 for Taft. Eisenhower was just 9 votes short of the nomination. Victory for the general came after Senator Edward Thye of Minnesota switched his state's 19 votes from favorite son Harold E. Stassen to the Eisenhower column. This triggered off as bandwagon effect, with many vote shifts coming in quick order. Dirksen stood firm and requested no change in how Illinois would record its votes—it would stay with Taft all the way. The final count was: Eisenhower—845, Taft—280. For the record, the Eisenhower nomination was made unanimous, but there was certainly anything but unanimity within the ranks of the Republican party on that momentous day.

General Eisenhower conferred with Senator Taft immediately after receiving the presidential nomination. Later, after accepting the nomination and addressing the convention, Eisenhower met with his floor leaders and advisors to decide upon a vice-presidential running mate. When a recommendation from Taft was received, it was that the vice-presidential nod should go to Everett Dirksen.[31] Unfortunately for Ev, the rancor and bitterness caused by his hastily prepared speech in the credentials fight made him unacceptable not only to Dewey and his followers but also to others. Governor William S. Beardsley of Iowa, whom one would assume would be for a fellow midwesterner on the ticket, heatedly contended, "All I have to say is that after what Dirksen said the other night, the people of Iowa wouldn't use him to wipe their feet on."[32] The choice, at Eisenhower's suggestion, with Dewey in agreement, went to Senator Richard M. Nixon of California. Only later did Ev find out that by being thrust into battle so quickly did he talk himself out of serious contention as Eisenhower's running mate. After Nixon was ratified by the convention as the GOP vice-presidential nominee, Dirksen was asked if party harmony could be restored sufficiently to prevent Taftites from sitting out the election. Characteristically Ev responded, "I always hope that all scars will be healed. I have seen them healed before."[33]

At his Denver headquarters, Eisenhower selected his staff and made plans for the ensuing campaign against the Democratic nominee for the presidency, Governor Adlai E. Stevenson of Illinois. One of the things uppermost in his mind was how to win the wholehearted support of stalwart men like Taft and Dirksen. An invitation was sent to each to meet with Eisenhower in Denver. Dirksen was the first of the two to attend. Following a cordial talk, Ev promised to campaign for Ike "with fervor."[34] Following the meeting, Dirksen issued a statement for fellow Republicans saying, "The time has come for unity. We must close ranks like a great crusading host."[35]

Upon returning to Washington, where as chairman of the Republican Senatorial Campaign Committee he needed to make plans, Dirksen received a letter from Robert Taft. The latter informed Ev of the invitation he had received from Eisenhower. The Ohioan confided: "I am a good deal concerned with the result of such a meeting. I don't want it used (with pictures) to prove that I have now been converted to the General's principles. I don't want it made to look as if I were abandoning the principles for which I have campaigned, or abandoning my friends to the purge that so many Eisenhower supporters seem to plan for them." Dirksen was asked to sound out Senator Frank Carlson of Kansas, an early Eisenhower supporter with whom Taft enjoyed a close friendship, to set up a meeting "where the General could give certain assurances (some of these might be made public and others not)." The assurances listed were five in number:

1. That he would reduce the budget for fiscal 1953 to sixty billion dollars. . . . I don't like to ask for specific assurances on foreign policy . . . but I think we do have a right to ask that the expense not be so great as to destroy a free system here at home.
2. That no spender like Paul Hoffman be appointed Secretary of State and that Dewey not be appointed Secretary of State.
3. That he intends to support the platform pledges on the Taft-Hartley Act and not angle for the votes of labor bosses. . . .
4. There ought to be no commitment to anything like the Brannan Plan or even a flat 90 percent guarantee. . . .
5. There should be a representation on approximately equal terms in the Cabinet of Taft supporters.[36]

"If this could be worked out, I would be glad to campaign vigorously for the ticket, and urge everyone to go along," Taft made it clear to Dirksen. "Otherwise, I will support it, of course, but I think I would confine my speaking to those Senators and congressmen in whose election I am interested."[37] It was obvious that Taft was still bitter over his defeat and meant to extract concessions from Eisenhower before giving wholehearted support to the GOP presidential ticket. Ev did relay Taft's message to Frank Carlson and a meeting between the Ohioan and Eisenhower was arranged for September 12 at Morningside Heights, the official residence of the president of Columbia University, the position Eisenhower held prior to his appointment as commander of NATO. After a two-hour breakfast session, in which Eisenhower gave verbal assurances that Taft's views would not be ignored, the Ohioan was impressed by his host's genial behavior and concilliatory attitude. Without insisting upon a public commitment by Eisenhower to any specific set of political principles, Senator

Taft held a press conference to announce his full support of the man who had defeated him for the GOP presidential nomination. Taft also urged his followers to do so.[38]

As was his longtime practice, Dirksen never let intraparty rivalries prevent him from giving wholehearted support to the entire GOP ticket. Dirksen spent many months on the campaign trail giving speeches in some twenty-five states. Basically he expounded upon the GOP slogan of "Communism, Corruption, and Korea" and made searing indictments of the Truman administration while praising Eisenhower as a great leader. Most of Ev's efforts, however, were dedicated to GOP candidates running for the Senate. In rendering assistance to senatorial candidates, Ev made no distinction as to whether they were in the Eisenhower wing of the party (formerly the Dewey faction) or the Taft camp.

The results of the 1952 election were gratifying to Republicans in that Eisenhower triumphed handily over Adlai E. Stevenson, but there was less to cheer about in terms of Senate races. When the 83rd Congress convened in January the GOP controlled the upper chamber by the extremely narrow margin of one. Robert A. Taft was chosen majority leader and most of the Ohioan's lieutenants were given positions of power. Newcomers in the Senate also included Democrat John F. Kennedy of Massachusetts, who had defeated Henry Cabot Lodge, and Republican Barry Goldwater of Arizona, who had defeated Ernest McFarland. Since the latter had been majority leader for the Democrats, his defeat necessitated the selection of another leader for the now minority party. The choice made was Lyndon B. Johnson of Texas, who was both an adept parliamentarian and an adroit politician. Ev would studiously observe LBJ's tactics and would learn much from them about Senate leadership.

The Republicans in the Senate had a difficult time adjusting to their new role as majority party. Having had to oppose for so long made it hard for them to propose. Thus more often than not the GOP members of the Senate tended to treat President Eisenhower as they had Roosevelt and Truman. Taft had already made known his fears that under Eisenhower "we may get a Republican New Deal which will be a good deal harder to fight than the Democrats."[39] GOP senators, for a change, felt a sense of power and wanted to limit executive authority, cut the budget, and curtail overseas commitments. As Ev put it to an Illinois reporter, the Republicans wanted to get the "Reds on the run"[40] at home, get the shooting stopped in Korea, and drastically reduce government expenditures all across the board.

In May of 1953 Dirksen, heading a subcommittee of the Appropriations Committee, toured Asia to assess the effectiveness of foreign aid. His congressional junket covered Formosa, Japan, Korea, Indochina, and the Philippines. In Nationalist China, Ev met with Chiang Kai-shek and in South Korea he had meetings with Syngman Rhee, U.S. Ambassador Ellis D. Briggs, and the commander of the Eighth Army, General Maxwell D. Taylor. His tour of the Far East convinced him that while foreign aid was needed, much of it was being wasted. He recommended a reduction of several billion dollars in foreign aid appropriations but was only successful in getting a cut of $700 million.[41]

At home, the lack of fear exhibited by some liberals regarding the threat of internal subversion bothered Dirksen. In his zeal to thwart communism Dirksen tended to overreact to a threat that probably was not as menacing as he believed it to be. He could not understand why liberal Democrats should defend men like Alger Hiss or others alleged to have had communist contacts. Hiding behind the Fifth Amendment seemed incongruous to him when the very people using it would dispose of all free speech if their totalitarian ideology ever prevailed in the country. He feared fellow travelers and felt disdain for those who got involved with subversive groups. Ev was also of the opinion that a housecleaning was needed in the State Department to get rid of those who had forged the American foreign policy leading to what he regarded as the infamous Yalta Agreement. It was for this reason that Dirksen was one of thirteen who voted against approving President Eisenhower's appointment of Charles E. Bohlen as U.S. Ambassador to the Soviet Union. On the Senate floor Ev explained: "Chip Bohlen was at Yalta. If he were my brother, I would take the same attitude I am expressing in the Senate this afternoon. He was associated with the failure. Mr. President, in the language of Missouri, the tail must go with the hide. I reject Yalta. So I reject Yalta men."[42]

As a member of the permanent Subcommittee on Investigations of the Senate Committee on Government Operations, of which Joseph McCarthy was chairman, Dirksen joined with the Wisconsinite in an attempt to investigate communist subversion in the government. In private President Eisenhower urged Dirksen "to influence Republican members on McCarthy's committee to observe proper procedure," but McCarthy continued unabated in his overbearing way, needlessly ignoring this advice. From the beginning President Eisenhower disliked McCarthy and his tactics. He sought to wean away supporters of McCarthy in such a manner as to isolate him. One of the members of McCarthy's committee who was especially courted was Dirksen. Ev received frequent invitations from the White House to join the president in informal settings.[43] Although not yet convinced McCarthy's investigatory efforts should be suppressed, Dirksen began to exert himself more and more in an attempt to moderate McCarthy's wild, witch-hunting tactics.

The dilemma facing Dirksen was hard for him to resolve. He agreed with McCarthy's objectives, namely, that subversives should be exposed and ferreted out of the federal government. The Illinois Senator was aware that such a difficult undertaking would bring severe criticism from some quarters. It was a dirty job, he believed, yet it had to be done for the good of the country. At times, however, McCarthy's tactics did not set well with him. Particularly offensive to Ev were the contemptuous attitude of the Wisconsinite and his abusive language when dealing with dissenting colleagues in the Senate. Dirksen also realized he had a responsibility to both the president and Republican party, so he worked as a compromiser in an effort to get both McCarthy and administration officials to make concessions. Within this context he sought to mediate between McCarthy and Eisenhower. Senator Dirksen should have realized, and to his discredit he did not, that McCarthy was not the type of man to yield anything to anyone under any circumstances. Thus in his loyalty to McCarthy's goals, Dirksen did a great disservice to the very results he wished to see accomplished.

The ultimate confrontation between McCarthy and the White House resulted because of the senator's roughshod methods of conducting an investigation regarding alleged communist infiltration into the U.S. Army. By March of 1954 it was apparent at 1600 Pennsylvania Avenue that sterner measures were needed to stop McCarthy. It was Dirksen who on March 16 helped work out an agreement whereby the Army-McCarthy hearings would be conducted by a special committee of the subcommittee. McCarthy would be on this special committee but would not be chairman of it, and therefore his power would be reduced. Dirksen also recommended that a Tennessee lawyer named Ray H. Jenkins be named the committee's counsel to guarantee the observance of proper procedure.[44] Once the hearings began, hundreds of eager spectators jammed the Senate caucus room. Klieg lights were everywhere so that the ever-present television cameras could bring each day's hearing to millions of viewers watching at home. From the very start the Army-McCarthy hearings were a hit on TV with daily programs of live dramatics from Washington.

Day after day and week after week the hearings dragged on. Robert T. Stevens, secretary of the army, alone occupied the witness chair for fourteen days. Dirksen, who was a member of the special committee, was aware that the day-by-day spectacle of a Republican-dominated committee investigating its own administration was not good politics. Neither was it good for the morale of the army. Ev consulted with Karl Mundt of South Dakota, chairman of the special committee, and with Charles Potter of Michigan and Henry Dworshak of Idaho, the other GOP members, as to how they could speed up the hearings. On May 3 Ev talked with army counsel John G. Adams and special counsel Joseph N. Welch to see if a compromise could be worked out. The plan was for each side to limit the number of witnesses it would call so that a definite termination date could be foreseen. This proposal was rejected both by Stevens and Welch. General Matthew B. Ridgeway, army chief of staff, had informed the White House of his intent to let the hearings turn into a showdown. Eisenhower agreed at this point to let McCarthy hang himself in public, no matter what the consequences were. Dirksen, however, was not made aware of this and presumed his efforts had administration backing.

Although the circus-like atmosphere of the Army-McCarthy

hearings gave it high ratings on TV, Dirksen saw no point in keeping it going. He again proposed a plan to cut the hearings short. He suggested that when Stevens finished his testimony, McCarthy would be called to take the stand in public sessions. Thereafter other witnesses would be examined in executive sessions. Ev presumed that without the posturing for television and excessive speechmaking the hearings would conclude quite rapidly. Dirksen put this proposal into the form of a motion. It lost four to three when Senator Mundt voted no. The chairman had done so only when the army objected to the plan.[45] The Democrats—John McClellan of Arkansas, Henry Jackson of Washington, and Stuart Symington of Missouri—all voted no. Politically they viewed the Army-McCarthy hearings as a kind of intramural fight within the GOP, to be exploited for all it was worth.

During the course of the protracted proceedings, Dirksen himself was prompted to take the stand as a witness. This came about because of army allegations that Roy Cohn, the McCarthy committee's original counsel, had sought preferential treatment for Private G. David Schine. The latter had been on the staff of the McCarthy committee when he was drafted. Adams, the army counsel, had approached Ev on January 22 to see if the senator could prevent the McCarthy committee from issuing subpoenas relative to its investigation of Fort Monmouth (this involved a confrontation between Senator McCarthy and General Ralph W. Zwicker over a dispute concerning the promotion and honorable discharge of an army dentist named Major Irving M. Peress who was alleged to be a communist). The implication left by Adams was that if McCarthy pursued his investigation, the army would reveal how Roy Cohn tried to get special treatment for his friend David Schine.

Under oath Dirksen testified, "Frankly, as I reconstruct the conversation in my office on that afternoon, Mr. Adams came to my office for the purpose of enlisting my influence to kill those subpoenas and to stop them. I can place no other interpretation upon that action." He continued, "The thing that stuck in my mind mainly was not the pressure" to stop the army hearings, Dirksen said, but the threat of blackmail by the revelation of "an alleged effort to secure preferred treatment for a private which certainly would not look good on the front page and might enmesh every member of the subcommittee if it could be established and that we might find ourselves charged with ... neglect of duty."[46] Subsequently, after this meeting with army counsel Adams, Dirksen suggested to McCarthy, Mundt, and Potter that if this accusation were true, Roy Cohn should be dismissed as the committee's counsel. Ev also thought it might be wise for the White House to give Adams his walking papers for trying to intimidate a Senate committee by unfair tactics of which the committee itself had been accused.

As the Army-McCarthy hearings proceeded, Senator McCarthy began to dig his political grave. His incessant interruptions on points of order, his rude badgering of witnesses and other members of the committee, and his contempt for law when stolen documents were used to bolster his case all served to destroy his image. Public opinion turned against McCarthy, who emerged not as a knight in shining armor but as a villainous TV knave in this courtroom-like setting. The public as a jury came to dislike McCarthy's crude, heavy-handed manners, and their verdict was one he could not reverse. The Army-McCarthy hearings ended on June 17. The great show was over, but the repercussions were yet to appear.

On July 30 Senator Ralph E. Flanders (R-Vt.) introduced Senate Resolution 301 which read, in part: "Resolved, that the conduct of the Senator from Wisconsin, Mr. McCarthy, is unbecoming a member of the United States Senate, is contrary to Senatorial traditions, and tends to bring the Senate into disrepute."[47] The Senate voted on August 2, by a vote of 75 to 12, with Dirksen voting no, to set up a select committee to conduct hearings on SR. 301. Vice-President Nixon subsequently announced the makeup of the committee. The Republican members included Arthur V. Watkins of Utah, who was made chairman; Frank Carlson of Kansas; and Francis Case of South Dakota. The three Democrats were Samuel Ervin of North Carolina; Edwin C. Johnson of Colorado; and John C. Stennis of Mississippi.

The Watkins committee commenced its hearings on August 31. SR. 301 was very vague, so the committee had to decide what specific actions on the part of McCarthy constituted evidence that the Wisconsinite had in fact acted in a manner unbecoming a senator, that his actions were contrary to senatorial traditions, or that he had actually brought the Senate into disrepute. This meant taking up McCarthy's unlawful acceptance and use of classified documents, his badgering of General Zwicker, and his abuse of fellow senators. Edward Bennett Williams, Senator McCarthy's counsel, claimed that whatever offenses he had committed, there were precedents in the Senate for all of them. Classified documents had been used before by senators, witnesses had been bullied by senators, and senators had hurled intemperate language at one another. In any case, it appeared the Watkins committee, acting in accordance with courtroom procedure and handling evidence judiciously, could not come up with a complete verdict of guilty. Nevertheless, even though a Senate committee is not a court of law, McCarthy's fate was sealed already because, politically speaking, he had alienated too many senators with his demagogic methods.

In Dirksen's judgment, the final recommendation of the Watkins committee went far afield from its assigned job. It had been set up to ascertain "the truth or falsity of the formal charges made by the Army on the one hand and the countercharges made by Senator McCarthy for himself and his associates on the other."[48] All other matters were irrelevant although not necessarily unimportant.

In its 40,000-word report issued on September 27, the Watkins committee recommended censure of McCarthy on two counts: McCarthy's behavior in 1951 and 1952 before the Senate Subcommittee on Privileges and Elections, and his abusive treatment of General Zwicker.

Senator Dirksen worked in two ways to head off a formal censure, which he did not believe was warranted in lieu of existing precedents. Although McCarthy did not exactly abide by any agreed-upon Marquis of Queensbury rules, Ev felt the Democrats were engaging in a political reprisal, not a nonpartisan reprimand. He tried to persuade McCarthy to make an apology and thus avert censure, but McCarthy flatly refused to do so. Barry Goldwater likewise made such an attempt and also failed.[49] Dirksen then worked with Karl Mundt and others to compose a compromise resolution which would slap McCarthy on the wrist but not actually censure him. Ev's "amendment in the nature of a substitute" read, in part, as follows:

> Reasonable doubt exists as to the authority of the Senate to censure or condemn a Senator for language or conduct in a prior session . . . that no rule presently exists under which censure or condemnation for the alleged language or conduct might be justifiably imposed; that a Senator is under no legal duty to appear before a Committee on invitation. . . .
>
> That there has been no violation of Senatorial tradition . . . that the Congress does have the right to examine into the applicability of an Executive Order or directive especially where the internal security of the nation be involved; that while abusive or intemperate language is to be deplored, it does not in the light of precedent warrant formal censure or condemnation. . . .[50]

Dirksen merged his proposal with one originally prepared by Karl Mundt. The Mundt resolution was voted down on December 1 by a vote of 74 to 15.

On December 2, 1954, the Senate voted on the two counts. The first charge related to McCarthy's failure to cooperate with the Senate Subcommittee on Privileges and Elections in a manner contrary to senatorial traditions and "is hereby condemned."[51] The second allegation dealt with the abuse of the Watkins committee which was deemed "contrary to Senatorial ethics and tended to bring the Senate into dishonor and disrepute, to obstruct the constitutional processes of the Senate, and to impair its dignity; and such conduct is hereby condemned."[52] The vote was 67 for condemnation with 22 against. The Democrats were solidly for it. Among the three Democrats absent and not voting was Senator John F. Kennedy, who was hospitalized for a back problem. His would have been an interesting vote, since his father was a rabid McCarthyite and his brother Robert had worked as a legal counsel for the McCarthy Committee. The Republicans were split evenly at 22 for and 22 against condemnation. Dirksen voted no as did Minority Leader Knowland.

President Eisenhower was elated over the outcome. He sent for Senator Watkins to tender his thanks. In his memoirs Eisenhower wrote, "I felt impelled . . . to express my appreciation to the man who was the hero of the episode. . . ."[53] Pro-McCarthyites were outraged. On Lincoln's birthday in Chicago, the right-wing Committee of One Thousand Republicans held a meeting. Wearing "I'm for McCarthy"[54] buttons, some 1,700 ultraconservatives met to praise McCarthy and damn Eisenhower. Speakers included Governor J. Bracken Lee of Utah, Senator George Malone (R-Nev.), General Robert E. Wood, Joseph McCarthy, and Everett Dirksen.[55] The only speaker who did not denounce Eisenhower was Dirksen. Ev quickly ascertained that this group, some of whom spoke of forming a third party, were far too extreme in their views. Dirksen publicly decried the idea of a third party as "pure nonsense"[56] and thereafter would never again appear on a platform with McCarthy. When McCarthy continued his personal vendetta against Eisenhower by smearing him whenever possible, Ev severed all relations with him. Long before McCarthy died on May 2, 1957, Dirksen no longer considered him a political ally or even an intimate colleague to be treated with respectful cordiality. It was also noteworthy that when Colonel Robert McCormick died on April 1, 1955, Ev did not rise in the Senate to deliver even a perfunctory eulogy. The colonel's *Tribune* had been far too harsh on Eisenhower, in Dirksen's judgment, and so he felt no compunction in not lauding someone who was unable to tolerate diverse viewpoints within the Republican party. Always a party loyalist, Ev saw his role as one who must mend political fences and work for political harmony within the GOP. With the demise of McCarthyism, one of the less-commendable periods in Senator Dirksen's political career had ended.

On March 1, during the Army-McCarthy hearings, President Eisenhower had invited Dirksen to have breakfast with him at the White House. Eisenhower later wrote about Ev, "He had already shown the potential of a strong Republican leader, and I wanted to enlist his help."[57] President Eisenhower had worked behind the scenes to promote McCarthy's downfall and he used this same quiet but steady manner to gain support for his legislative program. Just as he made key policy decisions by controlling head-strong individuals such as John Foster Dulles, secretary of state, and Ezra Taft Benson, secretary of agriculture, so he strove to win over significant leaders in Congress such as Everett Dirksen. This was accomplished with patient deftness and diplomatic tact. It demonstrated Eisenhower's skill in exerting leadership without appearing to be abrasively imperious. Not only did Senator Dirksen move toward the president's position on domestic and foreign affairs, but he also developed a personal fondness for Eisenhower. The latter was a direct result of Eisenhower's winning way as a man of goodwill.[58]

The overt courtship of Dirksen by Eisenhower continued after the McCarthy episode with Dirksen responding in a positive manner. This change in allegiance was reflected publicly on a "Meet the Press" television program on January 9, 1955, aired just one day after President Eisenhower gave his State of the Union message to Congress. Dirksen indicated he would give strong support for enactment of the administration's legislative program. Among Eisenhower's proposals were an increase in the minimum wage, extension of the Reciprocal Trade Agreements Act, federal aid to education, and federally financed public housing.

Dirksen defended his new pro-Eisenhower stance within the GOP, which meant giving legislative support to administration proposals he had heretofore opposed. At one point, William S. White of the New York *Times,* a panelist on the "Meet the Press" show, asked Ev the following question: "I would like to ask you what your comment is on the fairly general Democratic claim of yesterday that the President had sent up a Democratic program, in his message?" Dirksen replied, "Attitudes of parties must necessarily differ from time to time, depending on what conditions are in the country and in the world, and whether somebody finds great comfort in putting a particular political tag on it doesn't mean a great deal in my book." Under questioning as to whether he considered himself a conservative or liberal Republican Ev answered, "Labels don't mean much to me, but I do like to regard myself as a moderate. And if you will ever look up the word some time in *Webster,* you will find that a moderate is one who avoids both extremes. And so I try to avoid the extremes."[59] Other than on the Bricker amendment (more will be said about it later), which Eisenhower was against and he was for, Dirksen made it clear he stood with the president all the way. Significant, too, was Ev's hearty endorsement of Eisenhower for reelection in 1956. With Taft gone and McCarthy politically dead, Everett Dirksen now considered himself Eisenhower's loyal ally.

NOTES

1. Hans Küng, *Truthfulness: The Future of the Church,* trans. Edward Quinn (New York: Sheed and Ward, 1968), p. 43.

2. Margaret Chase Smith, *Declaration of Conscience* (Garden City, N.Y.: Doubleday, 1972), p. 28.

3. "Meet the Press" (NBC-TV), Sept. 11, 1951, script in R&R-EMDC.

4. "Excerpts from Commencement Address" by EMD to graduation class of DePaul University, Chicago, June 13, 1951, text in R&R-EMDC; *DePaul, the university magazine* (June, 1951), reprint in C-EMDC.

5. 82d Cong., 1st sess., S. 1702, June 19, 1951, text in LF-EMDC. See also Press Release, July 12, 1951, R&R-EMDC.

6. 82d Cong., 1st sess., S. 1720, June 22, 1951, text in LF-EMDC.

7. 82d Cong., 1st sess., S. 1849, June 13, 1951, text in LF-EMDC.

8. 82d Cong., 1st sess., S. 1971, Aug. 9, 1951, text in LF-EMDC.

9. Press Release, Mar. 17, 1951, text in R&R-EMDC.

10. Address by EMD to District Convention of Missouri Republicans, Springfield, Mo., Aug. 11, 1951, text in R&R-EMDC.

11. Robert Howard, "Dirksen Calls Korea 'World War 2-½,' " Chicago *Tribune,* Oct. 2, 1951, copy in C-EMDC.

12. Los Angeles *Examiner,* Oct. 2, 1951, copy in C-EMDC.

13. Reprint of *Congressional Record,* Apr. 25, 1951, in R&R-EMDC.

14. EMD, "Are Administration Foreign Policy Aid Policies Undermining America's Basic Strength?" *Congressional Digest* (Nov., 1951), reprint in IF-EMDC.

15. Ibid.

16. Ibid.

17. "Taft Is Favored in Private Poll, Dirksen Rated for Vice-President," Peoria *Star,* June 10, 1951, copy in C-EMDC.

18. "Taft Tops Ike in Secret Poll in House GOP," Chicago *Tribune,* Nov. 16, 1951, copy in C-EMDC.

19. "Club Founded to Send Dirksen to White House," Pekin *Times,* Aug. 14, 1951; "Boost Dirksen for President," *Illinois State Journal,* Aug. 16, 1951, copies in C-EMDC.

20. "Dirksen Gets Favorite Son Endorsement," Pekin *Times,* Oct. 18, 1951, copy in C-EMDC.

21. "Meet the Press" (NBC-TV), Sept. 11, 1951, script in R&R-EMDC.

22. "Name Dirksen as Taft Leader for Illinois," Chicago *Tribune,* Nov. 19, 1951; "Senator Dirksen Opens Illinois Campaign Office for Taft," Peoria *Star,* Dec. 4, 1951, copies in C-EMDC.

23. Telegram, EMD to Henry Cabot Lodge, Paris (NATO Headquarters), Apr. 6, 1952, copy in R&R-EMDC.

24. Introduction by EMD of Robert A. Taft to District of Columbia Republican Convention, Apr. 23, 1952, text in R&R-EMDC.

25. James T. Patterson, *Mr. Republican: A Biography of Robert A. Taft* (Boston: Houghton Mifflin, 1972), p. 548.

26. William J. Miller, *Henry Cabot Lodge, A Biography* (New York: James H. Heineman, 1967), pp. 247, 249.

27. *Official Proceedings of the Twenty-Fifth Republican National Convention,* 1952, copy in R&R-EMDC.

28. Ibid.

29. EMD to Thomas J. Smith, July 18, 1952, GGC-EMDC.

30. HCH to EMD, July 23, 1952, HCHL.

31. Patterson, *Mr. Republican,* p. 565.

32. Herbert S. Parmet, *Eisenhower and the American Crusades* (New York: Macmillan, 1972), p. 100.

33. Leonard Lurei, *The King Makers* (New York: Coward, McCann and Geoghegan, 1971), p. 245.

34. *Illinois State Journal and Register,* Aug. 4, 1952, copy in C-EMDC.

35. Pekin *Times,* Aug. 4, 1952, copy in C-EMDC.

36. Robert A. Taft to EMD, Aug. 6, 1952, Papers of Robert A. Taft, Library of Congress (Washington, D.C.), hereafter cited as Taft Papers-LC.

37. Ibid.

38. Parmet, *Eisenhower,* pp. 129-30. Frank Carlson reported about the meeting, "I know from visiting with Bob Taft that he felt well pleased over the outcome and certainly General Eisenhower the same." Frank Carlson to Merle J. Trees, Sept. 13, 1952, Papers of Frank Carlson (Kansas State Historical Society, Topeka).

39. Robert A. Taft to Herman Welker, Aug. 18, 1952, Taft Papers-LC.

40. Douglas Cornell, "Dirksen Raps 'Mess' Left by Democrats," Bloomington *Daily Pantagraph,* Sept. 20, 1953, copy in C-EMDC.

41. "Senator Dirksen to 'Listen, Learn,'" Chicago *Daily News,* June 2, 1953, copy in C-EMDC.

42. McNeil, *Dirksen,* p. 114.

43. The White House calendar indicates that prior to the Senate condemnation of McCarthy, Senator Dirksen was invited to join the president for breakfast five times, luncheon three, and twice to "off the record" meetings. In Papers of Dwight D. Eisenhower-DDEL.

44. Roy Cohn, *McCarthy* (New York: The New American Library, 1968), pp.131-32.

45. Ibid.; "G.O.P. Blocs O.K. Predicted by Dirksen," Chicago *Tribune,* May 9, 1954, copy in C-EMDC.

46. Quoted in Michael Straight, *Trial by Television* (Boston: The Beacon Press, 1954), p. 118.

47. Quoted in Richard H. Rovere, *Senator Joe McCarthy* (New York: World Publishing, 1966), p. 223. Senator Flanders, contrary to what anti-McCarthyites thought, agreed with McCarthy that the State Department was infiltrated with communists and fellow travelers, but he disliked the Wisconsinite's behavior. See Ralph Flanders oral history-DDEL.

48. "Senator Dirksen: Army Was Slow to Bring Charges," *U.S. News* (Sept. 10, 1954), reprint in IF-EMDC.

49. Barry M. Goldwater, *With No Apologies, The Personal and Political Memoirs of United States Senator Barry M. Goldwater* (New York: William Morrow, 1979), p. 61.

50. "An Amendment in the Nature of a Substitute Offered by Mr. Dirksen," text in R&R-EMDC.

51. Rovere, *McCarthy,* p. 230.

52. Ibid.

53. Dwight D. Eisenhower, *Mandate for Change, 1953-1956* (New York: New American Library, 1963), p. 400.

54. Parmet, *Eisenhower,* p. 383.

55. New York *Times,* Feb. 13, 1954, copy in C-EMDC.

56. Washington *Star,* Feb. 16, 1955, copy in C-EMDC.

57. Eisenhower, *Mandate,* p. 395. Eisenhower once wrote about Dirksen in his diary, "I asked him to be the 'verbal leader' of the middle-of-the-road philosophy (my philosophy) in the Senate." Eisenhower Diary Series, July 23, 1953, Dwight D. Eisenhower Library (Abilene, Kansas). Presidential Assistant Emmet John Hughes indicates that Eisenhower described his wooing of Dirksen and other Taftites as one of "persuasion—and conciliation—and education—and patience." See

his *The Ordeal of Power: A Political Memoir of the Eisenhower Years* (New York: Atheneum, 1963), p. 124.

58. Eisenhower was not the political incompetent that some historians have depicted. In their *Ezra Taft Benson and the Politics of Agriculture, The Eisenhower Years, 1953-1961,* the authors used an interpretation which depicted Eisenhower to be a strong and decisive president. For a discussion of this revisionist position, see Fred I. Greenstein, "Eisenhower as an Activist President: A Look at New Evidence," in *Political Science Quarterly,* 94 (Winter 1979-80): 575-99; Richard H. Immerman, "Eisenhower and Dulles: Who Made the Decisions?" *Political Psychology,* 1 (Autumn 1979): 3-20.

59. "Meet the Press" (NBC-TV), Jan. 9, 1955, script in R&R-EMDC.

5

Dirksen and Eisenhower: Modern Republicanism Wins a Mandate

IN A PRIVATE LETTER to Joe Bunting of the Bloomington *Pantagraph* in regard to a critical editorial, dated December 8, 1955, Everett Dirksen defended his past pro-McCarthy stance by stating, "With respect to my part in the McCarthy affair, I did what I esteemed to be my duty in the light of all the facts, and some of these facts will probably never be disclosed since certain confidences were involved." Dirksen then confided: "It is the best evidence of my continuing relationship with the President that I take pride in the fact that he has considered me as one of his top troubleshooters in the Senate. I have said very little about it because I recall my conversation with the President in which he asked me to serve in this capacity without asking any glory or headlines for such service."[1]

There was a definite shift in Dirksen's voting pattern commencing in 1955. Even though his support of administration measures was never lower than 75 percent, which was above the average of all the GOP members of the Senate, it continually increased from 1955 onward. In terms of percentage, his pro-administration voting record rose sharply from 75 percent in 1955 to 85 percent in 1956 and 95 percent in 1957.[2] Although Ev was never anti-Eisenhower per se while in the Taft wing of the party, his allegiance to the president became greater after Taft's death and McCarthy's political demise. Several reasons exist for this shift in position. Eisenhower was a very popular president, and it was politically wise for Republican members of Congress to attach themselves to his coattails in 1956. Other considerations made Dirksen adjust his outlook. Eisenhower was doing an excellent job both in promoting stable prosperity at home and peace abroad. The president deserved support. Thus when Eisenhower appealed to Ev for help because Knowland was an ineffectual minority leader, Dirksen responded positively. While the Californian was ideologically rigid and personally abrasive, Ev was flexible and friendly to all factions.

Although having arrived at opinions based on his own experience, Everett Dirksen nevertheless was tolerant of others and worked for agreement on commonly accepted points of view. He was willing to fight for personal beliefs, but he understood the necessity for accommodation in order to preserve party unity. During an interview on a radio program Dirksen asserted, "I pride myself on the fact that I am a good party man, and the reason I say that is not for selfish personal purposes, but rather I think the well-being of the country and its future is identified pretty well with a vigorous, virile two-party system." When asked if McCarthy should be read out of the party, Ev replied, "The Republican tent, as you know, is large enough to embrace a good many points of view. . . ."[3] On another interview show some time later, this time on television, Ev described himself politically as a "middle-of-the-roader." When queried about McCarthy, Dirksen answered, "He may express himself in a rather extreme fashion, but that doesn't mean that represents the viewpoint of the party, or anywhere near the majority of the party."[4] It was obvious that while Ev had parted company with McCarthy, he did not believe in purges to preserve ideological purity.

Part of Everett Dirksen's manner of keeping abreast of how federal agencies performed was to monitor them personally as closely as he could, especially as it pertained to the vast foreign aid expansion. On June 3, 1955, Dirksen and Earle Clements (D-Ky.) went on an overseas junket on behalf of the Senate Appropriations Committee. They would make stops in Asia, the Middle East, and Europe. What Ev saw on this firsthand inspection tour made a favorable impression on him. It was obvious to him that the Eisenhower administration was making effective use of both economic and military aid as funded by Congress. He was pleased with the way U.S. foreign aid was being administered, particularly the fine work of Mutual Security Director Harold Stassen. The latter had been much criticized in the Senate by McCarthy and William E. Jenner (R-Ind.). Dirksen returned from his inspection trip convinced that recipient countries were making good use of American aid, and that both military and economic assistance should be continued.[5]

When President Eisenhower requested a supplementary mutual security appropriation of $3,205,341,750 in 1955, Senator Dirksen led the fight to prevent it from being cut back. Since Minority Leader Knowland supported a drastic slashing of the requested amount, Ev became Eisenhower's floor leader to stymie this effort. On the floor Dirksen argued that well-administered foreign aid did not constitute "a giveaway" program but "is the most selfish program I know of." He sought to convince what he now considered his errant isolationist brethren that it was in the best interests of the United States to shore up the economies of underdeveloped countries. Ev defended the proposition that to "teach them a little know-how" would serve to prevent them from becoming the prey of communist imperialism. Ev admitted forthrightly to his colleagues that he had on previous occasions favored reducing foreign aid. "I remember the days when I used to attack this program. I did it with a great deal of verve and vigor. I take it back. Publicly and privately I take it back."[6] Following Dirksen's vigorous defense of the president's foreign aid program, Senator William Jenner of Indiana took the floor. Looking right at Ev, the confirmed isolationist said, "Somebody in the cloakroom told me he heard a whirring sound. I am sure that was Colonel McCormick turning over in his grave when the Senator made that statement."[7]

Speaking at a $100-a-plate dinner in Chicago to raise campaign funds for his 1956 bid for reelection, Dirksen sought to explain why it was necessary for him to be a flexible middle-of-the-roader. "If moderation is a mark of good public service," he maintained, "I have tried to avoid those extreme courses which have sometimes marked our national thinking in recent years, and to find the middle road in the belief that this course not only assures steady progess but provides the greatest good for the greatest number of our people."[8] At this particular fund-raising affair Ev collected $140,000.

The desire to be successful at the polls obviously inclines any candidate, whether consciously or unconsciously, to assume a public posture best suited to attract votes. This political stance is most frequently dictated by the general temper and tone of one's constituency. Everett Dirksen represented the state of Illinois in mid-America. Its downstate voters reflected a longtime aversion to big government and generally opposed what they perceived to be foreign aid giveaways. Dirksen's shift to a more internationalistic attitude, therefore, certainly could not be categorized solely as an opportunistic move aimed at winning favor with voters. To some extent he was going against public opinion at home. It was, rather, a recognition that the foreign policy needs of the nation had changed, and that circumstances in 1956 were quite different from those in 1950.

Democrats, who regarded Dirksen's reelection bid as a shameless exercise in hanging onto Eisenhower's coattails, also overlooked some other important factors. Dirksen had to work with Republican midwesterners in the Senate who were basically Taftites, but he personally never spoke ill of the president and certainly was never anti-Eisenhower as such.[9] In 1954 Ev campaigned for a GOP Congress on the basis that if the Democrats won, Eisenhower, a "gentle President," would be put "in a position of begging the opposition for a program for the welfare of 165 million people in the country."[10] Dirksen stated publicly he "thoroughly disagreed" with McCarthy that President Eisenhower was soft on communism.[11] The Illinois Senator quickly repudiated any attempt by an anti-Eisenhower cabal to form a new right-wing party. What had happened was a reoccurring process; namely, Dirksen was once again accommodating to political reality. Taft was the leader of his party when he came into the Senate; McCarthy was the last vestige of that power. Now the GOP leader was Eisenhower and Ev recognized the fact. Also at work was the "hidden hand leadership"[12] technique utilized by the president to exert a strong inconspicuous influence on Republicans to work as a team.

Senator Dirksen would demonstrate his ability to be a team man, but he never relinquished his option to act independently when conscience so dictated. There was a tension between his personal social philosophy and the growing need for raising domestic spending and increasing foreign aid. Ev was troubled over increased deficit spending, rising inflation, and continual growth of the federal bureaucracy, and he was likewise concerned that too much government interference with free enterprise would cripple initiative and stifle individualism.

Senator Dirksen gave a succinct summary of his social outlook in an address to a group of Masons in 1955. Speaking in New York City to his fellow lodge members, Ev inquired, "What other engine of human progress is there than this combination of man's indestructible soul and his fecund and imaginative mind?" Answering his own rhetorical question, Ev expounded, "The constant, intelligent, undramatic application of man's mind and soul to that which God placed in the universe is the wellspring of human progress." From this premise he deduced, "It is, therefore, man and man alone who can give us hope and dissolve the fears and vexations of this age." Ev had great faith in what just one determined person could do. "The human will is stronger than titanium or steel," he declared. "With these moral weapons at our command we cannot fail in the search for spiritual fission as one answer to the challenge of the nuclear age." He concluded his sermon-like talk by saying: "It is high time for us to go back to the one imperishable bench mark of civilization. That is you, the individual."[13]

On the legislative front Dirksen translated his personal convictions into legislative efforts to protect individual freedom, human rights, and the principle of self-determination for all peoples. Some of these attempts were futile in and of themselves and others too far ahead of the times. Dirksen had a strong pro-civil rights record in the House and Senate. In 1953 he submitted a bill, S. 1, for the creation of a federal commission on civil rights "to promote observance of the civil rights of all individuals; and to aid in eliminating discrimination in employment because of race, creed, or color."[14] Also in 1953 Ev and Senator John F. Kennedy (D-Mass.) co-sponsored Senate Resolution 35 upholding the right of self-determination for Ireland. On the floor of the Senate Dirksen defended the right of the Irish people to "make their own destiny."[15] Senator Dirksen's pro-Irish position was based on several factors. He visited Ireland while a soldier in World War I and sympathized with Irish desires for independence. Dirksen disapproved of the British suppression of the Easter Rebellion of 1916. His anti-British sentiment was fueled further because of Britain's role in imposing what he believed to be a Carthaginian peace on Germany via the Versailles Treaty and because of the British default on war debts to the United States. A final reason was his deep commitment to the principle of self-determination. In defense of this precept he was an early champion of nationhood for Israel, decried the existence of Soviet satellites after World War II, supported reunification of Korea, and later would justify American intervention in South Viet Nam to preserve that nation's independence. Finally, there was no public demand, and very little agitation in 1955 (even among women), for an equal rights amendment to the U.S. Constitution. Yet Dirksen sponsored such an amendment because he believed "equality of rights under the law shall not be denied or abridged by the United States or by any State on account of sex."[16] Ev, no doubt, might be considered old-fashioned by modern feminists, but his stand for equality of the sexes under law was ahead of the times.

There were other constitutional changes Dirksen wished to see attained. He cosponsored an amendment which would have divided the total electoral vote of each state in an exact ratio of the popular vote with the result "the person having the greatest number of votes for President shall be the President."[17] Ev sponsored another constitutional amendment which would have repealed the Sixteenth (income tax) Amendment. In its place would be an amendment stating that all taxes, duties, and excises "by income shall not exceed 25 per centum."[18] In addition no inheritance or gift tax could be increased except by a three-fourths vote of both houses of Congress. Arguing for a lost cause, since the times were not right for a tax revolt, Ev neverthless contended,

"Our present system of taxation, with its heavy progressive income and inheritance taxes, will eventually destroy this system and result in the substitution of some form of socialism."[19]

The Bricker amendment was probably the most controversial constitutional change proposed during the Eisenhower administration. Introduced originally by Senator John Bricker (R-Ohio) in 1952, it was reintroduced in 1953 carrying the cosponsorship of sixty-three other senators. Dirksen was one of forty-four Republicans backing it (with two opposed). The original version would have placed drastic limitations on the treaty-making power of the president. A treaty negotiated by the chief executive would not become internal law unless implemented by the specific enactment of appropriate legislation by Congress. Other prohibitions included the following restrictions: no treaty could abridge individual rights granted by the U.S. Constitution; no treaty could grant power to a foreign nation or international body to adjudicate rights of U.S. citizens; and all the above limitations applied also to executive agreements.

When President Eisenhower let it be known that he opposed it, Dirksen worked with others to tone down the language of the proposed amendment. No version was accepted by the Senate in 1953 since marshaling a two-thirds vote was not possible. In 1954 an even more modified version lost by one vote. In 1956 Dirksen fashioned yet another rendition of the Bricker amendment. Ev worked with Frank E. Holman, Eberhardt Deutch, and William Scheppe, all past presidents of the American Bar Association, to both simplify the language and remove many of the negative features. The key provision now read simply: "A provision of a treaty or other international agreement which conflicts with any provision of this Constitution shall not be of any force or effect."[20] The Dirksen-Bricker amendment was never brought up for a vote and thus it died. No attempts were made thereafter to revive it.

President Eisenhower's role in preventing adoption of the Bricker amendment was adroit and deliberately underplayed so as not to create a rift between himself and Senate Republicans. He would invite Bricker, Dirksen, and others to a White House breakfast or to an informal cocktail hour where he would assuage their concerns about the president usurping the treaty-making power.

It was through this technique that Eisenhower also won Ev's support for the St. Lawrence Seaway project. Dirksen had opposed it originally on the basis that it might hurt commerce in Chicago, but Eisenhower convinced him the nation as a whole would benefit from its construction. Through patience, tact, and persuasion Eisenhower likewise won Ev's support for other measures such as renewing the reciprocal trade agreements, federal aid to education, increasing Social Security benefits, and raising the minimum wage level. Eisenhower was working "quietly, in this office," he told a White House aide, to get Dirksen to think in positive terms and to help him reorient the GOP from its standpat position to one of proposing solutions to pressing national problems.[21] In 1954, for instance, Henry Cabot Lodge wrote Eisenhower telling him that in the campaign oratory of the midterm elections the Republican party was being characterized as "reactionary" while the achievements of "modern Republicans" were being ignored. The president replied to Lodge that he was "removing all identification marks from your letter and sending copies of its substance to Dick Nixon who is, so far as I know, speaking in more states than almost any other person. I think I shall also send one to Everett Dirksen, who, I believe is much in demand as a speaker. . . . Perhaps this will do some good."[22]

Ike's acceptance of Modern Republicanism as constituting his political philosophy was explicitly stated on November 7, 1956. In a victory statement after being reelected to the presidency, Eisenhower accepted his election to a second term as a mandate for Modern Republicanism. "America has approved of Modern Republicanism,"[23] he asserted. In his news conference of November 14, 1956, Eisenhower defined once more what he meant by Modern Republicanism. "It is a type of political philosophy that recognizes clearly the responsibility of the Federal Government to take the lead in making certain that the productivity of our great economic machine is distributed so that no one will suffer disaster, privation, through no fault of his own."[24]

Did Dirksen ever accept the label of Modern Republican? On a "Meet the Press" television program in 1957 he categorically described himself as a "moderationist." When asked specifically whether or not he subscribed to Modern Republicanism, he replied: "So tags are tags. It is like 'Modern Republicanism' . . . I am just an old-fashioned, garden variety of Republican, who believes in the Constitution and the Declaration of Independence, in Abraham Lincoln, who accepts the challenges as they arise from time to time, and who is not unappreciative of the fact that this is a dynamic economy in which we live, and sometimes you have to change your position."[25]

Democrats in Illinois were aware that defeating Senator Dirksen in the same year that Eisenhower was running for reelection would be a formidable task. Everett Dirksen's Democratic opponent in 1956 was Richard Stengel. He was a state senator from Rock Island and had served in the Illinois upper chamber for eight years. Being the second cousin of the famous Casey Stengel, manager of the New York Yankees, helped Richard, but he was still a relatively unknown figure in Illinois.

It was not Stengel whom Ev feared. What worried him was a political scandal uncovered by investigative reporter George Thiem of the Chicago *Daily News.* It was discovered that state auditor Orville E. Hodge, who won renomination and was also scheduled to be a delegate at the Republican National Convention, had been involved in embezzlement, forgery, and a confidence game, illegally taking from the state an amount of money totaling $1,571,364. Hodge pleaded guilty to all charges and was given a prison sentence ranging from twelve to fifteen years.[26] Fortunately for Governor William G. Stratton, also up for reelection, all of the money taken by Hodge was recovered. But Dirksen remembered what had happened to Scott Lucas when a scandal broke out just before election time.

Richard Stengel employed an array of tactics in his losing campaign against Dirsken. His primary ploy was to exploit the Hodge scandal. In an attempt to link Ev with the ignominious affair, Stengel brazenly claimed Dirksen was an "arch croney"[27] of Hodge. To ensure a continual flow of adverse publicity for the Republicans, the Democrats arranged for Senator J. William Fulbright (D-Ark.), chairman of the Senate Banking Committee, to hold hearings in Chicago ostensibly to see if new federal legislation was needed to prevent the reoccurrence of Hodge-type scandals. The forty-one-year-old Stengel continually attacked the sixty-year-old Dirksen as a reactionary mossback. Adlai E. Stevenson, again the Democratic presidential nominee in 1956, joined in this assault by calling Ev a "holdover from the nineteenth century."[28]

Another political tack utilized by Stengel was an attempt to drive a wedge between Ev and Eisenhower. The strategy was to depict Dirksen as a McCarthyite and an anti-Eisenhower Republican. In one of Stengel's widely used political ads the lead caption read, "Pardon us Mr. Dirksen—but your record is showing." It portrayed Ev as one who defended McCarthy, opposed the president's domestic program, and voted "against the foreign policy and our national defense programs of Presidents of both parties." The ad concluded, "Your record is bad, Mr. Dirksen, and we don't blame you for trying to hide it!"[29] Finally, Stengel challenged Ev to debate the issues with him, even as Dirksen had done with Scott Lucas. Ev declined, as did Lucas in 1950, since no incumbent with high visibility wants to give exposure to a relatively unknown opponent.

Dirksen, while confident, in no way took his reelection for granted. He spent the last ten weeks before election day averaging 200 miles a day in travel. Ev tried to blunt the repercussions of the Hodge scandal by telling voters "not to vote in a fit of anger."[30] His basic strategy was to identify himself with President Eisenhower as closely as possible. One of Ev's campaign ads read, "Ike Needs Him—You Need Him; Keep Everett M. Dirksen in Washington."[31] The Ike and Ev theme was also utilized on a bumper sticker. Using a red, white, and blue color scheme, the letters IKE within Dirksen's name were printed in a lighter shade. The result was an italicized IKE within the name D *I* R *K* S *E* N.[32] In his speeches Ev stressed how Eisenhower, with his support, had led the nation to an era of "peace and prosperity."[33]

The greatest help Dirksen received was from Eisenhower himself. The president drafted a special letter of praise, knowing it would be widely publicized. "Now that the session [of Congress] is over, I want to thank you most sincerely for the effective help you have so often given to the Administration in securing legislative approval of key measures we have advanced for the public good," he wrote. "In your case I have been especially pleased by the way you have responded when I personally called on you for special help in important legislation." The Eisenhower letter concluded with a specific election pitch to the voters of Illinois: "I know you will soon be engaged in a very active campaign for reelection. I hope that the people of your State will give you the opportunity to continue your service in the United States Senate."[34] Eisenhower not only endorsed Dirksen outright but came to Peoria, Ev's political back yard, to deliver a campaign speech. In introducing the president, Dirksen basked in the radiant popularity of Eisenhower through visual identification. The widely printed photographs of Ev and Eisenhower side by side, both smiling and with fingers indicating V for victory, were obviously good campaign material.

Limiting his campaign appearances to Illinois, Dirksen in many ways campaigned for himself by campaigning for Eisenhower. He extolled Eisenhower's record by emphasizing the fact that the president had ended the Korean War and brought about a prosperity based on a peacetime economy. Ev penned the following words for a press release: "But the Democrats have been making promises for twenty years. They promised to keep you out of war, but they didn't. They promised to create jobs, but they didn't—until the war came along. They promised to reduce taxes, but they didn't. It took two Republican Congresses to get any kind of tax reduction."[35] He asked women voters would they "rather trust their sons and husbands to the Republican administration headed by Eisenhower and Nixon, in peace or war, or to the Stevenson-Kefauver team?"[36] This type of appeal went over well in downstate Illinois where the traditional isolationist vote was the strongest.

As the 1956 senatorial campaign came down the home stretch, Dirksen had little doubt as to its outcome. About the only thing with which he was really concerned was, what would be the size of his margin of victory? When the final votes had been tallied, Dirksen's plurality over Stengel was an impressive 357,470. At the same time Eisenhower carried Illinois by a total of 847,845. Obviously Eisenhower's enormous popularity helped both Senator Dirksen and Governor Stratton to win reelection. But Ev had done well on his own, also. He pulled a winning margin of over 75,000 in Democratic Cook County and was one of the few Eisenhower-endorsed candidates for the U.S. Senate to triumph. Although the president's coattails helped because of ticket splitting, of the six incumbents christened by Eisenhower as Modern Republicans worthy of his special help, only two were reelected — Dirksen and John Sherman Cooper of Kentucky. Going down to defeat were Douglas McKay of Oregon, Arthur B. Langlie of Washington, James H. Duff of Pennsylvania, and George Bender of Ohio. Speaker Sam Rayburn (D-Tex.) was probably correct when he noted, "The election proved one thing, and that is the people like and want President Eisenhower, but they do not like or want the Republican Party as demonstrated by their votes in electing a Democratic Senate and House."[37] The Eisenhower blessing no doubt helped Ev, but it in no way ensured Dirksen's reelection had he not been popular enough in his own right to have his mandate renewed by the voters in Illinois.

NOTES

1. EMD to Joe Bunting, Dec. 8, 1955, Working Papers-EMDC, hereafter cited as WP-EMDC.

2. Figure 7.1 titled, "Overall Support of President Eisenhower, 1954-1960," in Jean Torcom Cronin, "Minority Leadership in the United States Senate: The Role and Style of Everett Dirksen" (Ph.D. dissertation, Johns Hopkins University, 1973), p. 289.

3. Radio interview on "Reporter's Roundup" (Mutual Broadcasting System) Mar. 21, 1955, script in R&R-EMDC.

4. "Youth Wants to Know" (NBC-TV), Jan. 20, 1957, script in R&R-EMDC.

5. Press Release, June 3, 1955, R&R-EMDC; Chicago *Daily News,* June 9, 1955, C-EMDC; Washington *Star,* June 26 and July 23, 1955, C-EMDC.

6. Chicago *Sun-Times,* July 23, 1955, C-EMDC.

7. *The Reporter* (Aug. 11, 1955), reprint in IF-EMDC.

8. "Dirksen Makes Formal Bid for 2d Senate Term," Chicago *Tribune,* Oct. 7, 1955, C-EMDC.

9. Gary W. Reichard, *The Reaffirmation of Republicanism, Eisenhower and the Eighty-Third Congress* (Knoxville: University of Tennessee Press, 1975), p. 204.

10. Robert Bendiner, "All Aboard for the Coattail Special," *The Reporter* (June 28, 1955), reprint in IF-EMDC.

11. Ibid.

12. Fred I. Greenstein, "Eisenhower as an Activist President: A Look at New Evidence," pp. 586, 597.

13. Address by EMD at the annual breakfast of the Masonic Lodge of New York, Astor Hotel, Mar. 20, 1955, text in R&R-EMDC.

14. 83d Cong., 1st sess., S. 1, Jan. 7, 1953, LF-EMDC.

15. *Congressional Record,* Jan. 16, 1953, S. 421, reprint in LF-EMDC.

16. 84th Cong., 1st sess., S. J. Res. 39, Constitutional Amendment, Feb. 9, 1955, LF-EMDC.

17. 84th Cong., 2d sess., S. J. 31, Constitutional Amendment, 1956, LF-EMDC.

18. 83d Cong., 1st sess., S. J. Res. 23, Constitutional Amendment, Jan. 16, 1953, LF-EMDC.

19. *Congressional Record,* Jan. 21, 1955, S. 451, reprint in LF-EMDC.

20. Text of Dirksen-Bricker Amendment, 1956, LF-EMDC; EMD to Gordon Shocket, Mar. 28, 1956, LF-EMDC; Washington *Post* and *Times Herald,* Mar. 13, 1956, LF-EMDC.

21. Hughes, *The Ordeal of Power,* p. 125.

22. Henry Cabot Lodge, *As It Was: An Inside View of Politics and Power in the '50s and '60s* (New York: W. W. Norton, 1976), p. 149.

23. *Public Papers of the Presidents of the United States, Dwight D. Eisenhower,* 1956 (Washington, D.C.: Government Printing Office, 1958), p. 1,090.

24. Ibid., p. 1103.

25. "Meet the Press" (NBC-TV), May 19, 1957, script in R&R-EMDC.

26. Robert P. Howard, *Illinois: A History of the Prairie State* (Grand Rapids, Mich.: William B. Eerdmans, 1972), pp. 549-50.

27. "Dirksen Hodge Pal: Stengel," Chicago *American,* Oct. 26, 1956, C-EMDC.

28. Dixon (Ill.) *Telegraph,* June 22, 1956, C-EMDC.

29. Chicago *Tribune,* Oct. 30, 1956, C-EMDC.

30. James A. Maxwell, "Nervous Men in Illinois," *The Reporter* (Nov. 1, 1956), IF-EMDC.

31. Copy of political advertisement, 1956, C-EMDC.

32. LD, *Mr. Marigold,* p. 147.

33. "Dirksen Stresses Peace and Prosperity Theme in Country," Savannah (Ill.) *Times-Herald,* Sept. 18, 1956, C-EMDC.

34. DDE to EMD, Aug. 9, 1956, C-EMDC.

35. Press Release, Oct. 8, 1956, R&R-EMDC.

36. Ibid.

37. Sam Rayburn to Kenneth D. McKellar, Nov. 12, 1956, Papers of Sam Rayburn.

Everett Dirksen as a senior at Pekin High
School (*Dirksen Center*)

Lieutenant Everett Dirksen in World War I
(*Dirksen Center*)

Everett Dirksen in 1950, while running for the U.S. Senate
(*Dirksen Center*)

Senator Everett Dirksen in 1951 on the Capitol steps with his wife, Louella, and his daughter, Joy (*Dirksen Center*)

Governor Thomas E. Dewey talking to Senator Everett Dirksen at
the 1952 Republican National Convention (*Dirksen Center*)

Senator Everett Dirksen delivering the presidential nomination
speech for Senator Robert A. Taft at the 1952 Republican National
Convention (*Dirksen Center*)

President Dwight D. Eisenhower conferring with Senator Everett Dirksen (*Dirksen Center*)

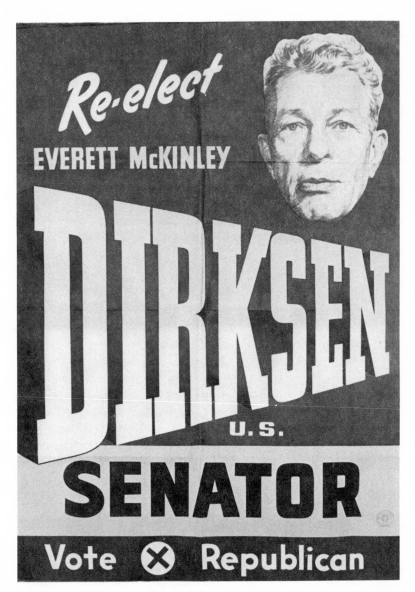

Campaign poster for Dirksen's successful 1956 reelection campaign (*Dirksen Center*)

Vice-President Richard M. Nixon in conversation with Senator Everett Dirksen (*Dirksen Center*)

GOP House Minority Leader Charles Halleck and Republican Senate Minority Leader Everett Dirksen during a telecast of the "Ev and Charlie Show" (*Dirksen Center*)

President John F. Kennedy signing the Nuclear Test Ban Treaty in 1963. Left to right (front row): Sen. John Pastore, Sen. J. William Fulbright, Hon. George Ball, Sen. Everett Dirksen, Sen. Leverett Saltonstall, Vice President Lyndon B. Johnson; (second row): unidentified, Hon. W. Averell Harriman, Sen. George Smathers (hidden), Hon. Dean Rusk, Sen. Hubert H. Humphrey, Hon. William C. Foster, Sen. Howard Cannon, Sen. Thomas Kuchel (*John F. Kennedy Library*)

President Lyndon B. Johnson huddling with Senator Everett Dirksen in the Oval Office of the White House (*Lyndon Baines Johnson Library*)

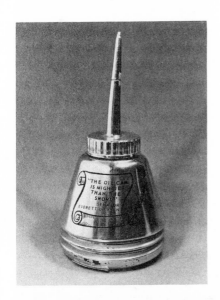

Miniature oil can kept on the desk of Senator Everett Dirksen to symbolize his role as a compromiser (*original in Dirksen Center; photo by Jack Carr*)

Telecast of GOP House Minority Leader Gerald R. Ford and Senator Everett Dirksen as the "Ev and Jerry Show" (*Dirksen Center*)

Cover photo on the dust jacket of Dirksen's last record album, issued posthumously by Bell Records and reprinted here by permission

Gravesite of Everett Dirksen at cemetery in Pekin, Illinois (*photo by Jack Carr*)

Bust of Everett Dirksen by sculptor Carl Tolpo in front of the Dirksen Center (*photo by Jack Carr*)

6

Dirksen as Minority Leader: A New Style of Leadership

THE POLITICAL FORTUNES of Everett Dirksen were at high tide when the 85th Congress convened in January of 1957. There was an opening in the GOP leadership hierarchy as a result of the defeat of Senator Eugene Millikin of Colorado. Millikin, an anti-Eisenhower Republican whom the president virtually ignored during the 1956 election, held the post of chairman of the Republican Senate Conference. Whoever held this position presided over the party caucus. The status of Senator William Knowland of California, the minority leader, also complicated the situation. Knowland harbored presidential ambitions. He had made his availability known in 1956, when for a time it appeared as if Eisenhower physically would not be able to run for reelection. In a not very secret fashion Knowland had already made plans to seek the presidency in 1960. Thinking the Senate a poor platform from which to launch his campaign, he planned to seek the governorship of California in 1958. Being governor, he reasoned, would automatically give him control over a large delegation and make him a prime contender for the GOP presidential nomination when Eisenhower vacated the White House four years hence.

With these ambitious plans in mind, Knowland wanted to pick his successor while he had the opportunity. Usually the whip, or assistant leader, gained an advantage by having the inside track to become minority leader when the incumbent retired or was defeated. The problem was that Leverett Saltonstall of Massachusetts, representing the eastern-liberal-internationalist wing of the GOP, currently held the post of party whip. Knowland, himself an arch-conservative-isolationist, worked with Styles H. Bridges of New Hampshire (also of the Old Guard) to rearrange the structure of party leadership. Bridges was chairman of the Republican Policy Committee. Their strategy, which succeeded, was to persuade Saltonstall, ostensibly for the sake of party harmony, to step down as whip and accept the chairmanship of the Republican Senate Conference. Then Knowland and Bridges sponsored Dirksen as their candidate for whip. This ploy worked and Dirksen was selected as the new whip. It was paradoxical that the legatees of the Taft wing engineered Ev's election to assistant minority leader at the time when Dirksen was so closely identified with Eisenhower's policies.

General reactions to Dirksen's ascendancy into the GOP leadership ranks were very positive within GOP circles. He was acceptable to all shades of Republicans because of his pleasant personality, tolerance of all viewpoints, and his reputation for hard work. When asked his opinion about Ev's election, President Eisenhower replied, "I have never denied that Senator Dirksen and I have had some strong differences, but he has turned into a very valuable lieutenant when I called on him for help."[1] Ev, in turn, acknowledged his pro-Eisenhower stance by telling a reporter, "I am on friendly terms with the President."[2] In Illinois, leading Republicans talked openly about Ev being the heir apparent to Minority Leader Knowland.[3] Dirksen, as whip, gained valuable experience for the minority post. In fact, because Knowland was so preoccupied with his presidential ambitions, Ev often played the role of acting minority leader. Realizing that his future opportunity depended upon maintaining his stance as a broker between the conservatives and liberals within his party, Dirksen kept his political fences well mended. "I see myself to be a middle-of-the-roader," Ev told an interviewer on television, "and since we do not put restrictions upon the members of our party, I suppose they can be catalogued as a little more liberal or a little less liberal, but I still like the term 'Republican' very much."[4]

By mollifying both wings of his party Dirksen remained on good terms with each while leading the fight for White House proposals. Ev was prompted more and more to grasp the reins of leadership when Knowland would drag his feet or openly oppose portions of the president's programs. As a party leader Ev increasingly submerged his personal views in favor of measures proposed by the administration. To the press Senator Dirksen continued to describe himself as a "moderationist."[5] Not wanting to become identified too strongly with either the conservatives or liberals, he walked a tricky middle road. Asked if he were a Modern Republican on a radio interview, Dirksen again deftly eschewed a label by answering, ". . . I simply have to think of myself as a Republican and I believe most of the party members will do likewise." Dirksen, it is noted, then made it clear he would support the administration. "I try, of course, to support the President of the United States because he is the party leader," Ev explained. "I think I have supported the Administration policies pretty well."[6]

The leadership model adopted by Dirksen was a combination of the best traits of Robert Taft and Kenneth Wherry. Taft's brilliance lay in the fact that he had such detailed knowledge of pending legislation. Wherry's effectiveness stemmed from his likeable personality. Dirksen's tools of the trade as a leader were his mastery of details, open candidness, cordiality, concern for the principles espoused by his colleagues, and the ability to persuade without being obnoxious. Ev's favorite saying was, "The oil can is mightier than the sword."[7] The passage of scripture which he most often quoted was from James 5:16: "Confess your faults one to another, and pray for one another, that ye may be healed. The effectual fervent prayer of a righteous man availeth much." On his desk Dirksen had a wooden plaque with the inscription, "Oh, Lord, the sea is so great and my ship is so small."[8] A leader so inclined as Dirksen to take into consideration the feelings of others, to deprecate his own role, and to utilize wit and humor evoked from his colleagues much affection and good will.

As a legislative leader, Dirksen was adept at blunting the edges of controversy, building coalitions, and widening the areas of agreement. Senator Jacob Javits (R-N.Y.), one of the most liberal Republicans in the upper chamber, aptly described his approach to Dirksen: "He can be amenable. He knows how to develop an amalgam of views among thirty-two high-powered prima donnas on the Republican side. Yet he can be stubborn, and we hope we don't run into the blunt end of his stubbornness. The best posture with him is always to come clean, to deal with him, because that is the way he responds most."[9]

Increasing fame and political power over the years did have their effect on Dirksen. He loved the limelight and at times tended to make his personal views on certain issues the public position of the party. After coming from the White House, Ev could, and did on occasion, exhibit a bit of vanity by depicting himself as the president's sole spokesperson. And what a performance Dirksen could put on for the press! Sitting on top of his desk with newspeople crowded around, Ev could regale them with his repartee. For instance, when asked about rumors that Vice-President Nixon had approached him to form a Nixon-Dirksen duo for the 1960 presidential election (which was not true), Ev obfuscated his reply in a flow of vague rhetoric to make it appear there might be some substance to the story.[10] Frequently he was asked how certain pieces of legislation were faring. If he had little or nothing to report, Ev resorted to humor as a way of evading a direct answer. In effect, he would say, "I am doing my best." With a wide grin he would then amplify upon the situation with a witty anecdote. One such story Ev told involved a man convicted of committing several crimes. He was sentenced to fifty years on the first count, forty years for the second, thirty years for the third—all to run consecutively. When the full significance of this sentence fell on the offender he looked in piteous bewilderment at the judge and said, "Judge, honestly, I don't believe I can serve that long." The judge, puzzled for a moment, then said, "My good friend, just do the best you can."[11]

In 1958 events took place which made it possible for Dirksen to make his move for the position of minority leader. William Knowland, as expected, did not seek reelection to the Senate. Not to seem overly eager, Dirksen issued a perfunctory statement that he would not actively campaign for the position of GOP minority leader. He made his availability known but, seemingly, would let the job seek him. Yet no one climbs up the ladder of political preferment with one's hands in one's pockets. Neither did Ev. He called in all of his political "IOUs." To broaden his appeal to liberal Republicans, Dirksen indicated that he favored "more active participation" by all GOP Senators in strategy conferences "so as to develop fully the party viewpoint on all issues."[12] Ev also announced publicly he favored a more equitable distribution of committee assignments for Republicans with less seniority. When the GOP Senate caucus met in January of 1959, prior to the opening of Congress, Dirksen confidently predicted, "I have the votes."[13]

The liberal Republicans, led by Senator George Aiken of Vermont, promoted the candidacy of Kentucky's John Sherman Cooper to challenge Dirksen. Clifford P. Case of New Jersey, speaking for the GOP liberals, claimed that Dirksen's stance "does not represent what we believe the party should stand for."[14] Ev was aware of the liberal revolt against him and had taken steps to circumvent it. First, he stressed his pro-administration voting record. In the last Congress Ev was in support of President Eisenhower 88 percent of the time in contrast to Cooper's 76 percent. Second, Ev spread the word he would support Thomas Kuchel of California, one of the liberals, for the post of whip. Third, Dirksen solemnly pledged to give the liberals, most of whom had less seniority than members of the Old Guard, better committee assignments. Fourth, and the final trump card, Ev let it be known the White House backed his candidacy.[15] When the vote was taken on January 7, 1959, Ev won over Cooper by a tally of 20 to 14. Although the sixty-three-year-old Everett M. Dirksen had been in the Senate only eight years and was eighteenth in seniority, he was now the new GOP minority leader.

The White House was pleased with what transpired not only in the Senate but the House. Charles Halleck of Indiana had deposed Joseph Martin of Massachusetts as House minority leader. Ev and Charlie, as they would become known, liked each other. They were both from small towns, were pragmatic, and displayed the flexibility needed for their respective roles as legislative leaders. Eisenhower had frequently grumbled to his presidential aide, Sherman Adams, how he disliked the weekly meetings with Knowland and Martin. The latter two, in his view, were too negative and reactionary. Ev and Charlie were vastly different.

By and large, they supported Eisenhower's programs, gave sound advice, and remained loyal even over issues they might personally have opposed. Eisenhower so liked Ev and Charlie that he once commented to Sherman Adams that the weekly leadership meetings "have become a pleasure, something I actually look forward to."[16]

John Eisenhower, who served as his father's White House aide, testified to the intellectual growth of Everett Dirksen. When the Soviet Union prompted its East German satellite to issue threats about absorbing West Berlin, John commented, "I was a bit astonished to observe how little some of the legislators actually knew about the Berlin situation." He then elaborated on Dirksen's good performance. "As the morning went on, moreover, his grasp developed remarkably. Finally he put together his recommendations for a public statement: (a) we have explored the situation and will maintain our rights and responsibilities to the people of Berlin; (b) we have agreed to stand firm but are willing to negotiate; and (c) our military capabilities are adequate for our particular position in the world." John concluded his observation with this tribute to Dirksen: "These constituted to my mind about as good a summary of a U.S. public position as had been drafted by anybody."[17]

True to his word, Dirksen did reassign younger Republicans, most of whom were in the liberal or moderate wing of the GOP, to better committee assignments. In order to induce older Republicans with more seniority to yield up at least one of their choice committee assignments, Ev set the example by giving up his seat on the important Appropriations Committee. Thus liberals such as Kuchel got on Appropriations; Case on Labor; Carlson on Foreign Relations; and Javits on Banking. Ev made it a regular policy thereafter to see to it that every freshman senator got at least one important committee assignment. Again Dirksen set the example, in 1961 for instance, when he gave up his own seat on the Labor Committee so that newly elected John Tower of Texas could have it. In this manner Ev won the friendship of new members while getting an IOU to be collected later.

The year 1959 was momentous for Everett Dirksen in more than one way. It was the year he and his wife moved from their eighth-floor Berkshire apartment into their newly constructed home. Ev and Louella purchased a three-and-one-half acre plot in Louden County between Leesburg and Sterling, Virginia, about a one-hour drive from the Capitol. It was a wooded tract over-looking the Potomac River. Louella designed the house and Ev helped clear the ground. The house was built ranch style of stone and redwood, with a huge fireplace. It had a full-length picture window overlooking the beautiful riverbank. The house contained a second fireplace in the master bedroom, a study for Ev, and a grand piano used for regular sessions of singing old-fashioned ballads. Ev took delight in personally planting many shrubs and trees. Every year he would put out both a vegetable and flower garden. To attract birds to his yard, Dirksen built dozens of birdhouses. Ofttimes they were simple, made of coffee cans, and other times they were elaborate. One such birdhouse was a min-iature, scaled version of Mt. Vernon. Ev and Louella called their home "Heart's Desire."[18] In the garden was a plaque that read:

> The kiss of the sun for pardon
> The song of the birds for mirth;
> One is nearer to God's heart in a garden
> Than anywhere else on earth.[19]

There is no doubt that Dirksen would not have been able to survive the rigors of legislative leadership without the solace of Heart's Desire. Up at sunrise, he would putter in his garden when the weather permitted. Each morning before going to his Senate office he would spend at least fifteen minutes in his flower garden in silent prayer and meditation. He drew spiritual strength and physical renewal from his close contact with nature. Many times he would recuperate from illnesses with almost miraculous speed when at Heart's Desire. His first illness was a mild heart attack in 1957, but his recuperation was remarkable.[20] Being a constant coffee drinker, hot or cold, and a three-pack-a-day smoker, he was a frequent sufferer from ulcers. Temporarily he would switch to Sanka coffee, take Maalox by the bottle, and cut down on his smoking. Soon he would be back into the old pattern. The pres-sures of his office were always there, but time spent in his garden always seemed to refresh him and bring his health back to normal.

In 1959 Ev suffered from chest pains and again was forced to spend more time in his garden for relaxation. Dirksen went on a diet, reducing from 220 pounds to 180. President Eisenhower, who had formerly been a chain-smoker, told Ev regarding cigarettes, "I've been watching you and you've been leaning mighty heavy on those things. You ought to cut down."[21] Dirksen promised to stop smoking as Eisenhower had done. For weeks he would not carry cigarettes with him, but he would beg them from colleagues until it became a joke. Soon he was back to normal with a perpetual cigarette in his hand. In later years even when suffering from emphysema, to the point where he kept a bottle of oxygen in his office, Dirksen still could not quit smoking. It was a lifelong habit which he never did conquer.

While much of the business of the Senate was relatively routine, punctuated at times with partisan furor, some issues by their very nature were highly controversial without regard to party alignment. One of the most explosive and tension-filled issues to come before the Senate was civil rights. To Dirksen it was a moral issue and not one which gained him political support back home. In fact, it would hurt him, since his stronghold was downstate Illinois. The bulk of the state's black population lived in Chicago and, since the time of the New Deal, most were Democrats. Thus Ev had nothing to gain politically from pushing civil rights. Nevertheless in 1960, now minority leader, he led the fight for President Eisenhower's request to enact legislation to increase substantially the powers of the nearly impotent Civil Rights Commission that had been established in 1957. On February 8 Ev introduced the administration's proposal "to provide for the federal enforcement of civil rights."[22] Working with Majority Leader Lyndon Johnson, who was posturing for his party's presidential nomination, Dirksen agreed to hold around-the-clock sessions to terminate a southern filibuster. The debate had been going on for more than seven weeks, yet Ev was of the opinion that no filibuster should prevent a vote on the measure. As the twenty-four-hour sessions commenced, Ev sagely noted, "All of us are standing up well under this ordeal thus far but eventually the flesh must ride herd on the spirit."[23]

As one who perpetually represented the minority party in the

Senate, Dirksen was not one to condemn easily or seek thoughtlessly to break a filibuster. It was often the only weapon a minority possessed and Ev would make use of it himself in the future. On the Senate floor Ev admitted he had always favored prolonged debate. "I will confess my sins in public any old time." Senator Richard Russell, who had yielded temporarily to Dirksen, angrily replied, "Mr. President, I refuse to yield for that long a time to anyone."[24] Tempers flared as the eighteen Southern Democrats launched their 125-hour around-the-clock filibuster. Dirksen slept intermittently on a couch, sipped cup after cup of coffee, and when awake chain-smoked cigarettes between roll calls. When the southern Democrats could no longer continue their ordeal, the final vote for passage of the Civil Rights Act of 1960 was 71 to 18. Ev delivered all of the Republican votes in its favor. The new law levied criminal penalties for "threats of force"[25] or interference with court orders; made the possession of explosives a federal crime; made it illegal to flee a state to avoid prosecution; provided that election records be preserved for twenty-two months; and gave the commissioner of education authority to provide for desegregated schooling of sevicemen's children. Another step, albeit small, had been taken on the road toward achieving meaningful civil rights for all individuals. At the leadership conference at the White House, President Eisenhower congratulated Ev and other GOP leaders for their successful efforts. Senator Saltonstall noted that pro-Democratic newspapers were giving "much credit to Senator Johnson whereas much of it really belonged to Senator Dirksen."[26]

Ev Dirksen would be involved in more civil rights battles in the future. His statesmanship in this field was based on true concern for moral principles and individual rights. To a constituent who disagreed with his pro-civil rights stand Ev wrote, "I labor under no delusion whatsoever because political life has taught me long ago to be realistic, but there are some things one can glean from a devotion to American history and one of these is that sooner or later a moral cause will come out on top." He then went on to lecture his racist constituent. "The Constitution Preamble states that the people of the United States do ordain and establish this Constitution," contended Dirksen. "It does not say 'we the people with white skins or brown skins or black skins,' but all of the people."[27]

In a similar letter to his longtime friend, General Robert E. Wood (the former head of Sears, Roebuck and Company and one of the founders of the America First Committee), Ev once lectured, ". . . let me say that this is an issue which among other things has a deep moral aspect and there is a duty on the part of Republicans to do their full share if they hope to be worthy of the Republican tradition and particularly the imprint left upon this party by a humble man named Abraham Lincoln."[28]

As minority leader, Everett Dirksen had developed a close rapport with Lyndon B. Johnson. As the majority leader, LBJ controlled far more votes than did Dirksen, but on an issue such as civil rights there would have been no way for the Texan to have overcome the filibuster of southern Democrats without help from the GOP. LBJ told one of his aides that his chief concern was "keeping Dick [Richard] Russell [of Georgia] from walking across the aisle and embracing Everett Dirksen."[29] Ev liked LBJ personally and their relationship developed into a very close and intimate friendship that would endure all through Johnson's tumultuous period as president of the United States. As a professional politician, LBJ expected Ev to defend President Eisenhower and fight for his programs. When the Senate recessed in 1959 LBJ wrote Ev: "Of the leaders with whom I have served, there have been none who can wield the partisan stiletto with quite the gusto and the zest that you do. But even though the stiletto cuts deep, it never stings. I have an idea that we will always be friends, even though we will pursue separate paths."[30] On his "Your Senator Speaks" program, Dirksen described LBJ as being "aggressive, he's wiry, and is a very skillful leader." Ev also praised Johnson's resourcefulness and parliamentary agility. "Now and then of course we have to scowl at each other as you say, in the political turmoil, and also as a matter of conviction in dealing with these problems that come before us," Dirksen explained to his constituents in Illinois. "But I do pay testimony to him as a very able, and a very skillful Majority Leader of the Senate."[31]

During the last two years of the Eisenhower administration Ev displayed strong and effective leadership. On a "Face the Nation" television program in 1959 Minority Leader Dirksen asserted: "I have considered myself as the one who carries the flag for the administration, and I proceed to do it and to justify it as best I can and I think under every circumstance it can be justified."[32] Dirksen had done wonders in getting the GOP to close ranks on important issues such as civil rights. At the close of the 1959 session of the Senate, Alexander Wiley of Wisconsin, a former McCarthyite, wrote Ev, "You had a great part in sort of bringing the 'battlers at both ends' together into one Republican group."[33] Leverett Saltonstall of Massachusetts also congratulated Dirksen: "I believe much of the stimulus and energy that came to the Republican minority was due to your leadership. You worked hard. You worked intelligently, and you cooperated with every Republican Senator as well as with the majority leadership."[34] Even Vermont's George Aiken, who had led the liberal fight against Ev's election as minority leader, now conceded to Dirksen, "The Republican side of the aisle has functioned with more harmony this year than I have ever before known."[35]

At the close of the 1960 session of the Senate, Dirksen could again be proud of his record as minority leader. He had taken the lead in getting Eisenhower's defense budget approved; securing enactment of the Landrum-Griffin Labor Management Reform Act; getting approval of the Antarctica Treaty; helping to get through a stronger civil rights act; supporting amendments to Social Security for increasing health benefits to the aged; and pushing through a public housing bill acceptable to the president. Ev defended Eisenhower's stand on preserving fiscal responsibility and helped prevent the Democrats from using government spending to woo the electorate in the upcoming presidential election.

Once again Dirksen's role as minority leader was acclaimed by his GOP colleagues. John Sherman Cooper, whom Ev had defeated for his post, wrote Dirksen: "It has been a great privilege to serve under your leadership . . . you have made a magnificent record."[36] Jacob Javits of New York sent a commendatory letter which said, "I shall long remember with great appreciation your continuous cooperation during the civil rights fight, and your wonderful support on the health bill."[37] Freshman Senator Hiram L. Fong of Hawaii also lauded Ev with these words: "Our party's impact was great, a fact owning to your legislative skill and inspiring leadership in a most strenuous and taxing assignment."[38]

To foster unity and make known his appreciation to rank-and-file Republicans of whatever persuasion, Dirksen let his GOP colleagues know he prized their cooperation. He especially thanked the powerful Bourke B. Hickenlooper of Iowa. Ev made known his gratitude to the Iowan for his help and then noted: "Whatever divergence of views we may have were always advanced with good grace and full understanding. This complete freedom of expression is truly one of the great hallmarks of Republican faith. The record we leave is one of which we can be proud, and the cohesive spirit which has marked our common endeavors throughout the Session will be a strong weapon and a firm manifest to the country that we can function effectively as a party."[39] In this manner Dirksen promoted unity without necessarily demanding uniformity of thought.

Considering the spread within the GOP ranks from an ultra-conservative such as Barry Goldwater to an ultraliberal like Jacob Javits, it was amazing how many times Dirksen could get the support of both wings of his party. A study of the first session of the 86th Congress commissioned by Dirksen was quite revealing. The survey tallied the votes on 89 divided leadership issues (89 of 215 roll calls where the majority and minority leaders took opposite positions). If one isolates five representative conservatives and five representative liberals, a comparison can be made as to the group over which Ev had the most influence. By adding four Democrats the record illustrates how well Dirksen handled Republican liberals considering the way their counterparts in the Democratic party voted. The five conservative or moderate Republicans selected are John J. Williams of Delaware, Roman Hruska of Nebraska, Bourke B. Hickenlooper of Iowa, Barry Goldwater of Arizona, and Leverett Saltonstall of Massachusetts. They are paired against the following five GOP liberals (of varying persuasions): Thomas Kuchel of California, Margaret Chase Smith of Maine, George Aiken of Vermont, John Sherman Cooper of Kentucky, and Jacob Javits of New York. The Democrats selected are Paul Douglas of Illinois, Hubert H. Humphrey of Minnesota,

Mike Mansfield of Montana, and Lyndon B. Johnson of Texas. The results of the survey are contained in the chart below.[40]

Rank order	Vote with minority leader	Vote against minority leader	Absent	Name
1	89	0	0	Dirksen (R-Ill.)
2	81	4	4	Williams (R-Del.)
4	76	13	0	Hruska (R-Neb.)
8	73	9	7	Hickenlooper (R-Ia.)
9	72	5	12	Goldwater (R-Ariz.)
17	63	24	2	Saltonstall (R-Mass.)
30	48	32	9	Kuchel (R-Calif.)
31	47	42	0	Smith (R-Me.)
34	44	40	5	Aiken (R-Vt.)
40	39	45	5	Cooper (R-Ky.)
42	38	49	2	Javits (R-N.Y.)
49	17	72	0	Douglas (D-Ill.)
89	3	86	0	Humphrey (D-Minn.)
94	2	86	1	Mansfield (D-Mont.)
98	0	89	0	Johnson (D-Tex.)

While a higher percentage of the GOP conservatives and moderates followed Dirksen's leadership, it was noteworthy that Republican liberals came nowhere near Democratic liberals in opposing the minority leader.

The three leading contenders for the 1960 Republican presidential nomination were Vice-President Nixon, New York Governor Nelson A. Rockefeller, and Senator Barry Goldwater of Arizona. Everett Dirksen was never close to Nixon either as a senator or when the latter was vice-president. Politically, Ev viewed Nixon as a compromise candidate standing between the Goldwater conservatives and Rockefeller liberals. Since the New York governor was a powerful figure in eastern Republican circles, Dirksen viewed him at this time as an excellent candidate for the vice-presidency. In an interview on national television in 1959 Ev indicated a Nixon-Rockefeller ticket "would be a very happy thing for the party."[41]

Upon journeying to Chicago for the 1960 Republican National Convention, Dirksen stepped from the plane at O'Hare Airport and in his inimitable style smiled and announced, "I am happy to be back here in the broad, fertile bosom of Illinois in the resurrection of spring."[42] Ev was surprised to find that Governor William G. Stratton and the Illinois delegation were booming Dirksen for the vice-presidency.[43] No doubt Governor Stratton was eyeing Ev's Senate seat in case the junior senator was named to second place on the presidential ticket. Nixon might have done well to choose Dirksen as his running mate, but instead he gave the nod to UN Ambassador Henry Cabot Lodge. As it turned out, Ev would have been a much better campaigner. Ev's only role at the convention was to introduce President Eisenhower. Dirksen told the assembled delegates in exalted tones, "It has been my privilege to be a part of his team and help carry the flag, and I am proud and honored to present him."[44]

Normally, after the Republicans chose Nixon and Lodge and the Democrats selected Kennedy and Johnson, there would have been a short hiatus before the fall campaign started in earnest. But Lyndon Johnson saw to it that the Senate had only recessed, not adjourned, so there was a short rump session in 1960. It was now Dirksen's role as the leader of the loyal opposition to see to it that the Democrats did not make political capital out of it as Harry Truman had done in 1948 by calling a special session on "Turnip Day." In fact, it was Ev's intention to make the session boomerang, if possible, to the detriment of John F. Kennedy. The wise old pro had some parliamentary tricks up his sleeve that would make young JFK realize he was up against a master politician.

NOTES

1. "New Whip in Senate," New York *Times,* Jan. 4, 1957, C-EMDC.

2. Chicago *Daily News,* June 1, 1957, C-EMDC.

3. "Boom Dirksen for Knowland Post in G.O.P.," Chicago *Tribune,* Jan. 21, 1957, C-EMDC.

4. "Youth Wants to Know" (NBC-TV), Jan. 20, 1957, transcript in R&R-EMDC.

5. "Meet the Press" (NBC-TV), May 19, 1957, script in R&R-EMDC.

6. "Reporter's Roundup" (NBC-TV), Sept. 16, 1957, transcript in R&R-EMDC.

7. Penny, *Dirksen,* p. 131. These words were inscribed on a 6¾ inch white plastic replica of an oil can presented to Senator Dirksen by the chairman of the board and president of the National Can Corporation. The presentation read, "Presented in tribute to a great statesman . . . ," Memorabilia Collection-EMDC, hereafter cited as MC-EMDC.

8. Fred Bauer, ed., *Ev, The Man and His Words* (Old Tappan, N.J.: Hewett House, 1969), p. 13.

9. Penny, *Dirksen,* p. 15.

10. Charles B. Cleveland, "Mentions Dirksen for Vice-President," Chicago *Daily News,* Jan. 30, 1958, C-EMDC.

11. Address to Sons of St. Patrick, Mar. 17, 1958, text in R&R-EMDC.

12. "Dirksen Seen Choice for Minority Leader," *Congressional Quarterly* (Nov. 14, 1958), reprint in IF-EMDC.

13. "Senator Dirksen Challenged as Leader," *U.S. News and World Report* (Jan. 2, 1959), reprint in IF-EMDC.

14. Ibid.

15. "Ike Acts to Nip GOP Senate Split," Chicago *Daily News,* Dec. 17, 1958, C-EMDC.

16. Sherman Adams, *Firsthand Report: The Story of the Eisenhower Administration* (New York: Harper and Brothers, 1961), p. 26.

17. John S. D. Eisenhower, *Strictly Personal* (Garden City, N.Y.: Doubleday, 1974), p. 225.

18. LD, *Mr. Marigold,* p. 152.

19. Bauer, ed., *Ev,* p. 88.

20. LD, *Mr. Marigold,* p. 155.

21. "Great White Father's Smoke Signals," *Chicago American,* n.d., C-EMDC.

22. 86th Cong., 2d sess., S. 301, text in LF-EMDC.

23. "Fails to Reach Rights Accord in Conference," Chicago *Tribune,* Mar. 3, 1960, C-EMDC.

24. "Potomac Patter," Washington *Daily News,* Mar. 5, 1960, C-EMDC.

25. "Rights Bill Passed by Senate, 71 to 18," Washington *Post,* Apr. 9, 1960, C-EMDC.

26. Legislative Leadership Meeting, Apr. 26, 1960, Republican

Congressional Leadership File, Dwight D. Eisenhower Library, hereafter cited as RCLF-DDEL.

27. EMD to Richard C. Patton, May 7, 1962, GGC-EMDC.

28. EMD to Robert E. Wood, June 1, 1959, Robert E. Wood Papers-HCHL.

29. Harry McPherson, *A Political Education* (Boston: Little, Brown, 1972), p. 130.

30. LBJ to EMD, Sept. 14, 1959, RCLF-DDEL.

31. "Your Senator Speaks," Jan. 26, 1959, script in R&R-EMDC.

32. "Face the Nation" (CBS-TV), June 21, 1959, script in R&R-EMDC.

33. Alexander Wiley to EMD, Sept. 14, 1959, RCLF-DDEL.

34. Leverett Saltonstall to EMD, Sept. 14, 1959, RCLF-DDEL.

35. George Aiken to EMD, Sept. 15, 1959, RCLF-DDEL.

36. John Sherman Cooper to EMD, Sept. 6, 1960, GGC-EMDC.

37. Jacob K. Javits to EMD, Sept. 12, 1960, GGC-EMDC.

38. Hiram L. Fong to EMD, Sept. 2, 1960, GGC-EMDC.

39. EMD to Bourke B. Hickenlooper, Aug. 31, 1960, Papers of Bourke B. Hickenlooper-HCHL, hereafter cited as Hickenlooper Papers.

40. Report, "Accumulated Rank Position Entire Senate Membership Based on 89 Divided Leadership Issues," Adam Stricher to EMD, Jan. 15, 1960, WP-EMDC.

41. "Face the Nation" (CBS-TV), June 21, 1959, script in R&R-EMDC.

42. John Dreske, "How Stratton 'Created' Boom," Chicago *Sun-Times,* July 27, 1960, C-EMDC.

43. "Stratton Plugs for Dirk," Chicago *Daily News,* July 22, 1960, C-EMDC.

44. "Dirksen Hails President As Man of Peace," Chicago *Tribune,* July 20, 1960, C-EMDC.

7

Dirksen and Kennedy:
The Loyal Opposition
Versus the New Frontier

WHEN THE SENATE reconvened after the national conventions were over in 1960, Majority Leader Lyndon B. Johnson, his party's vice-presidential nominee, was placed in the unusual position of having to play second fiddle to John F. Kennedy, who headed the Democratic ticket. Vice-President Richard M. Nixon, the GOP presidential candidate, was in a better position to remain in the background and let Minority Leader Dirksen handle the parliamentary maneuvering. With their huge majority the Democrats presumably could enact the many promises contained in their 1960 party platform. These promissory planks pledged revision of the immigration law; less reliance on military assistance and more emphasis on foreign aid; an increase in the growth of the economy without inflation; tax reform; a rise in the minimum wage to $1.25 per hour; increased farm price supports to 90 percent of parity; provision for more financial assistance to local communities; creation of a peace corps; less reliance on nuclear weaponry and more stress on maintaining strong conventional military forces; steps to end the "missile gap"; and enactment of a civil rights bill to strengthen the attorney general's power in the area of filing civil injunction suits in federal courts.[1]

Senator Dirksen took delight, for instance, in pointing out to JFK how, as a senator from Massachusetts, he had vigorously supported the farm policy of Agriculture Secretary Ezra Taft

Benson which called for flexible price supports. In 1956, when the Soil Bank measure was being debated, Kennedy said, "To those of my colleagues who call upon me to support the 90-percent program . . . as a means of stabilizing farm income during the current farm recession, I can only point to the decline in farm prices and income which has taken place during the operation of that 90-percent program."[2] Ev chided JFK by saying, "Obviously the Senator is uncomfortable over the fact that his party platform commits him to return to rigid farm price supports . . . which his own voting record and numerous speeches place him squarely on record against such a course." Dirksen concluded his chastisement with a jibe at Kennedy's youth by teasing, "But I suppose boys will be boys."[3]

The Democratic platform, to Dirksen, was a document that "promises everything to everybody all the time."[4] Since the Democrats' civil rights plank was the very item the southern Democrats had deleted from the Civil Rights Act of 1960, which was Eisenhower's proposal, Ev decided to put Kennedy on the spot. He instructed Kenneth Keating of New York and Hugh Scott of Pennsylvania, two liberal Republicans, to introduce a civil rights bill that would empower the attorney general either to use court injunctions or to initiate civil suits to end segregation. Dirksen announced in mock seriousness, "They will give the Democrats a chance to adopt their own platform. That is the acme of unselfishness."[5] Obviously the civil rights bill had no chance of passage, since there would not be time to break the filibuster inevitably conducted by southern Democrats when such measures came up. What Ev demonstrated was that the Democrats too had widely divergent wings in their party and the voters should be apprised of that fact.

Humor was Dirksen's basic verbal tool to attack Senator Kennedy's proposed New Frontier program. When the proposal to raise the minimum wage to $1.25 per hour came up on the floor, it ran into as much opposition from southern Democrats as from Republicans. Ev was for raising it to $1.10 an hour but opposed too high a jump lest it create more unemployment. Knowing it would not secure enough votes to pass, Ev commented: "Oh, that's a happy demise. But we shall not attempt to lay it to sleep by giving it a semantic injection."[6] Dirksen even poked fun at himself. While trimming a tree in his yard at Heart's Desire, Ev accidently fell to the ground. Displaying a scar on his arm he joshed, "I sawed myself off a limb."[7] Likewise, Ev joked sardonically over a parliamentary maneuver he was using to sidetrack the Democrats' many proposals by saying: "The tabling device when I use it is always good and justified. When someone else uses it I have to examine it on its merits."[8] Dirksen bantered about his frequent submission of amendments as a tactic to delay proceedings. He quipped, "Being of the modest, offenseless, noncombatant type, I will defer to the superior judgment of any Republican who tries such a dastardly move."[9] The myriad displays of Dirksenian wit drew many reporters to the galleries who normally would have ignored such Senate repartee. Catching Ev on his way to the Senate chamber one reporter inquired: "Should we cover? Are you going to say anything good?" Ev tossed back the remark, "Oh, I don't know how good it will be, but it will be quotable."[10]

Following the disastrous rump session of the Senate, in which the Democrats could not agree on much of anything, Dirksen issued a press release facetiously charging that the Kennedy-Johnson duo fled from Washington, D.C., because it was "the Boot Hill of the New Frontier, where the Democratic platform lies buried after they gunned it down during the special session of Congress." In the same droll vein he continued his assault. "Most of the heavy spending proposed in the New Frontier was rustled from a book by Henry Wallace written in 1934 and curiously enough called the 'New Frontier.' " The Kennedy-Johnson version, he added, "can best be described as 'out where the waste begins.' " Referring to JFK's 35 percent record of absenteeism from the Senate in 1960, Ev amusingly called it the equivalent of playing hookey. "We call his the emptiest saddle on the New Frontier."[11] JFK's absence from the Senate was because of his entry into many state primaries. Once when returning from such a speechmaking tour, Kennedy complained to Ev of a sore throat and hoarseness. Dirksen, who liked JFK very much personally, gave him some advice on how to speak by using the diaphram rather than putting all the stress on his vocal cords. Kennedy followed this advice and was no longer troubled by inflammation of the vocal cords or laryngitis.

Everett Dirksen's warm feelings for John F. Kennedy and his genuine affection for Lyndon B. Johnson were manifested eloquently in what might be called one of the classic speeches ever given in the Senate. Ev was the speaker who gave it. Mingling humor with serious thoughts Dirksen spoke on the last day of the special session:

> I wish our distinguished compatriots who seek higher political office everything good—up to a point. I have always been amazed to see what a difference sixteen blocks can make. I extend the Senators who are candidates the warm hand of fellowship. We want to keep them here. I want to keep them here. It would be lonesome without my distinguished friend the Majority Leader, and my distinguished friend from Massachusetts. . . .
>
> My affection is as high as the sky and it is as deep as the sea— and I do not want sixteen blocks to intervene. We shall be charitable and gracious, there will be no malice; but we will pursue our responsibility as an opposition party and do our best. . . .

Ev concluded his farewell to JFK and LBJ with the peroration: "So, au revoir. We shall see you on the home diamond somewhere; and when it is all over, on the morning of November 9, all the healing waters will somehow close over our dissidence, and we shall go forward as a solid phalanx once more."[12]

When stumping the country for the Nixon-Lodge ticket, Senator Dirksen gave countless speeches. It all went for naught when the final tally came in. The narrowness of Kennedy's victory caused much consternation for Ev. He was particularly distressed over Nixon's loss of Illinois by a slim margin of 8,849 votes. This cost Nixon twenty-seven electoral votes and the presidency. Since Cook County was the bailiwick of Mayor Richard J. Daley's Democratic political machine, with its reputation for tampering with the ballot box, Dirksen, as well as former President Eisenhower, sought to persuade Nixon not to concede defeat.[13] A spot recount in Chicago had turned up 2,512 uncounted votes for Nixon. But despite this evidence, for some personal reason, Nixon turned down the idea of challenging the outcome of the 1960 presidential election.

When Everett Dirksen returned to Washington, D.C., there were only thirty-six Republicans in the Senate matched against sixty-four Democrats. To his advantage was the fact the veteran Lyndon Johnson was no longer majority leader. As vice-president, LBJ would not be running the Senate. That job went to Mike Mansfield of Montana. Senator Mansfield was a quiet-mannered, self-effacing man who did not indulge in the arm twisting and wheeling-dealing tactics of his predecessor. Mansfield's weakness as a floor leader indirectly enhanced Dirksen's prestige and power. The death of H. Styles Bridges (R-N.H.) in 1961, a powerful leader of the Old Guard, and of Robert S. Kerr (D-Okla.) in 1963, next to LBJ the most dominant figure in the Democratic ranks, also contributed to Dirksen's rise as a virtuoso performer in the Senate. As the undisputed leader of the loyal opposition, Ev indicated at the outset of the 87th Congress he was not going to play the role of a blind obstructionist. "We are not going to oppose just to be opposing," Dirksen explained. "We want legislation passed, and our aim will be to modify Mr. Kennedy's proposals."[14]

It was not a happy occasion when Everett Dirksen and Charles Halleck, the minority leaders of their respective chambers, met with President Eisenhower in January of 1961. The transition of power was all but completed. Only the inaugural remained. In his last meeting with Ev and Charlie, Eisenhower made an important recommendation. The Republican party, he noted, "must have a voice while it's out of power." The president suggested that this mode of expression be "based on the collective judgment of the congressional leaders."[15] As a result of this advice, Dirksen took the lead in forming the Republican Joint Congressional Leadership Conference. The first meeting was held in Ev's Senate office on January 24, 1961. Present, in addition to himself, were Senator Leverett Saltonstall, chairman of the Republican Caucus; Senator Styles Bridges, chairman of the Republican Policy Committee; Representative Charles Halleck, House minority leader; Representative Leslie Arends, House whip; Representative John W. Byrnes, chairman of the House Policy Committee; Representative Charles B. Hoeven, chairman of the House Conference; Representative Clarence J. Brown, ranking GOP member of the

House Rules Committee; Senator Thurston B. Morton, outgoing Republican national chairman; Representative William E. Miller, incoming Republican national chairman; Bryce Harlow, former aide to President Eisenhower; and Mark Trice, who served as secretary. Absent that day was Senate Whip Thomas Kuchel, who would be in attendance thereafter.

The initial meeting of the Republican Joint Congressional Leadership Conference was called to order by Senator Dirksen. It was decided that future meetings would be held weekly the day after the majority leadership met with President Kennedy. They would alternate between Dirksen's and Halleck's offices. It was agreed also that from time to time guests would be invited, such as ex-President Eisenhower and former Vice-President Richard Nixon. All policy decisions were to be made by this group, and its results were to be disseminated to Republican members of Congress. Following the weekly meetings there was to be a televised press conference, at which time "Senator Dirksen and Congressman Halleck should have full and free latitude in informing the press as to matters taken up and decided at the meeting."[16] The latter decision set the stage for what became known as the "Ev and Charlie Show,"[17] so named by reporter Tom Wicker of the New York *Times.*

As spokespersons for their party, Dirksen and Halleck would appear before the television cameras to make statements as to the position of the Republican party on the various issues of the day. Then the press conference would be opened up to questions from reporters. From the outset the "Ev and Charlie Show" was an instant success. Dirksen, in particular, found television a forum much to his liking. Ev was fitted with a pair of large, horn-rimmed glasses (without lenses) to hide the lines under his eyes. But his massive head, tousled hair, infectious smile, and charismatic stage presence all contributed to make him a national TV star. In his uniquely mellow tones Ev would gently needle the Democrats, shoot off witty gibes, or sternly lecture the president as a father would talk to his son. Richard Strout of the *Christian Science Monitor* called the "Ev and Charlie Show" "a cross between the Huntley and Brinkley NBC news broadcast and an old-fashioned minstrel show." JFK dubbed Ev and Charlie the "Untouchables," after a popular television series of the time.[18]

There is no doubt that Dirksen loved the klieg lights, the crowd of reporters around him (sometimes numbering over a hundred), and the attendant publicity of being chief spokesperson for the GOP. In his jocose style, he intrigued newsmen with his quips and rambling anecdotes. During the campaign JFK claimed there was a "missile gap" between the United States and the Soviet Union, because of the Russian sputnik being launched. After becoming president, Kennedy admitted no such gap existed. Dirksen promptly dubbed it JFK's "yap-gap."[19] There had been Democratic criticism of Eisenhower's playing golf too much rather than being at his desk. Ev said of JFK's playing golf, "I thoroughly approve of the President playing golf. You want to keep him fit . . . I want him to be able all the time to tee off on Khrushchev whenever it is necessary." Concerning President Kennedy's antirecession program, Ev, at one press conference, described it as "but a snowflake on the bosom of the Potomac."[20] Kennedy got a big laugh from one of Ev's jokes relative to the president's habit of using a rocking chair to soothe his injured back. Dirksen quipped, "I like rocking chairs. They give you a sense of motion without any danger."[21]

Some Republicans, particularly the younger liberals, were critical of Dirksen for what they thought was his cornball humor. Cartoonists, such as Herblock, had a partisan field day in creating clown caricatures of Ev and Charlie. In one such cartoon Herblock had Halleck asking Dirksen, "In 10,000 words or less Ev . . . is it true you're verbose?"[22] In another cartoon Dirksen and Halleck were depicted as vaudevillians with hats and canes in which Ev asked, "Should we recognize the Outer Mongolians?" Charlie replied, "I wouldn't recognize one if I saw him."[23] Dirksen did not take offense at all. He was used to self-deprecating humor and realized it was not an attack on his ego. In fact, the publicity raised his visibility to a national level, making him a kind of venerable institution.

Liberal pundits tended to lampoon the "Ev and Charlie Show," but conservative columnists regarded it as an effective instrument for the loyal opposition to reach a national audience. Peter Edson, in his sydicated column, catalogued some of the political results achieved by Dirksen and Halleck. They included forcing the Kennedy administration to cancel the deal whereby tractors were to be traded to Fidel Castro for prisoners; securing a unanimous Senate resolution against seating Red China in the UN; nullifying attempts at "back door" financing of foreign aid; getting the number of export licenses for trade with the Soviet Union reduced; and preventing diplomatic recognition of Outer Mongolia. It was primarily due to Dirksen and Halleck that Republicans solidly backed Kennedy during the missile crisis in Cuba and during the period of extreme tension when East Germans built the Berlin Wall. While playing their roles as leaders of the loyal opposition there was "little carping at President Kennedy himself."[24] William Edwards of the Chicago *Tribune* maintained: "For the first time in political history, a minority party had discovered an effective channel for voicing a unified policy of opposition to administration policies. Its effect upon congressional votes is conceded by Democratic leaders."[25]

Everett Dirksen genuinely liked reporters and they, in turn, regarded him as good copy. When the word was out that "Ev is up," meaning giving a speech on the Senate floor, the reporters flocked to the galleries to watch his performance. His friendliness and informality made him a favorite of the press. Sitting on his desk Buddha-style, with reporters crowded into his office, or even when facing television cameras, Ev could be very open and forthright. He put it this way: "I try to be candid, and if for any reason I had to pull a punch, I left it up to the press and TV and said 'Look, you will get me in trouble, but I will answer you anyway if that is the way you want it.' "[26]

Within the GOP, Dirksen was applauded by former President Eisenhower for his positive stance as the leading spokesperson for the Republicans in Congress. At a testimonial for Ev in Chicago, Eisenhower lauded Dirksen for being a "superb, loyal, courageous, and resourceful leader." He furthermore praised Ev for willingly volunteering to "carry the flag" or pick up the "hot poker" during his administration. He also extolled Ev's virtues as a patient leader: "I have never seen him angry. I have never seen him petulant. I have never seen him chagrined. Nor have

I ever seen him scold a colleague over a vote." Acknowledging Dirksen's oratorical prowess, Eisenhower noted, "How long would it be regarded as a significant gift unless it was coupled with facts, knowledge, conviction, and hard work." He ended his acclaim by saying to Ev, "I greet you as a loyal, true-blue team player, and I pay my personal tribute to you as a great American."[27]

President John F. Kennedy was, in his turn, highly appreciative of Dirksen's statesmanship when it came to crucial matters of domestic and foreign policy. In his role as minority leader and chief GOP spokesperson, Ev did criticize the New Frontier. JFK expected such criticism because his domestic policies were at variance with much that Dirksen stood for. Ev was leary of the welfare state aspects of Kennedy's programs, the increased deficit spending, and the attempts to increase the size of the federal bureaucracy. This did not mean Senator Dirksen intended to use his power to block all of Kennedy's proposals. The minority leader stated it this way: "It should be remembered that the minority has the same stake in the well being of the whole country as the majority, and in consequence you have to refine the role of the minority so that it will include these things—to support those proposals that the administration might offer if, in our judgment, they are in the interests of the country and if they're sound." In times of international crisis Dirksen definitely believed the GOP should rally behind the president. In such times, Ev believed, "we cannot as a minority show a disunited spirit to the world. We must make it manifest to the whole wide world and particularly those countries that are on the imperial march that this country is united behind the President, once policy has been set."[28]

There were those within the GOP who regarded Dirksen as being "soft on Kennedyism."[29] The right-wing Liberty Lobby seemed to view Ev as some sort of crypto-liberal who sold out to JFK. But, as Robert D. Novak argued in the *Wall Street Journal,* the minority leader's cooperative attitude was in the self-interest of the Senate Republicans. It got concessions not obtainable thrugh sheer partisan opposition. The conclusion reached about Dirksen's leadership was that it "has proved far more effective than [that of] his immediate predecessors."[30] The conciliatory attitude assumed by Everett Dirksen made it easy for JFK to seek the minority leader's help. Ev once observed: "John Kennedy was easy to talk to. When he had difficulties, he had no hesitation about calling me up for help. He always felt free to talk with me."[31]

It was particularly in the realm of foreign policy that Senator Dirksen gave great support to John F. Kennedy. During the Bay of Pigs fiasco and the subsequent missile crisis in Cuba, the GOP minority leader did not take partisan advantage of these situations to censure the president for his foreign policy failures. Rather, Ev backed JFK and actually stifled criticism from the GOP side of the aisle. This does not mean that Dirksen closed his eyes to mistakes. He was critical of Kennedy for not getting rid of Fidel Castro when he had the opportunity. Ev also exposed the attempted cover-up of the fact that four American flyers had been killed in Cuba.[32] When a dangerous situation developed in Berlin over the wall constructed by the East Germans, it was Dirksen who announced, "Let it be clearly understood that President Kennedy has the complete support of the Republican leadership in Congress in the Berlin crisis."[33] In a remarkable speech in which he described the bond of friendship between Polish-Americans and their beloved relatives in Poland, Ev created a receptive mood for the Senate to remove foreign aid restrictions it had imposed upon that country the day before.[34] Dirksen also spoke up in defense of JFK's policy with regard to Laos and Vietnam. In agreeing with the domino theory, Senator Dirksen supported assistance to these countries to prevent them from becoming communist-dominated. "If they succumb," Ev asked, "what about the other countries like Cambodia and Burma and Indonesia?"[35]

There were many Kennedy administration proposals that would never have passed had it not been for Everett Dirksen's bipartisan support. The Telstar Communications-Satellite bill was stymied by a filibuster led by Senators Wayne Morse (D-Ore.) and Paul Douglas (D-Ill.). Ev persuaded enough Republicans to vote for cloture to end the dilatory talk-fest and thus permit the bill to be voted upon. It then passed easily. In the case of the United Nations Bond Purchase bill, to buy UN bonds up to $100 million, Dirksen secured twenty-two GOP votes for the measure to ensure a wide margin of passage since a big vote was needed to make a good influence on world opinion. Most Republicans wanted to oppose the creation of the Peace Corps. Ev reasoned with his colleagues in Congress that the GOP "should not take a negative approach to this program." He pointed out that "it does have appeal to young people as well as the churches."[36] Likewise, Dirksen supported the space project to land a man on the moon; increased expenditures for civil defense; and a civil rights bill, cosponsored with Majority Leader Mike Mansfield, aimed at eliminating discriminatory literacy tests used in qualifying voters to participate in federal elections. As Ev announced, "We propose to help Mr. Kennedy put it through Congress, if the Democrats can put their own ranks in order."[37]

Perhaps the most appeciated support by Dirksen was his action in helping to secure ratification of the Test Ban Treaty. This treaty would stop the testing of nuclear devices in the atmosphere, but it needed a two-thirds vote in the Senate. While the negotiations with the Soviet Union were being carried out in Geneva, Senator Dirksen had been urging JFK to order resumption of U.S. atmospheric tests. When Kennedy did indicate such tests might resume if the Soviets stalled much longer, Ev then queried, "Is President Kennedy's commendable stand of March 2, [1962] on resumption of atmospheric testing being watered down at Geneva to a point where our nuclear supremacy will be gravely endangered?"[38] Five months later Dirksen argued publicly that American nuclear supremacy should be maintained at almost any price so as to remain a deterrent to war. Speaking for the joint Republican congressional leaders, he vowed, "We believe we should complete our current series of tests. We believe we should start a new series if necessary to maintain our nuclear supremacy."[39] In the summer of 1963, when JFK unilaterally announced suspension of all atmospheric testing by the United States, Ev contended such a self-imposed moratorium was a "grave" mistake lest it give the Soviets a nuclear advantage.[40]

Assessing Dirksen's stand on the Test Ban Treaty when it was presented to the Senate in the fall of 1963 for ratification, it would appear, by virtue of his own pronouncements, that he would oppose its approval. But Ev was going to change his mind. JFK took great pains to have him briefed, particularly on the dangers of radiation fallout resulting from atmospheric testing. The treaty forbade testing in the ocean or outer space but not underground; therefore, the U.S. could continue to test nuclear weapons without fear of radiation. Such testing on the part of the Soviet Union also could be carefully monitored. Dirksen became convinced the treaty actually was in the self-interest of the American people. His task then was to persuade hard-line Republicans to change their minds and support ratification. When the Senate Foreign Relations Committee gave the treaty its approval by a 16-1 margin, Dirksen at this time indicated only a subtle shift in his stance by announcing, "I have said I would wait until all the evidence was in."[41] In leading others, timing is an important factor. Ev bided his time and began building his case. In his own mind Dirksen was certain of the need for prohibiting nuclear testing in the atmosphere. What he had to do was to present a series of arguments in such a manner as to justify a switch in the position of his hard-line colleagues. In a carefully prepared brief, Dirksen set forth a number of well-thought-out reasons why GOP Republican senators should join him in voting for ratification. He pointed out that in the 1960 GOP platform, Republicans themselves had called for suspension of nuclear testing in the atmosphere. Failure to ratify, contended Dirksen, would give the communists a "very effective weapon for propaganda" and mark the U.S. as "warmongers before the nations of the world." Any deviation from the treaty by the Russians would, Ev reasoned, "indeed firm up the moral position of the United States in the eyes of the world." This treaty, he attested, would be "in the interests of peace." Ev maintained, furthermore, that lessening Cold War tensions was a wise step in view of the ferment "in Vietnam and Korea, in Malaysia and Ceylon, in Burma and the Middle East, or the Berlin Wall." Finally, he insisted, even without atmospheric testing the U.S. would retain its nuclear arsenal, since "we are fully assured of a program that will keep us strong in the nuclear field."[42]

Everett Dirksen received important backing from former President Eisenhower, but he knew by conducting a straw vote that not enough Republicans would cast votes for approval to ensure

Senate ratification of the Test Ban Treaty. In a White House meeting with JFK, Ev suggested a tactic aimed at helping reassure some of his GOP colleagues that implementation of the treaty would not in any way undermine U.S. nuclear superiority. Dirksen gave Kennedy a draft of a statement directed at Majority Leader Mansfield and himself in which specific reassurances were given by the president relative to the maintenance of a preeminent nuclear position vis-à-vis the Soviet Union. JFK readily accepted the idea. He realized the doubting Thomases in the Senate had to be convinced and that implementation of the treaty would not be detrimental to the strategic superiority held by the U.S.

President Kennedy soon thereafter sent a letter to Dirksen and Mansfield, which was immediately made public. It read in part, "I am deeply appreciative of the suggestions which you made to me on Monday morning that it would be helpful to have a further clarifying statement about the policy of the Administration toward certain aspects of our nuclear weapons defenses, under the proposed test ban treaty now before the Senate."[43] Several specific assurances were given by JFK: underground testing would continue; a strong U.S. military posture would be maintained; vigilance would be pursued in detecting violations; peaceful development of atomic energy would continue; and signing of the treaty by communists nations such as East Germany would not imply diplomatic recognition of them on the part of the United States.

Senate ratification of the Test Ban Treaty, however, remained in doubt right up to the end. Dirksen had been deluged with over 250,000 pieces of mail, most of it opposing approval of the treaty. Only three other issues in his career up to this time had generated as much controversy: the 1940 Neutrality Act with its cash-and-carry provision, the MacArthur firing, and the McCarthy censure.

With great political courage, Ev set about to write a speech favoring ratification of the treaty. It had to be the kind of speech that might yet persuade one or two senators whose votes were needed to get the required two-thirds vote. He also personally appealed to holdouts within the ranks of the GOP. These appeals were gentle in nature but included the gamut from reasoning and pleading to simply calling in an IOU. It was always amazing that

Ev could use the *you owe me* appeal to such great effect. He was the most called-upon senator in terms of giving speeches. Ev was a national figure and when he came into another senator's state to campaign for him, it had a tremendous impact on voters. Having Dirksen campaign for you was tantamount to having the president (if you were a Democrat) come into your state as far as Republicans were concerned. Despite chronic ulcers and perpetual fatigue, Dirksen would help out his colleagues when they were in trouble at the polls. This earned for him a solid *good guy* reputation. Thus Ev did not hesitate, when issues were in doubt, to remind recalcitrant GOP cohorts of services rendered on their behalf.

When Senator Dirksen took the floor on September 11, 1963, to speak on the treaty, the galleries quickly filled. "Ev is up," went the call. Quietly, almost in a whisper, Dirksen announced: "At the outset, let me say I shall support the treaty. It is no easy vote." Knowing that other senators were also receiving much mail, possibly reflecting public opinion against ratification as did his, he sought to justify his position. "I feel that I must follow a type of formula laid down by Edmund Burke, the great parliamentarian and Prime Minister of Britain, when he said it was his business to consult with the people, but it would be a betrayal of his conscience and a disservice to them if he failed to exercise his independent judgment." Again knowing that some doubting senators were not yet sure whether the treaty was a good or a bad thing, Dirksen quoted Abraham Lincoln: "The true rule in determining whether to embrace or reject anything is not whether it have any evil in it but whether it have more of good than of evil. There are few things wholly evil or wholly good." Having justified using independent judgment and having established a logical rationale for accepting some evil with the good, Dirksen then closed with an emotional argument. "I want to take the first step," he asserted. "I am not a young man; I am almost as old as the oldest member of the Senate," admitted Dirksen. "One of my age thinks about his destiny a little," Ev said somberly. "I should not like to have written on my tombstone, 'He knew what happened at Hiroshima, but he did not take a first step.' "[44] The Test Ban Treaty was subsequently approved by an 81 to 19 vote.

Although JFK was beholden to Everett Dirksen for many legislative triumphs, he also realized Ev conscientiously opposed many of his domestic policies. Committed to fiscal responsibility as practiced by Eisenhower, Ev was apprehensive over the large budget deficits incurred by Kennedy. "Maybe the decade of the '60s will be the deficit decade," maintained Dirksen.[45] Regarding Kennedy's 1962 State of the Union message, which contained many costly proposals, Dirksen responded, "The prime factor in inflation is excessive government spending, particularly when it entails deficit spending."[46]

Balancing the need to stay at his post as minority leader, to prevent or modify the wasteful and costly aspects of New Frontier welfarism, with the state of his own health, Everett Dirksen faced a crucial decision. In 1962, the sixty-six-year-old Everett Dirksen had to decide whether or not to seek reelection to a third term in the Senate. He was bothered periodically by ulcers and had a history of abdominal pains caused by tension. Ev had also suffered from attacks of kidney stones, complained of heart palpitations, and on several occasions had to be hospitalized for "acute exhaustion."[47] His wife Louella advised Ev to retire, but after every illness Ev bounced back again and quickly resumed his heavy work load. Dirksen really had no intention of quitting. He entered the GOP primary in Illinois knowing his duties as minority leader would give him very little time for campaigning. His opponent was Harley D. Jones, a Chicago lawyer. When the primary votes were tallied, Ev easily defeated his challenger by a margin of 611,196 to 93,701. This would have been a comforting victory but for the fact the Democratic candidate for his seat, Representative Sidney Yates of Illinois, won over his primary rival by an equally large plurality.

Representative Sidney Yates was a formidable opponent for Dirksen. Yates had been slated by Mayor Richard J. Daley, head of the Cook County Democratic Organization, after UN Ambassador Adlai E. Stevenson refused an offer to run. Yates had been promised a federal appointment if he lost, so the fifty-two-year-old veteran congressman decided to tackle Ev. Yates was a liberal New Frontiersman with a 97 percent pro-Kennedy voting record in the House. He was known as a good campaigner and witty storyteller. His endorsement by organized labor ensured him adequate funding for the ensuing senatorial campaign.

On the eve of his reelection campaign, Senator Dirksen got an unsolicited boost when *Time* magazine ran a feature article on his career with his picture on the cover. In the magazine's highly readable prose style, Ev was described as a "big-handed, big-boned man with a lined cornfield face and greying locks that spiral above him like a halo run amok." It continued:

> He speaks, and the words emerge in a soft, sepulchral baritone. They undulate in measured phrases, expire in breathless wisps. He fills his lungs and blows word-rings like smoke. The sentences curl upward. They chase each other around the room in dreamy images of Steamboat Gothic. Now he conjures moods of mirth, now of sorrow.[48]

In rapturous tones the article went on: "They call him 'Irksome Dirksen,' 'the Wizard of Ooze' 'the Liberace of the Senate,' and 'Oleaginous Ev.' They claim he was born with a golden thesaurus in his mouth, that he marinates his tonsils in honey."[49] Actually, the latter witticism had an element of truth since Ev did massage his throat not with honey but with cold cream.[50] This was a daily ritual, odd as it may seem. The cover story on Dirksen went on to detail his record, his shifts in stands, and some negative aspects of his political philosophy, but overall it was a publicity man's dream, so Ev ordered thousands of reprints for use as campaign handouts.

In Illinois, Sidney Yates had already mounted a strong campaign against Dirksen. "I won't let him pussyfoot on any issue," Yates vowed. "To use his expression, I will 'ventilate' his record."[51] Already, early in his campaign, Yates had to counter the widely spread rumor that JFK did not really want to see Ev defeated. Yates kept publicizing the fact that Dirksen's voting record was only pro-Kennedy 26 percent of the time compared to his own 97 percent record. He was the "Kennedy man"—not Dirksen.[52] According to Yates, his GOP opponent was "just a chronic againster,"[53] In the midterm elections, Yates charged, "Let the Republican Party follow the servile pattern of the Ev and Charlie

Show. If it does, the inevitable result of party defeat and despair can be foretold."[54]

The two most difficult obstacles for Yates were Dirksen's enormous prestige and the fact the JFK did not really want to see Ev defeated. If Dirksen were not reelected, Bourke Hickenlooper of Iowa, who had succeeded Styles Bridges as chairman of the Republican Policy Committee, was a good bet for minority leader. He was an ultraconservative, a hard-liner against any kind of détente with the Soviet Union and much less willing to make any compromise or accommodation with the Democrats on any issue. The indications of Kennedy's feelings became obvious during the campaign. For instance, it was leaked in 1962 that the president would appoint to federal office several individuals recommended by Dirksen. Among these nominees was Bernard Decker, a Republican, who would be appointed to the northern Illinois federal court vacancy instead of the choice of senior Democratic Senator Paul Douglas. This obviously was a political sop to Dirksen and a slap in the face to both Senator Paul Douglas (D-Ill.) and Sidney Yates. Douglas lodged a protest with Lawrence F. O'Brien, special assistant to the president, complaining, "The Republicans are still making capital on Senator Dirksen's alleged pull at the White House in comparison to Yates."[55]

The political coup de grace for Sidney Yates came three days after the president made his appearance at a fund-raising banquet in Chicago. At 8:00 in the morning on October 23 Senator Dirksen got a phone call from the White House telling him an Air Force jet was ready to fly him back to Washington. The Cuban missile crisis made it imperative for JFK to confer with the leaders of Congress, and this included Ev as minority leader. From October 23 to 25 Dirksen was in the capital. After a few days in Washington, Ev told JFK he had to get back to his campaign in Illinois. Kennedy replied in an offhand manner, "Why, Ev, what are you worried about? You've got it in the bag."[56] Dirksen quipped to the president, "That was a nice speech you gave for Sid Yates in Chicago. Too bad you caught that cold making it."[57] The latter referred to the alibi Press Secretary Pierre Salinger handed out to reporters when Kennedy abruptly canceled his campaign tour to return hastily to the capital.

Always the fox, Dirksen was smart enough to let this JFK remark leak to the press and soon it was on the front pages of newspapers all over the state of Illinois. Yates tried to refute the story by calling Dirksen's comment "an outright and contemptible lie." The doomed Democrat charged, "This proves once again that Dirksen will do anything to get elected, even to the point of manufacturing quotations by the President of the United States."[58] Later, in his memoirs, Paul Douglas revealed how incensed he was when he wrote, "I was dispirited that the administration should treat so shabbily a good candidate who supported the forward-looking practices of our Democratic Party."[59]

There were two interesting footnotes to the 1962 election. The first episode involved the two candidates. When defeated candidate Sidney Yates received an appointment as the U.S. member on the UN Trusteeship Council from President Kennedy, Dirksen took time out to say a good word for him to ensure his quick confirmation by the Senate.[60] Ev did not take offense at some of the harsh campaign barbs thrown at him by Yates. It was part of the game of politics.

The second episode involved Senator Paul Douglas, who was very angry at the outcome of the election. Immediately following the election he fired off a letter to the president containing a blistering memorandum. It both denounced the pending appointment of Bernard Decker to the federal bench and excoriated the Senate Democratic leadership for having "actually supported Dirksen for reelection." Indirectly, Douglas's memo also upbraided the White House for its role in overtly helping to reelect Dirksen. The senior senator from Illinois contended the Decker nomination, if approved (it was), would confirm rumors of White House "support for Dirksen." In the same manner Douglas rebuked Mike Mansfield and Hubert Humphrey for their "glowing praise" of Dirksen just before the election. Douglas criticized the way in which Mansfield permitted Dirksen to report to the Senate the nomination of Arthur Goldberg to the U.S. Supreme Court; the acceptance of Dirksen's key amendments to the tax bill (which Douglas opposed); and the announcement on the morning of the election that Mansfield and Dirksen would make an around-the-world trip in the president's plane to crisis areas.

Getting even closer to 1600 Pennsylvania Avenue in his series of stinging rebukes, Douglas enumerated other evidence as to why the impression was given that the president did not want Dirksen defeated: on the morning of the Illinois primary, newspaper photographs showed Ev and JFK sitting side by side at the opening of the baseball season; when portions of the East Front of the Capitol were dedicated, the television cameras depicted Ev embracing JFK; during the missile crisis a special jet plane was sent to pick up Ev; and during the campaign "some high White House sources indicated to newsmen that Yates had little chance of winning and that Dirksen was not in trouble." It was Douglas's contention that "for months the word has been that there was a deal to elect Dirksen and not to push Yates."[61] Senator Douglas got no denial or explanation from the White House. He was essentially correct in his assessment of what had taken place.

Senator Dirksen's political association with JFK was professional while his personal relationship was one of father-like affection and admiration of a fellow senator who had ascended to the presidency. It was while preparing for Thanksgiving festivities in 1963 that Senator Dirksen heard the tragic news of President Kennedy's assassination at Dallas, Texas. He was fond of JFK as a colleague and frequently lapsed into calling him Jack even when Kennedy was President. JFK respected and admired Ev. They were both pragmatic and professional politicians. Both had a sense of humor and both were willing to compromise. It was a sad sight for Dirksen to see the bronze casket unloaded after having been flown in from Dallas. He was forced by grief to turn his head in disbelief. After returning to his Senate office from the airport, Ev groaned, "I still can't believe it has happened. I am stunned, shaken."[62]

The holiday was a somber one as Dirksen worked on a tribute to be given in the Senate. On November 25 Ev took the Senate floor to pay his last respects. "Here we knew his vigorous tread, his flashing smile, his ready wit, his keen mind, his zest for adventure," Ev attested. "Here with quiet grief we mourn his departure." Dirksen recalled with sadness how he had given the president a turkey just three days before the "evil deed." Ev vouched, "He was his own profile in courage." In his soft voice

Dirksen intoned the final peroration: "The *te deums* which will be sung this day may be wafted away by the evening breeze which caresses the last resting place of those who served the Republic, but here in this Chamber where he served and prepared for higher responsibility, the memory of John Fitzgerald Kennedy will long linger to nourish the faith of all who served that same great land."[63] Now Lyndon B. Johnson was president of the United States. He too had been in the Senate with Everett Dirksen for many years. When a reporter asked Dirksen whether he could work well with LBJ, Ev replied, "We have been friends for over a long period of time and I served as Minority Leader when he was Majority Leader and we always managed somehow to compose our differences and at the same time make the points, so far as our party responsibility was concerned."[64] In the ensuing years the bonds of friendship between Ev and LBJ would grow even stronger during the tumult and fury of the days that lay ahead.

NOTES

1. Democratic Platform, 1960, *National Party Conventions, 1831-1972* (Washington, D.C.: Congressional Quarterly, 1976), p. 100.

2. Senate Speech, Mar. 5, 1956, in *John Fitzgerald Kennedy, A Compilation of Statements and Speeches Made During His Service in the United States Senate and House of Representatives* (Washington, D.C.: Government Printing Office, 1964), p. 384.

3. "Dirksen Rips 'City Boy' Kennedy's Farm Blast," Chicago *Tribune,* Aug. 3, 1960, C-EMDC.

4. Washington *Post,* Sept. 30, 1960, C-EMDC.

5. Carroll Kilpatrick, "Dirksen Expounds on 'Dog-Days' Session," Washington *Post,* Aug. 19, 1960, C-EMDC.

6. Ibid.

7. Ibid.

8. Ibid.

9. John Dreiske, "Senator Dirksen Is Still His Loveable Old Self," Chicago *Sun-Times,* Aug. 12, 1960, C-EMDC.

10. Washington *Daily News,* Aug. 20, 1960, C-EMDC.

11. Press Release, Sept. 26, 1960, R&R-EMDC. The Henry Wallace referred to by Dirksen was a renowned New Dealer who served as

FDR's secretary of agriculture from 1933 to 1940, and held the office of vice-president from 1941 to 1944. For more information on Wallace's political philosophy see our *Henry A. Wallace of Iowa: The Agrarian Years, 1910-1940* (Ames: Iowa State University Press, 1968), and *Prophet in Politics: Henry A. Wallace and the War Years, 1940-1965* (Ames: Iowa State University Press, 1970).

12. Everett M. Dirksen and Herbert V. Prochnow, *Quotation Finder,* pp. 43-44.

13. Jack Bell, "Recount Upset Still G.O.P. Hope," Chicago *American,* Nov. 13, 1960, C-EMDC.

14. Jack Bell, "Dirksen Plans Helpful Policy," Washington *Post,* Dec. 19, 1960, C-EMDC.

15. "Ev and Charlie: GOP End Men," *Newsweek* (Apr. 24, 1961), IF-EMDC.

16. Minutes of the first meeting of the Republican Joint Congressional Leadership Conference, Jan. 24, 1961, RCLF-DDEL.

17. Henry Z. Scheele, *Charlie Halleck: A Political Biography* (New York: Exposition Press, 1966), p. 207.

18. Ibid., p. 208.

19. Victor Lasky, *J.F.K.: The Man and the Myth* (New York: Macmillan, 1963), p. 510.

20. *Newsweek* (Apr. 24, 1961), reprint in IF-EMDC.

21. Ibid.

22. Philadelphia *Evening Bulletin,* May 24, 1961, C-EMDC.

23. Washington *Star,* July 15, 1961, C-EMDC.

24. Peter Edson, "The Ev and Charlie Show," Washington *Daily News,* Sept. 7, 1961, C-EMDC.

25. William Edwards, "GOP Creates New Weapon to Unify Opposition's Voice," Chicago *Tribune,* Oct. 8, 1961, IF-EMDC.

26. "Issues and Answers" (ABC-Radio and TV), Jan. 23, 1961, script in R&R-EMDC.

27. Testimonial to Senator Everett M. Dirksen, Sept. 16, 1961, text of Dwight D. Eisenhower's speech in R&R-EMDC.

28. "Dirksen of Illinois," *The Christian Science Monitor,* June 7, 1962, IF-EMDC.

29. Theodore C. Sorensen, *Kennedy* (New York: Harper and Row, 1965), p. 391.

30. Robert D. Novak, "Dirksen's Dilemma," *Wall Street Journal,* Mar. 9, 1962, IF-EMDC.

31. Lewis J. Paper, *The Promise and the Performance: The Leadership of John F. Kennedy* (New York: Crown, 1975), p. 172.

32. Ralph de Tolendano, *RFK: The Man Who Would Be President* (New York: G. P. Putnam's Sons, 1967), p. 261.

33. Statement by EMD, July 21, 1961, Republican Joint Congressional Leadership Conference, text in R&R-EMDC.

34. Stephen Horn, *Unused Power: The Work of the Senate Committee on Appropriations* (Washington, D.C.: Brookings Institution, 1970), p. 145.

35. "After Sixteen Years," radio and TV speech, July 31, 1961, script in R&R-EMDC.

36. Minutes of the Republican Joint Congressional Leadership Conference, Mar. 16, 1961, RCLF-DDEL.

37. Statement by EMD, Jan. 30, 1962, RCLF-DDEL.

38. Statement by EMD, Mar. 22, 1962, text in R&R-EMDC.

39. Statement by EMD, Aug. 16, 1962, text in R&R-EMDC.

40. Statement by EMD, June 13, 1963, text in R&R-EMDC.

41. "Summary on the Test Ban Treaty," Sept. 3, 1963, text of radio and TV speech in R&R-EMDC.

42. Press Release, Sept. 11, 1963, R&R-EMDC. The position set forth by Dirksen also represented the thinking of former President Eisenhower. See Thomas F. Soapes, "A Cold Warrior Seeks Peace: Eisenhower's Strategy for Nuclear Disarmament," *Diplomatic History* 4 (Winter 1980): 57-71.

43. JFK to EMD and Mike Mansfield, Sept. 10, 1963, copy in Central Files, John F. Kennedy Library, hereafter cited as CF-JFKL.

44. *Congressional Record,* Sept. 11, 1963, reprint in R&R-EMDC.

45. William Moore, "Dirksen Sees Deficit Decade with Kennedy," Chicago *Tribune,* Mar. 30, 1961, C-EMDC.

46. Statement by EMD, Apr. 12, 1962, text in R&R-EMDC.

47. "Ailing Dirksen Enters Hospital for Observations," Chicago *Sun-Times,* July 15, 1961, C-EMDC.

48. "The Leader," *Time* (Sept. 14, 1962), reprint in R&R-EMDC.

49. Ibid.

50. LD, *Mr. Marigold,* p. 260.

51. Washington *Post,* Jan. 7, 1963, C-EMDC.

52. Chicago *Daily News,* Feb. 11, 1962, C-EMDC.

53. Chicago *Sun-Times,* Mar. 2, 1962, C-EMDC.

54. St. Louis *News-Gazette,* Mar. 11, 1963, C-EMDC.

55. PHD to LFO, Aug. 30, 1962, CF-JFKL.

56. Peoria *Star,* Oct. 27, 1962, C-EMDC.

57. David Detzer, *The Brink: Cuban Missile Crisis, 1962* (New York: Thomas Y. Crowell, 1972), p. 181.

58. George Tagge, "Yates Hurls 'Lie' At Story He Can't Win," Chicago *Tribune,* Oct. 27, 1962, C-EMDC.

59. Paul H. Douglas, *In the Fullness of Time: The Memoirs of Paul H. Douglas* (New York: Harcourt Brace Jovanovich, 1972), p. 574.

60. "Dirksen Backs Yates for UN Trusteeship Post," Chicago *Sun-Times,* Mar. 7, 1963, C-EMDC.

61. PHD to JFK with memorandum, Nov. 9, 1962, Paul H. Douglas Papers, Chicago Historical Society.

62. Jim Bishop, *The Day Kennedy Was Shot* (New York: Funk and Wagnalls, 1968), p. 576.

63. "Remarks made by Senator Everett M. Dirksen on the floor of the U.S. Senate, November 25, 1963, on the death of John Fitzgerald Kennedy, 35th President of the United States," text in R&R-EMDC.

64. "Interview on NBC Program 'LBJ Report No. 1,' " Nov. 25, 1963, script in R&R-EMDC.

8

Dirksen and Johnson:
Two Brother Artisans
in Government

FOR TWO SUCH divergent characters as Everett M. Dirksen and Lyndon B. Johnson, the strong bond of friendship that held them together was indeed a fascinating case of political symbiosis. Indication of this unique closeness and camaraderie was revealed by Lady Bird Johnson in her reminiscences. She recalled leaving her husband and Ev engaged in earnest conversation in the west hall of the White House one afternoon. They were, in her apt way of putting it, "two brother artisans in government" enjoying each other's company. Upon returning several hours later Lady Bird found the pair still there, leaning over head to head, chattering away as if time meant nothing. She overheard Dirksen say slyly, "You don't mind if we denounce you once in a while, do you Lyndon? You can explain that better than when someone on your side of the aisle denounces you." Her own thought on seeing these two political pros, although partisan foes, interspersing gentle banter with their serious discussion was simple enough. Lady Bird observed, "There is something terrifically right about watching them talk to each other."[1]

While Dirksen's relationship with JFK had been a cordial one, with Ev's role being more of a paternal senior senator toward a junior colleague, his relations with LBJ were those of a close and intimate professional peer. Dirksen and Johnson knew and respected each other from the days when both were in the House of Representatives, but their real friendship developed steadily and grew stronger only as they worked with each other in the Senate. This collaboration started when Ev was GOP whip and LBJ was Democratic majority leader. Later, when Dirksen became minority leader, their contacts increased daily and their mutual admiration for one another deepened into one of fraternal trust and affection. When LBJ became president in 1963, Ev remained the Texan's trusted congressional confidant and White House crony. This special relationship became an important factor in the manner in which Dirksen reacted publicly to the policies of the Johnson administration, especially those relating to the international scene.

The modus vivendi worked out by Ev and LBJ, initiated when the president was also in the upper chamber, was based upon a mutually agreed upon set of premises. They were enunciated by Dirksen as follows:

> The Senate is a public institution; it must work; it's a two-way street; and that requires the efforts of both parties. One party cannot do it on its own because if the opposition, or minority party, wanted to be completely obstructionist you could tie up the Senate in a minute, even with a handful of people. So we fully understood each other, that that's how it had to be. And that's the reason I got along exceptionally well with Senator Johnson.[2]

Dirksen went on to explain that whereas he and LBJ "took precious care to avoid a real collision," it did not signify the total absence of marked disagreements or exchanges of "harsh language." Occasionally this did take place. Yet, despite political differences and the necessary byplay of partisan politics, each agreed the Senate had to remain a "viable instrument" geared to "function for the interest of the country."[3]

In his memoirs, LBJ wrote this assessment of Ev, his brother compatriot: "Dirksen could play politics as well as any man. But I knew something else about him. When the nation's interest was at stake, he could climb the heights and take the long view without regard to party. I based a great deal of my strategy on this understanding of Dirksen's deep-rooted patriotism."[4]

George E. Reedy, LBJ's aide and onetime press secretary, also affirmed the closeness that existed between Johnson and Dirksen. As to the "personal esteem" in which the president held Ev, Reedy observed: "I can attest to this as I knew both men quite well. . . . They understood each other, trusted each other, and both were masters of what I consider the highest art of politics—working sensibly with political adversaries but without sacrificing political principles." Although "poles apart on domestic issues," asserted Reedy, they developed a "close affinity" while LBJ served as majority leader and Dirksen was minority leader. Reedy, who later became Nieman Professor of Journalism at Marquette University, recalled: "I was present at a number of conferences between the two men and it was obvious that they understood each other so well that they practically communicated by ESP. It took very little conversation for them to arrive at agreements on what they could do together and where they had to walk separate paths."[5]

President Johnson's trust and confidence in Everett Dirksen was indeed well placed. When asked once by a reporter what his role would be as minority leader relative to LBJ's administration, Ev answered, "Well, the role of the Republican Party, or any minority party for that matter, would be one of constructive opposition, not blind opposition, and by 'constructive opposition' I mean you accept the things that are good for the country, you try to amend or modify proposals that in your judgment and in the judgment of the Party are not good and if they contain more of evil, shall I say, than of good, then you reject them. But always you try to follow a constructive line."[6]

Senator Dirksen was a frequent visitor at the White House and was much consulted by President Johnson. It sometimes appeared that Dirksen, not Mike Mansfield the Democratic majority leader, was the personal pipeline through which the White House communicated its wishes to the Senate. On any given day Ev's phone could ring and have President Johnson on the other end. This occurrence sometimes took place several times during a day. LBJ might simply inquire as to Ev's health, argue over an amendment, beg for help on an upcoming vote, offer Ev some private information, or render thanks for rounding up Republican support for a presidential proposal. Once in a while the president would chide his not-so-servile chum for attacking him on the Senate floor. On one occasion, after being the recipient of Dirksen's well-phrased criticisms, President Johnson asked, "Now, why did you say that, Everett?" Dirksen replied in mock seriousness: "Well, Mr. President, you remember I am the leader of your opposition. And when three dogs come at you, you have to feed them some hamburger."[7]

In 1964 Ev was sixty-eight years old. He was afflicted with numerous ailments and yet remained a pivotal figure in the Senate. In that year alone he had to wear a brace for a back sprain, needed a blood transfusion because of a bleeding ulcer, suffered discomfort from cardiovascular malfunction, and received treatment for his worsening emphysema. President Johnson, who himself had been struck down by a massive heart attack while Senate majority leader, worried constantly about Ev's health. He needed Dirksen's help and realized it would be impossible for him to control Congress without Ev's assistance. Yet Senator Dirksen seemed indestructible despite his numerous illnesses. The Illinoisan learned to live with his infirmities by shrugging them off with the statement that "most of the important work of the world has been done by people who weren't feeling well."[8]

By temperament and design (because he led the minority party in the Senate) Everett Dirksen's mode of leadership differed distinctly from that of LBJ. Dirksen was far more subtle in the manner in which he exerted influence on colleagues. Unlike his Texas counterpart in the White House, Ev did not have prestigious favors or federal patronage to parcel out. He would not, moreover, wield the stick or twist arms to force recalcitrant senators into line. To keep from being overwhelmed by Democrats, since they had a sixty-seven to thirty-three advantage in membership, Ev battled with a Fabian strategy to avoid decisive defeat. To keep his own troops in line Dirksen utilized gentle persuasion, patient urging, and moral suasion. He was never argumentative, eschewed coercion, and avoided arousing ideological passions that might prove to be divisive. Considering the circumstances under which Ev had to operate he was sure, as he told a reporter, "you get more votes with an oilcan than you can get with a baseball bat."[9] To preserve party unity, Dirksen was not above dishing out blandishments and applying the soothing balm of honeyed words to those individuals whose key motivator was a flattered ego.

Even when unified, the GOP ranks were so thin compared to the number of Democrats it was necessary for Dirksen to maximize their effectiveness at all times. This was done by steering clear of direct confrontations when such moves meant sure vanquishment. To assure some GOP influence on legislation, Ev resorted to negotiation, compromise, and shrewd use of the amendatory process to modify measures that could not be defeated. Dirksen often had to be satisfied with a slice; a fourth of a loaf; a half a loaf; and once in a while no loaf at all. When possible, he made deals to gain concessions. In 1963, for instance, Ev agreed, after a series of meetings with LBJ, to pledge GOP support for the next year's budget after Johnson agreed to keep it below the $100 billion figure.[10] This was, according to previous projections, a cut of $7.7 billion. It was the best victory Dirksen could attain considering the thinness of his ranks.

Whenever Ev was forced to enter into a prearranged deal, his prime criterion was the "fact that the final objective was the good of the country and its people."[11] This line of logic did not always satisfy ideological purists within the Republican party. They insisted upon total and uncompromising opposition in terms of their doctrinaire beliefs rather than compromise in order to have some impact on what emerged from Congress. Time after time Dirksen demonstrated the ability to convince most of his colleagues of the wisdom of being pragmatic and effective rather than being ideologically pure and impotent.

Timing is important in politics and Senator Dirksen seemed to have a built-in radar when it came to knowing how people felt and when the appropriate time had arrived to move on important legislation. This acute sense of timing pertained to the prevailing feelings of the general public as well as the mode of thought pervading the minds of his colleagues in the Senate. At his annual birthday party in January 1964, where key members of his party were in attendance, Dirksen made some cogent, politically inspired, philosolphical observations. In a series of instructive utterances, seemingly unrelated, Ev outlined why action or inaction is more appropriate at any given time. He averred,

"One thing is eternal. That is change." He then noted, "One thing is certain—progress is the steadfast undramatic application of human life upon what is here." And finally Ev warned: "There is a time for everything and a season for every purpose. When we forget this, our efforts often prove fruitless and abortive."[12]

The issue Senator Dirksen was alluding to was civil rights. The circumstances surrounding passage of civil rights legislation during the Eisenhower administration made for limitations in both its scope and legal implementation. The pressure of the civil rights movement, which had been mounting since the 1950s, now demanded further action in the 1960s. In effect, Dirksen was saying to his GOP colleagues that this was the time for men and women of good will to move another step forward in the direction of making sure that all individuals secured the privileges and protections of the U.S. Constitution regardless of race or color. Ev sensed that it would be perilous for the nation to delay the solution of this issue any longer.

In 1964 LBJ was likewise convinced of the necessity for securing passage of the stalled civil rights bill. Southern Democrats had sounded the death knell to President Kennedy's measure by threatening a filibuster in the Senate. It was obvious to Lyndon Johnson that a cloture vote would be necessary before this piece of legislation could be enacted. To stop debate took a two-thirds vote of those present. In addition to southerners, who traditionally thwarted civil rights measures by their dilatory tactics, there were many Republicans loathe to vote cloture simply because the filibuster had always been a potent weapon for a minority. Everett Dirksen himself was not above using it, or a threat of one, to further GOP objectives. Since sixty-seven votes were needed to invoke cloture, the Democrats, who had the votes to pass a civil rights bill once the filibuster was broken, needed Republican votes to force an end to debate.

In this situation, Everett Dirksen, as minority leader, held the key to success or failure relative to the enactment of a civil rights bill. In discussing strategy with Attorney General Robert F. Kennedy, brother of the slain president, LBJ reminded Kennedy, "The person who you're going to get the votes from, really in the last analysis, is Everett Dirksen."[13] Senator Hubert H. Humphrey of

Minnesota, the Democratic whip and longtime civil rights advocate, likewise conceded that "the key to cloture remained Everett Dirksen." Although they were political foes with totally different voting records, Humphrey and Dirksen were also genuine friends. To ensure Ev's cooperation, Hubert gallantly deferred to his colleague from across the aisle by giving him center stage and showering him with public accolades. "But mostly," Humphrey wrote about Dirksen in his memoirs, "when you scraped away everything else, he had a sense of history and his place it it."[14]

The support given by Senator Dirksen to invoke cloture in 1964 was truly an act of statesmanship. Ev's actions were dictated solely by his deep concern for furthering civil rights and not by political expediency. Dirksen had never been the recipient of Chicago's black vote, which was predominantly Democratic, and there was certainly no organized white pressure for civil rights legislation from downstate. In fact, agitation by blacks, plus some rioting, had caused the rise of a white backlash among some middle-class Americans. At best, Ev sensed a greater acquiescence among whites for civil rights than heretofore, but in no way would he benefit at the polls by what was really an act of political courage.

It was up to Dirksen to deliver about four-fifths of the GOP vote to choke off the filibuster. How could this be achieved? There were six Republicans who were adamantly opposed to voting cloture. They were John Tower of Texas, Barry Goldwater of Arizona, Edwin L. Mecham of New Mexico, Milward L. Simpson of Wyoming, Wallace F. Bennett of Utah, and Milton B. Young of North Dakota. Pitted against them on the other end of the political spectrum were the liberal Republicans from the Northeast. These included such senators as Jacob Javits of New York and Clifford Case of New Jersey. These two solons had large black urban constituencies with which to contend. The crucial swing group was composed of Senators from relatively sparsely populated midwestern states with small numbers of blacks, who neither viewed civil rights as a burning issue nor wished to suspend debate at this time. Representative of this group were Bourke B. Hickenlooper of Iowa, Len B. Jordan of Idaho, Karl E. Mundt of

South Dakota, and Carl T. Curtis and Roman L. Hruska, both of Nebraska.

It was this swing group which Ev had to convert en masse to his cause. They were generally conservative men of conscientious sensitivity who, while not liking racial discrimination as such, did not really approve of the idea of condoning massive federal intervention. Dirksen understood the thinking of his fellow midwesterners and set about to make the proposed civil rights bill acceptable to his skeptical, fence-sitting GOP colleagues. Dirksen's office became the headquarters for hammering out a compromise measure. In and out of his Senate office went Majority Leader Mansfield, Hubert Humphrey, and Deputy Attorney General Nicholas Katzenbach. Each worked with Ev on a package of civil rights amendments to make the final measure one with which midwestern Republicans could live. Dirksen was a true master at finding just the right language in the wording of an amendment to give it the widest acceptance possible. Slowly but surely Dirksen was making progress. Mike Manatos, an administrative assistant to the president, who was assigned specifically to help Dirksen in any way, reported to Lawrence O'Brien, the legislative liaison between the White House and Congress, that "the attitude is most encouraging as it applies to Dirksen and his group."[15] When asked by a reporter how things were coming along, Ev answered in his inimitable way, "We have been beating out the iron upon the anvil of discussion."[16]

What Dirksen did to broaden support for the civil rights bill was to moderate, but not emasculate, certain controversial provisions contained in the measure. For example, an Equal Employment Opportunities Commission was created to act as a conciliatory agency to preclude mandatory intervention by the Department of Justice. Likewise, local agencies within a state were given ninety days to handle complaints about job discrimination first before a final federal involvement would take place. The provision for cutting off federal funds as punishment for not fostering integration in public schools was limited to the school district or districts involved—not to an entire state. Ev made the overall bill palatable to his conservative cohorts by carefully fashioning the language. In one section, for instance, it was indicated in specific terms that an employer would be guilty of violating the law only if he or she intentionally practiced discrimination in hiring and firing. The power of the federal government to investigate both interference with voting and vote frauds was altered to delete the latter since it had nothing specifically to do with civil rights as such. Hence, the denial of voting, but not vote fraud cases in general, was cause for federal investigation. Dirksen deliberately refashioned the administration's civil rights bill to permit legal remedy to emanate first from local and state governments before federal intervention would take place. This introduction of local initiative to forestall federal action made the civil rights measure acceptable to those Republicans heretofore unalterably opposed to it.

Nothing Dirksen did, however, could satisfy southern Democrats. Ev told reporters: "Dick Russell, [Senator Richard Russell (D-Ga.), the leader of the southern filibuster] says the Attorney General has nailed my skin to the barn door to dry. Well, nobody has hung up my conscience and my sense of history to dry. Pardon me for the sermon."[17]

Debate had been going on for over two months when Senator Dirksen took the floor for his final speech before joining with Mike Mansfield to move acceptance of the filing of a cloture petition. There were a few GOP senators still equivocating on the issue and Ev meant to win over their votes. "For myself," he spoke, "I have but one purpose and that is the enactment of a good, workable, equitable, practical bill having due regard for the progress made in the civil rights field at the state and local level." To bolster his case Ev quoted Victor Hugo's entry in his diary made on the night he died: "Stronger than all the armies is an idea whose time has come." Dirksen went on to contend: "The time has come for equality of opportunity in sharing government, in education, and in employment. It will not be stayed or denied. It is here." Ev then used a story to make a point: "Years ago, a professor who thought he had developed an uncontrovertible scientific premise submitted it to his faculty associates. Quickly, they picked it apart. In agony he cried out, 'Is nothing eternal?' To this one of his associates replied, 'Nothing is eternal except change.' " Finally, Dirksen argued it was time to invoke cloture so a civil rights bill could be enacted. "It is essentially moral in character. It must be resolved. It will not go away."[18]

On June 12, after a sixty-seven-day talkathon conducted by southern Democrats, the Senate voted for cloture by a vote of seventy-one to twenty-nine. Dirksen delivered twenty-seven of his thiry-three votes on the GOP side of the aisle. It was a remarkable feat. Ironically, one of the Republicans voting both against cloture and the final civil rights act was Senator Barry Goldwater, who was soon to be the Republican presidential nominee. Ev had spent much time trying to persuade Goldwater to join him, but the doctrinaire Arizonan would not budge from his position that the civil rights bill was unconstitutional. Years later Sentor Goldwater explained, "Senator Dirksen talked with me about the Civil Rights Act, pointing out that my voting against it would be a political mistake, but when I explained to him the constitutional reasons I had for opposing it, he understood it and that was the end of it." Goldwater went on to comment: "There was never any friction between the two of us. I held him in great respect. In fact, there was almost the feeling of father to son. He never tried to get me to support any legislation other than just a friendly word or two and he always understood my position."[19]

The Civil Rights Act of 1964, so skillfully midwifed by Senator Dirksen, was enacted by a vote of seventy-three to twenty-one. In its final version the measure forbade discrimination in public accommodations; outlawed literacy tests; authorized the attorney general to bring suits when local agencies failed to provide suitable remedies; extended the life of the Civil Rights Commission; provided for termination of federal funds for programs where discrimination was permitted; and created the Equal Employment Opportunities Commission.

Everett Dirksen was the hero of the hour. Liberals lauded him, the press praised him, and Lyndon Johnson was indebted to him. LBJ later wrote of Ev's key role: "In this critical hour Senator Dirksen came through, as I had hoped he would. He knew his country's future was at stake. He knew what he could do to help. He knew what he had to do as a leader."[20] Larry O'Brien, as President Johnson's legislative liaison lieutenant, had spent many hours with Ev. He wrote to Dirksen, "Your always reasoned and courteous approach to the problems at hand had made our working relationship a most agreeable one — although possibly not the unalloyed pleasure it could have been were we members of the same political party."[21]

Ev had never before received any recognition, let alone political support, from the black community in Chicago. In fact, civil rights protesters had picketed his home and office while he was leading the fight for cloture. But after the Civil Rights Act of 1964 was passed, the Chicago *Defender,* a leading black newspaper, editorialized:

> Even in the high noon of our sharpest criticism of Senator Dirksen, we recognized his intellectual honesty, his rare talents, and the skills he can summon in defending his position on the ultra sensitive race issue.
>
> We must confess that in the past we have misunderstood his motives. Today, however, we doff our hats to him for the grand manner of his generalship behind the passage of the best civil rights measure that has ever been enacted into law since Reconstruction.[22]

There were some ultraconservatives on the race issue within the Republican party who disagreed with Dirksen on civil rights. Back in Ev's home state, there was such a coterie of Republicans definitely opposed to either breaking the filibuster or enacting a civil rights bill. Important among this group was General Robert E. Wood, former president of Sears, Roebuck and Company and a founder of a once-powerful isolationist organization known as the America First Committee. He was very active in Illinois politics and was not bashful about letting Dirksen know that instead of leading the fight against the southerners, the minority leader should be their close political ally. In rebuttal of Wood's assertions, Ev contended the future of the GOP did not lie "in the Deep South" and, secondly, "when you can get more than 80 percent of the Senate Republicans to concur in which I have done I doubt whether I can be far wrong."[23]

Senator Dirksen dared to take a tough stand against the segregationists in Illinois because he had renewed his credentials with this right-wing element by being an early supporter of Senator Barry M. Goldwater for president. It was Ev who originally persuaded the Arizonan, then a member of the Phoenix City Council, to run for the U.S. Senate in 1952. Dirksen was also instrumental in getting Goldwater the chairmanship of the Senate Republican Campaign Committee, a position which allowed the westerner to become widely known throughout the rest of the country. When Goldwater entered the presidential race in 1964 those Republicans in Congress representing the Midwest and Far West tended to regard the outspoken conservative from Arizona as the legatee of the Taft mantle. Liberal Republicans, of course, viewed Goldwater as a reactionary if not an outright right-winger. Leaders in the anti-Goldwater camp included Governor Nelson Rockefeller of New York, Governor William W. Scranton of Pennsylvania, and former Senator Henry Cabot Lodge, then U.S. Ambassador to South Vietnam.

In January 1964, Harold E. Rainville, Dirksen's special assistant and head of his Chicago office, notified General Robert Wood that effective but quiet efforts were being made to further Goldwater's presidential ambitions. Relative to Dirksen's intentions, Rainville confided to Wood, "You may be sure that his interest and his activities are now, as they were in 1952, with a conservative of the Taft or Goldwater stripe. As a matter of fact, with his knowledge I have been working rather closely with the Goldwater people and I think more than any one person have done as much as possible to line up a solid delegation to the convention."[24] The extent of support in Illinois for Goldwater became evident on April 14 when the Arizonan received 64.5 percent of the vote in the GOP primary.

The Goldwater blitz hit high speed in California on June 2, when the Arizona senator narrowly defeated Governor Rockefeller in the California primary. Governor Scranton, who had won only his own state's presidential primary, and that by a write-in vote, made a belated effort to prevent Goldwater from being nominated. Part of his strategy was to get large delegations to withhold their votes from Goldwater by giving them to favorite son candidates. Scranton informed Dirksen, "You'd make a great favorite son."[25] Ev refused to go along with this political ploy, knowing full well the game was already over. Since Goldwater had gone the primary route and won, Dirksen said, "Barry has earned his spurs . . . he travelled the length and breadth of this land."[26] Liberals who had so recently applauded Dirksen were now critical of his support for Goldwater, but Ev felt he had to endorse his Senate cohort with enthusiasm—not reluctance—to sustain his credibility with the party's right-wing faction. "Too long have we ridden the grey ghost of me-tooism," Dirksen announced. "When the roll is called, I shall cast my vote for Barry Goldwater."[27]

Because of his primary victories, Barry Goldwater was the titular head of the Republican party, yet the shortly-to-be presidential nominee refused to accept the principle of compromise so expertly practiced by Dirksen. Wrapped in his own narrow set of principles, Goldwater voted his personal conscience without considering the overall political fortunes of the GOP. One of Barry Goldwater's unrestrained characteristics was to speak and vote in the Senate on the basis of doctrinaire principles without any concern for political fallout. With no forethought, seemingly, for public reaction, Goldwater was one of only six Republicans to vote against both cloture and the civil rights bill. Although Goldwater regarded Dirksen as his "wise counselor, my most constructive critic . . . [and] my loyal friend,"[28] the soon-to-be GOP presidential nominee adamantly refused to go along with Ev and support civil rights.

Thus it was that even after Senator Dirksen won new laurels for the Republican party in orchestrating passage of the Civil Rights Act of 1964, the party was severely hurt anyway by Goldwater's nay vote. The GOP could hardly boast and claim credit for its enactment and appeal to black voters with pride when its own presidential candidate repudiated it by a negative vote. To overcome, or at least in an attempt to nullify, the adverse repercussions of Goldwater's recorded vote against the Civil Rights Act, Dirksen worked with Representative Melvin Laird (R-Wis.), chairman of the Platform Committee, to include a plank relative to future enforcement of the law. Thus the GOP platform, paradoxical as it may seem, included a pledge that Republicans could be depended upon for "full implementation and faithful execution of the Civil Rights Act of 1964."[29]

Everett Dirksen also figured prominently in securing two planks in the platform calling for constitutional amendments—one to permit prayers in public schools and the other to allow states having bicameral legislatures to "apportion one House on bases of their choosing, including factors other than population."[30] More will be said about both later, but suffice it to indicate at this juncture that Dirksen favored more consultation via referenda with the general public on the need for amending the U.S. Constitution. Dubbed by others the "Dirksen Doctrine,"[31] it was Ev's contention that Congress should not unilaterally resist any change nor should an activist Supreme Court initiate change on its own simply by a subjective reinterpretation of the Constitution. Rather, according to Dirksen's political credo, the state legislatures— through ratification—or the people—through a constitutional convention—should be given more opportunities to make known their will. Ev felt his effort during the Eisenhower administration to secure adoption of a constitutional amendment giving the vote to eighteen-year-olds was thwarted somewhat undemocratically when Congress refused even to approve it so that state legislatures might consider it. Dirksen wanted the "country to think about it."[32] Thus he was firmly convinced that giving the states an opportunity to approve or reject constitutional amendments was far more beneficial to the democratic process than merely relying upon the more remote representation of Congress or the legal ingenuity of the Supreme Court.

Everett Dirksen had two official tasks at the 1964 Republican National Convention, held at the Cow Palace near San Francisco. His first stint before the microphone was to read a message sent by former President Herbert C. Hoover. The aged Iowan, who would be ninety years old in another month, was too infirm to be present personally. Ev had known Hoover ever since the latter's role in reorganizing the executive branch of the government during the Truman and Eisenhower administrations. It was a delight for Dirksen to say some kind words about the elder statesman whom Ev called the "Grand Old Person of the Grand Old Party."[33] After all the proceedings were over, Senator Dirksen sent the hoary Hoover an official gold convention badge with this felicitation: "I was truly honored by the assignment to present your message to the Republican Convention in San Francisco and I am delighted that they gave you such a great ovation which you richly deserved."[34]

The second job Ev had at the convention proved to be more of a chore than he originally bargained for. While still in the process of persuading Barry Goldwater to join with the preponderant majority of his colleagues in voting for the Civil Rights Act of 1964, Dirksen had agreed to nominate his fellow senator for the presidency at the upcoming Republican National Convention. Dirksen found it difficult to write a nominating speech because of his candidate's highly individualistic voting record and long history of expressing his views so frankly as to be impolitic. Ev's final product was not a typical "the man who" type of nominating speech, but more the folksy injunction that "one cannot make a silk purse out of a sow's ear." Like a lawyer seeking to emphasize the best attributes of his client, Dirksen prepared an address whose primary purpose was that of portraying Goldwater as a straightforward man of conscience, a fearless figure with true moral courage, and one willing to fight for the preservation of constitutional principles as he understood them.

It was late afternoon on July 15 when the roll call of states began to elicit from delegation chairpersons their desires to place names in nomination. When Alabama yielded to Illinois, this gave Everett Dirksen the opportunity to speak first. Goldwater's name would therefore be the first to be placed in nomination. Goldwaterites were jubilant as Ev mounted the rostrum. Preliminary votes taken on a series of floor fights over the platform indicated that Goldwater's followers were in total command of the convention. Among those delegates opposing the Arizonan's nomination there existed not just a feeling of having lost the fight to name the nominee, but a pervasive attitude of defeatism. Dirksen was well aware that most non-Goldwaterites felt that with the Arizona senator heading the ticket the GOP was doomed to defeat at the outset.

The tone of the nominating speech delivered by Everett Dirksen was dictated by the circumstances, which forced Ev to make it one long apologia laced with appeals for party harmony. At the beginning Dirksen implored his audience, "Let neither doubt nor defeatism impair our forces or our strength." In an attempt to

conjure up a sympathetic image for his candidate Dirksen depicted Goldwater in the framework of a "rags to riches" char-
acterization. He therefore told the delegates: "He is the grandson
of a peddler." There were some who snickered at the seemingly
demeaning portrait (he got critical mail), but in general Goldwaterites liked the imagery which described their hero as the son
of an immigrant who became a self-made man. Goldwater himself
liked the descriptive phrase. No sooner had Dirksen created a
symbolic likeness of an Horatio Algerish figure than he began to
offer a tortured but plausible explanation for Goldwater's many
political faux pas. "It is common experience that quoting only
a part of what a man has said has become truly a favorite indoor
sport," Ev maintained. "By this standard no man ever lived, no
hero was ever born but by some utterance, some vote, some
opinion can be decimated."[35]

Whatever good will Dirksen garnered for Goldwater with his
carefully calculated nominating speech soon vanished when Goldwater, as the GOP presidential nominee, gave his acceptance
speech. Ev winced in anguish and liberal Republicans seethed
with anger when the Arizonan uttered these needlessly intemperate and divisive words: "Anyone who joins us in all sincerity
we welcome. Those who do not care for our cause, we don't
expect to enter our ranks in any case. And let our Republicanism,
so focused and so dedicated, not be made fuzzy and futile by
unthinking and stupid labels. I would remind you that extremism
in the defense of liberty is no vice. And let me remind you also
that moderation in the pursuit of justice is no virtue."[36]

Dirksen was well aware that Goldwater's tactless rhetoric,
whether deliberately provocative or not, added fuel to the already
raging fires of disunity. Some liberal Republicans were so disenchanted they indicated their intention of walking out of the convention to go fishing. In political parlance this meant they were
going to sit out the campaign. Upon returning to Washington,
D.C., Senator Dirksen took it upon himself to play the role of
peacemaker. As spokesperson for the Republican Joint Congressional Leadership Conference, of which Goldwater was now a
member, Ev prepared a statement saying that "Republicans are
already at work resolving their differences." This type of pacific

pronouncement really constituted a bit of political whistling in the dark, but it was the kind of public statement that had to be made for the good of the party. While admitting to the role of "underdog," it was also stated that the GOP was "determined to carry the vital issues of our times to the American people." Since a great deal of politics revolves around posturing and image making, LBJ was portrayed as a "clever and determined politician." Goldwater, on the contrary, was depicted as a man possessing "strong and deep convictions and a moral fiber" making it possible for him to "solve our pressing problems of human relations at home" and stop the "ever-spreading cancer of communism abroad."[37]

Unfortunately, through his careless choice of words, Barry Goldwater soon created for himself the trigger-happy image of a reckless two-gun westerner ready to engage in an atomic shootout with the communists. One such gaffe was an ill-thought-out remark making it appear that the Arizonan believed a NATO commander should have the full authority to decide if an atomic weapon was to be used in battle. At a meeting of the Republican Joint Congressional Leadership Conference, Everett Dirksen sought to mitigate the adverse political effect by helping draft a damage-control type statement. To soften the impact of Goldwater's remark, it was made to appear probable that NATO commanders already did have stand-by authorization for use of atomic weaponry. Therefore President Johnson was called upon "immediately to make clear to the American people the truth in this matter—whether or not the United States Commander in Europe has or has not been given authority to use tactical nuclear weapons in time of dire emergency, and also whether or not this authority was given under the two previous presidents."[38] Actually, both Dirksen and Goldwater already surmised that NATO commanders, while having atomic weapons at their disposal, never possessed carte blanche authority to use them. A local decision to deploy nuclear arms would have needed Pentagon confirmation subject to presidential approval.

The aspect of the 1964 campaign that made it impossible for Goldwater to erase the warmongering image he had acquired was his basic agreement with LBJ on foreign policy. The president simply denied that he, as commander-in-chief, had given any authorization for use of atomic weaponry to field commanders. Beyond that LBJ did not give any public indication of how far he meant to escalate the conflict in Vietnam. Goldwater did not attack the president for allegedly conducting an undeclared war because he also supported military intervention on the part of the United States. He believed the U.S., as the leader of the Free World, should fight for South Vietnam's right of self-determination. Therefore, Goldwater could not use a campaign strategy of creating the impression the Republicans were the peace party and the Democrats the war party.

Everett Dirksen's inclination to give all-out support to presidents in time of military confrontation likewise made it impossible for him to launch an all-out attack on LBJ's Vietnam policy. Dirksen had supported FDR in 1941, Truman in the Korean War—despite using it as a campaign issue in 1950 and although he was critical of the limited, so-called no win, way the UN police action was carried out—and JFK in the 1962 Cuban missile crisis. Not wanting to criticize LBJ on foreign policy, lest it be interpreted in Hanoi as a sign of disunity, Dirksen forefeited the opportunity to make the Vietnam War a significant election issue.

There were additional reasons why the electorate in 1964 was not fully informed, via open debate, on the exact nature of the course on which the U.S. was embarking in Vietnam. The first stemmed from a secret meeting Goldwater had with LBJ. At this meeting, requested by the GOP presidential nominee, the hawkish Arizonan told the president: "The war in Vietnam is a national burden. The people are already divided. The legitimacy of our presence is being criticized. My views on this matter are clear and, I think, well known. I asked to see you because I do not believe it is in the best interest of the United States to make the Vietnam War or its conduct a political issue in this campaign. I have come to promise I will not do so."[39]

The second reason the future conduct of the war in Vietnam was not fully debated resulted from bipartisan support of the so-called Gulf of Tonkin Resolution. Following reports that North Vietnamese destroyers and torpedo boats had mounted attacks on U.S. naval vessels in the Gulf of Tonkin, President Johnson called in the leaders of Congress, including Goldwater and Dirksen, to ask for congressional authority for him to respond in some manner. With little discussion, the Southeast Asia Resolution, usually referred to as the Gulf of Tonkin Resolution, was approved by a vote of 88 to 2 in the Senate. Approval in the House of Representatives was achieved by a 416 to 0 vote. Stirred by patriotic fervor and wanting to display national unity in the midst of an election, Congress authorized the president to "take all necessary measures to repeal any armed attack against the forces of the United States" and "to take all necessary steps, including the use of armed force, to assist any member or protocol state of the Southeast Asia Collective Defense Treaty requesting assistance in defense of freedom."[40]

Despite the limitations placed on him by physical infirmity, the Republican minority leader tried to stay on the campaign trail in order to canvass for much needed votes. Although he was known as a GOP workhorse, because of a back injury Senator Dirksen did less campaigning in 1964 than in any other previous presidential campaign. Dirksen came to the conclusion long before the votes were counted that the Goldwater-Miller ticket would be beaten by the team of Johnson and Humphrey. In fact, LBJ, knowing he would win big, jokingly suggested to Ev that the Illinoisan rest and spend the summer "looking after flowers."[41]

Even Everett Dirksen was taken aback by the landslide proportions of LBJ's win over Goldwater. For the Republican party the election was an unmitigated disaster. Overall, the GOP won only seven seats in the Senate to twenty-eight for the Democrats. That meant in the new Congress there would be only thirty-two Republicans in the Senate to face sixty-eight Democrats. Ev's troops in the upper chamber were severely decimated by the Goldwater fiasco.

There were many postmortems as to the cause of the overwhelming defeat suffered by the GOP. In writing to a friend in Illinois, Dirksen asserted, "One authentic and I believe incontrovertible thing can be said, and that is the Republicans were put on the defensive at the very outset of the 1964 campaign, and kept there." He decried the fact that the GOP record simply got "lost in the melee." The Republicans, Ev reasoned, should have taken credit for enacting the Civil Rights Act and the Test Ban Treaty; for attempting to make "foreign aid more selective"; for seeking "deeper economies"; for trying to block court reapportionment; for working for a Freedom of Information law; for fighting against "federal centralization"; and for seeking to kill a "bogus farm bill." It was time, urged Dirksen, "to quit fighting among ourselves" and to return "the emphasis on the national interest as distinguished from group interest because this is the source of friction and cleavage." Ev concluded by writing, "I believe the time has come for a little less provincialism in our thinking."[42]

The first task faced by Dirksen was to help restore some modicum of balance within the GOP by seeing to it that the zealous and extremist Goldwater faction did not retain control over the party. Ev led the way in reorienting the Republican party away from Goldwaterism. Since Goldwater's Senate term expired in 1964, he was no longer in the upper chamber. The Arizonan had never been invited to sit in on meetings of the Republican Joint Congressional Leadership Conference and his position as chairman of the National Republican Senatorial Campaign Committee was given to Thurston B. Morton of Kentucky. Dirksen worked with others to get Dean Burch, a Goldwaterite from Arizona, replaced as national chairman by the more moderate Ray C. Bliss of Ohio. Ev likewise led the movement in the Senate to denounce the frenzied right-wing fringe represented by the John Birch Society. In explaining how he was going about expurgating John Birchers from the party, Dirksen informed former President Dwight D. Eisenhower, "In response to a question from the press, Jerry Ford and I asserted that this Society has no connection with the Republican Party, that the publicly expressed attitude of the Society on such matters as the UN, civil rights, your record and that of John Foster Dulles in meeting the threat of communism is irreconcilable with the stand taken by the Republican Party, and that there is no room in the Republican Party for the John Birch Society."[43] In justifying the wisdom of the moves to rid the party of its emotional fanatics, Ev commented, "The rule of reason always comes into its own."[44]

It was somewhat predictable that as Goldwater's influence on the GOP quickly declined, Senator Dirksen's power continued to increase. This was the result of a series of circumstances. In the House of Representatives the veteran Charlie Halleck was replaced as minority leader by the younger Gerald Ford of Michigan. In the newly named "Ev and Jerry Show," replacing the "Ev and Charlie Show," the senior status of Dirksen was soon evident. Ev was the leading figure in determining party policy in Congress. He very much dominated press conferences and stood as the unrivaled spokesperson for the Republican party on the national scene. That factor, which contributed most to Dirksen's unchallenged hegemony over the party, was due to the complete absence of a rival leader. Goldwater was in temporary exile in Arizona. Richard Nixon, who had lost his bid for the governorship of California in 1962, withdrew to New York to practice law. Former President Eisenhower, in ill health and advanced in age, spent more time at Gettysburg and became less involved in politics. Thus, during the Johnson administration Dirksen was in fact at the pinnacle of his political power.

In reacting to the "Declaration of Denver," a resolution of the Republican Governors' Association adopted at Denver, Colorado, on December 5, 1965, calling for a party conference, Dirksen, with Ford's help, organized the Republican Coordinating Committee (RCC). Membership on the RCC included former Republican presidents and presidential nominees, the Senate leaders, House leaders, representatives of the Republican Governors' Association, GOP national chairman and representatives of the national committee, and a representative of the Republican State Legislators' Association.

As the dominant voice of the Republican party in Congress, Everett Dirksen sought to restore some ideological equilibrium to the GOP stand on domestic and foreign policy issues. Quickly and effectively, Dirksen used his position as minority leader to free the party from control by an extremist element and thus set the stage for moderates to restore party harmony. Ev stepped on some toes in the process. When asked by a television interviewer if the Goldwaterites were permanently alienated, Dirksen replied optimistically, "Time is a great healer."[45] To his longtime friend Walter Trohan, political editor of the Chicago *Tribune,* Ev also wrote privately, "What a difficult world this would be if the healing touch of time did not soften the spirit."[46]

Soon after Lyndon B. Johnson was inaugurated for his second term, Everett Dirksen appeared on a television interview program viewed in the area of the nation's capital. Commenting on his role as party leader, Dirksen drew an analogy between being a politician and being a thespian. "To begin with, you deal with people," Ev explained. "You are in front of people in political life even as you are on the stage, and out of it there must develop a poise, a certain presence, a capacity for putting your thoughts in words, in poignant expression, so that it is conveyed to people and persuades them and in that respect there is complete identity between the theater and, I think, political life." Asked what he had learned about government during his career in Congress, Senator Dirksen responded, "I think you learn certain things which somehow fill out your philosophy as a legislator and I pretty much agree with this kind of language—that this free government is like an old waterlogged scow; it doesn't move very far at one time, but it never sinks and maybe that is the reason we have a free government today."[47]

With a new Congress having just convened and the GOP reduced substantially in its ranks by the Goldwater debacle, Ev was determined to keep the ship of state afloat as best he could. Party fortunes were important to him, but even more vital was the need to keep the government heading in a direction to best serve the long-range domestic and foreign policy needs of the nation. That was the ultimate objective of the politics and statecraft practiced by Everett Dirksen, the redoubtable minority leader of the diminished Republican party. At this particular time in American history, Ev knew the advocates of big government, deficit spending, and increased welfare-statism were in the driver's seat. It would be his thankless task to attempt to stem the advance of the Great Society juggernaut with the small band of GOP survivors left in the upper chamber.

NOTES

1. Lady Bird Johnson, *Lady Bird Johnson: A White House Diary* (New York: Holt, Rinehart and Winston, 1970), p. 237.

2. Oral history memoir of EMD, May 8, 1968, Lyndon B. Johnson Library, hereafter cited as LBJL.

3. Oral history memoir of EMD, Mar. 21, 1969, LBJL.

4. Lyndon Baines Johnson, *The Vantage Point: Perspectives of the Presidency, 1963-1969.* (New York: Holt, Rinehart and Winston, 1971), p. 158.

5. George E. Reedy to authors, May 20, 1980.

6. "Meet the Press" (NBC-Radio and TV), Jan. 24, 1965, script in R&R-EMDC.

7. Hugh Sidey, *A Very Personal Presidency: Lyndon Johnson in the White House* (New York: Atheneum, 1968), p. 80.

8. W. G. Henry, "Dirksen Prevails Despite Illness," Columbus (Georgia) *Ledger-Enquirer,* Aug. 29, 1965, C-EMDC.

9. "Dirksen Seeks Unity," Chicago *Daily News,* June 25, 1964, C-EMDC.

10. Presidential News Conference, Dec. 7, 1963, *The Johnson Presidential Press Conferences* (New York: Earl M. Coleman Enterprises, 1978), 1:3.

11. "Close Up" (ABC-TV), Feb. 7, 1965, script in R&R-EMDC.

12. "Some Observations by the Honorable Everett M. Dirksen, Minority Leader of the Senate of the Occasion of his 68th Birthday Anniversary," Jan. 4, 1964, text in R&R-EMDC.

13. Arthur M. Schlesinger, Jr., *Robert Kennedy and His Times* (New York: Ballantine Books, 1979), p. 696.

14. Hubert H. Humphrey, *The Education of a Public Man: My Life and Politics* (Garden City, N.Y.: Doubleday 1976), p. 276.

15. Memorandum, Mike Manatos to Larry O'Brien, May 6, 1964, Files of White House Aides, No. 39, LBJL.

16. Loudon Wainright, "The View from Here," *Life* (June 5, 1964), reprint in IF-EMDC.

17. New York *Times,* June 20, 1964, C-EMDC.

18. *Congressional Record,* June 19, 1964, reprint in IF-EMDC.

19. Barry M. Goldwater to authors, June 2, 1980.

20. LBJ, *Vantage Point,* p. 159.

21. Larry O'Brien to EMD, Aug. 17, 1964, Files of White House Aides No. 39, LBJL.

22. Chicago *Defender,* June 20, 1964, C-EMDC.

23. EMD to General Robert E. Wood, June 1, 1964, Robert E. Wood Papers, HCHL, hereafter cited as REWP-HCHL.

24. Harold E. Rainville to General Robert E. Wood, Jan. 31, 1964, REWP-HCHL.

25. "Dirksen Seeks GOP Unity," Chicago *Daily News,* June 25, 1964, C-EMDC.

26. Rowland Evans and Robert Novak, "Barry Goldwater Captures Dirksen," Washington *Post,* July 1, 1964, C-EMDC.

27. "Republicans: Some Facts of History," *Time* (July 10, 1964), reprint in IF-EMDC.

28. Goldwater, *With No Apologies,* p. 225.

29. *National Party Conventions, 1831-1972* (Washington, D.C.: Congressional Quarterly, 1976), p. 105.

30. Ibid.

31. Richard H. Rovere, *Affairs of State: The Eisenhower Years* (New York: Farrar, Strauss and Cudahy, 1956), p. 215.

32. Ibid., p. 210.

33. "A Message from the Honorable Herbert Hoover, Delivered by Senator Everett M. Dirksen, July 14, 1964," *Proceedings of the Republican National Convention, 1964,* p. 68, hereafter cited as PRNC-1964.

34. EMD to HCH, July 22, 1964, PPP-HCHL.

35. "Speech Nominating Barry M. Goldwater for the Presidency," July 15, 1964, text in R&R-EMDC.

36. PRNC-1964, pp. 418-19.

37. Text of statement in minutes of Republican Joint Congressional Leadership Conference, July 29, 1964, RCLF-EMDC.

38. Ibid., Sept. 23, 1964.

39. Goldwater, *With No Apologies,* pp. 192-93.

40. "Southeast Asia Resolution," Aug. 7, 1964, text in LF-EMDC.

41. Jack Valenti, *A Very Human President* (New York: W. W. Norton, 1975), p. 305.

42. EMD to Harvey Gross, Jan. 19, 1965, GGC-EMDC.

43. EMD to DDE, Sept. 30, 1965, RCLF-EMDC.

44. Nick Thimmesch, *The Condition of the Republican Party* (New York: W. W. Norton, 1968), p. 55.

45. "Meet the Press" (NBC-Radio and TV), Jan. 24, 1965, script in R&R-EMDC.

46. EMD to Walter Trohan, Mar. 22, 1965, Walter Trohan Papers, HCHL.

47. "Close Up" (ABC-TV), Mar. 22, 1965, script in R&R-EMDC.

9

Dirksen Versus the Great Society and Supreme Court

THE 89TH CONGRESS of 1965 rivaled the New Deal era's 73rd Congress in the enormous quantity of social and economic legislation enacted. In the first session President Lyndon B. Johnson submitted 87 measures of which 84 were passed; in the second session 113 proposals were sent to Congress from the White House of which 97 were approved. The bill for taxpayers attached to this floodtide of Great Society legislation was $157.5 billion. Once again, just as he had done during both the New and Fair deals, Everett Dirksen sought to moderate the deficit spending for massive federal programs so that they would not become either a wasteful bureaucratic morass or a costly political spoils system.

Ev worried over the fact that LBJ's budget was $31 billion more than Eisenhower's last one, with some $32 billion having been added to the national debt by Kennedy and Johnson. Dirksen also pointed out publicly that President Johnson "has failed to reassure the American people and the Congress concerning inflation, the war in Vietnam, and its future tax program." The tug of war between guns (defense spending) and butter (social and economic expenditures) was beginning to take place. Dirksen realized the Vietnam War was "escalating, but the administration has not informed the American people how bad it will get nor how costly it will become."[1]

Two aspects about the Great Society disturbed Dirksen a great deal. First, it was rapidly enlarging the size of the federal bureaucracy while simultaneously increasing governmental centralization. Second, it led to unbalanced budgets, inflation, and higher taxes. Relative to the first objection, Ev told a group of businessmen that he was troubled by the "deeper and deeper intrusion of federal power into the affairs of the people." He bemoaned the fact that "today we are indisputably in the welfare state."[2]

To demonstrate forcefully to the Senate how the federal bureaucracy tended to embroil everything under its control by issuing reams of regulations, he held up a ninety-three page booklet entitled, *Interpretation Bulletin on Overtime Compensation.* It was supposed to explain a portion of the Fair Labor Standards Act. Ev tore it apart page by page and scotch-taped it together to make a long roll. With a dramatic flair he had a Senate page unroll it while he held onto one end. It extended down the aisle for sixty-five feet. In dismay Ev told his Senate colleagues, "This is something merchants must familiarize themselves with to make sure they're not breaking the law." Dirksen continued his visual demonstration by having other pages unroll additional government regulatory material until all the aisles were strewn with long rolls of regulations. Raising his voice in indignation, Ev said to those senators present: "Gentlemen, just look at this. Small businesses, where the husband runs the shop and the wife does the books, cannot possibly cope with it." When Senator Frank Lausche (D-Ohio) examined one set of forms and admitted he could not understand them, Dirksen averred, "Interpret them? Why, seventy-six trombones and seventy-seven Philadelphia lawyers could not do it!"[3]

"Fiscal solvency," declared Dirksen on another occasion, "is one of the great issues of the time." Anticipating runaway inflation, he predicted "the whole business of spending, of waste in government is going to catch up with us sooner or later."[4] Most Democrats rejected Ev's warning since for a long time they had become accustomed to spending more money for multifarious programs than the government actually took in. Since the days of the New Deal, liberals justified deficit spending via Keynesian economics. According to John Maynard Keynes, deficits were permissible during depressions as pump-priming mechanisms. What liberals forgot was Keynes's injunction to balance budgets

and accrue surpluses in times of prosperity. Ever since the time
of Franklin D. Roosevelt, the only true practice of Keynesian
fiscal policy was during the Eisenhower administration.

Although it was not politically popular at the time, Senator
Dirksen called for fiscal responsibility and a more gradualistic
approach to reform. To Ev, the Great Society was a misguided
attempt at creating an immediate, utopian "blueprint for para-
dise."[5] Furthermore, it was being put together in a piecemeal
fashion without adequate, overall coordination. The future economic stability of the nation was being mortgaged by unrealistic
and ineffective policies that attempted to solve problems too
simplistically by hastily extemporizing massive programs. Dirksen
thus maintained that LBJ's War on Poverty was "erratic, costly,
and misdirected" and needed thoughtful "review and reap-
praisal."[6] Dirksen's caveat that the stability of the economy was
being seriously undermined was ignored as was his call for sub-
stantial reductions in government expenditures. His criticisms of
these hurried programs with such colossal price tags were shrugged
off as being the petty strictures of an overly frugal worrywart.

In addition to his disquietude over the evils of big government
and ever-increasing deficits, Everett Dirksen was also alarmed by
the growing activism of the U.S. Supreme Court. The nation's
highest tribunal, led by Chief Justice Earl Warren, entered into
controversial areas where heretofore it had abstained from rendering decisions. In addition to the chief justice, who had been
appointed by President Eisenhower in 1953, the "dominant
majority"[7] of the so-called Warren Court included Hugo L. Black,
William O. Douglas, William J. Brennan, Jr., Arthur M. Goldberg,
Abe Fortas, and Thurgood Marshall. The two dissenters who
tended to oppose the activist legal philosophy of the Court were
John M. Harlan and Felix Frankfurter.

In 1962, the U.S. Supreme Court issued a six to one decision
in the case of *Engle v. Vitale.* In the majority opinion, written
by Justice Black, the regent's prayer of the state of New York
was ruled unconstitutional. This prayer simply read as follows:
"Almighty God, we acknowledge our dependence upon Thee,
and we beg Thy blessing upon us, our parents, our teachers, and
our country."[8] The high court maintained that separation of church

and state as prescribed by the First Amendment to the U.S. Constitution prohibited the recitation of such a prayer in public schools. The First Amendment says: "Congress shall make no law respecting an establishment of religion or prohibiting the free exercise thereof." The Court ignored the positive part about "free exercise" and instead focused on the negative "make no law" aspect. It then applied the prohibition about establishing a religion to the various states via the Fourteenth Amendment. Senator Dirksen not only disagreed outright with the Supreme Court's legal reasoning on this particular issue of prayer in public schools, which had a long-standing tradition in many states, but also feared the moral repercussions of this judicial edict forbidding children from participating in public prayer.

Not only did the U.S. Supreme Court involve itself in the church-state issue in 1962, it also entered into the area of re-apportioning state legislatures. In *Baker v. Carr* (1962), a six to two decision in which Justice Brennan wrote the majority opinion, the Warren Court ruled that discriminatory apportionment of seats in state legislatures could be corrected by the federal courts. Writing for the majority two years later (in a six to three vote), Chief Justice Warren rendered his "one-man, one-vote"[9] decree in *Reynolds v. Sims* (1964). This decision made it mandatory for states to base the apportionment of seats in both houses of a bicameral legislature on population.

Senator Dirksen was very upset upon reading the decision promulgated by the Warren Court. He regarded it as being tantamount to an arbitrary ukase of an imperial court. Hitherto, the Supreme Court had never meddled in political questions involving the right of states to determine the constituent makeup of their respective legislative bodies. Dirksen was deeply distressed at both the antiprayer stance of the Supreme Court and its interference in state apportionment procedures. To him, they seemed harmful to the well-being and value system of rural America with which he sympathized. Also violated, he thought, was the principle of divided and limited power as set forth in the U.S. Constitution. Ev spent the rest of his senatorial career trying to overturn these decisions through constitutional amendments.

Relative to the ruling of the Warren Court on reapportionment,

Senator Dirksen joined immediately with the two Democratic senators from Mississippi, James Eastland and John C. Stennis, to cosponsor S. 3069. It would have provided for a "temporary stay of proceedings in any action for the reapportionment of any State legislative body."[10] The strategy of this move was to cause a delay long enough to forge a Midwest-South coalition of members of Congress from states with large rural and small-town constituencies. Ev's move to stall the restructuring of state legislatures failed to pass because Democrats and Republicans from large urban areas joined forces to defeat it.

With no other recourse, Senator Dirksen sponsored S. J. 2 in 1965, which provided for the following amendment to the U.S. Constitution: "The people of a state may apportion one house of a bicameral legislature using population, geography, or political subdivisions as factors, giving each factor such weight as they deem appropriate."[11] In defending his proposed constitutional amendment, Dirksen argued that it was not the legal prerogative of the Supreme Court to dictate to the various sovereign states as to the makeup of their legislative bodies. He contended that there was neither legal precedent nor congressional legislation authorizing the federal courts to tamper with the makeup of state legislatures.

At the heart of Dirksen's opposition to reapportionment based on the one-person, one-vote principle was a deep-seated fear that bicameral legislatures would come under the complete control of urban areas. This would mean a corresponding decrease of political power in the rural and small-town segment of the population Ev represented.

The first obstacle for Dirksen's constitutional amendment was the Senate Judiciary Committee. At first it killed Ev's proposal. To induce President Johnson to help him by putting pressure on wavering Democrats belonging to the Judiciary Committee, Dirksen announced he would forthrightly conduct an extended debate (a euphemism for filibuster) to tie up the administration's immigration reform bill. This was a measure to eliminate the discriminatory national origins provision, a proposal Ev actually agreed with and ultimately did vote for. It was not long before LBJ got his old Senate crony on the phone. The President told

Dirksen, "You can't do that to me." Ev replied to LBJ, "I love Caesar, but I love Rome more."[12] Johnson got the message. When the Senate Judiciary Committee took up the Dirksen amendment for reconsideration, it was Senator Thomas Dodd (D-Conn.) who switched his vote. The latter had gotten a personal phone call from LBJ insisting he reverse his position. The Dirksen proposal subsequently received a nine to seven vote for approval, which meant it had cleared the first legislative hurdle.

Having his constitutional amendment on the Senate calendar was one thing but getting it on the floor for a vote was another. Everett Dirksen was a clever enough tactician to realize he needed a parliamentary device to force a vote on his proposal. Ev knew just what he had to do. It was in this day-by-day maneuvering that he was at his best. There were always some perfunctory resolutions awaiting Senate approval. Usually they were called up with only a few members present on the floor. If the majority and minority leaders were in agreement, they would be passed quickly by a voice vote. Informing Majority Leader Mike Mansfield of his intent, and getting the go-ahead from the Montanan, Dirksen cleverly attached his constitutional amendment to an innocuous resolution in support of "National American Baseball Week." When the baseball resolution was routinely brought up for action, it gave Ev an opportunity to seek a vote on his constitutional amendment as a substitute for the original resolution.

Once on the floor, Dirksen moved the adoption of his constitutional amendment. This triggered a heated debate. During the course of the deliberations it came to Ev's attention on the Senate floor that Vice-President Hubert Humphrey was lobbying against it. Dirksen made a beeline to his office and immediately phoned the White House. Ev asked President Johnson what was going on. Had not the President promised to be neutral? LBJ claimed to know nothing about Humphrey's interference. Dirksen shot back, "Well, call him up and give him hell."[13] When the roll was called, the final tally was fifty-seven to thirty-nine in Ev's favor, but this was seven votes short of the needed two-thirds vote. All but three Republicans supported Dirksen and, of course, he received the votes of many Democrats who agreed with his proposal to permit at least one house of a bicameral legislature to be apportioned on some basis other than population.

"Unlike old soldiers, a basic issue neither dies nor fades away,"[14] Ev said doggedly after losing his battle in 1965. Defeat that day did not mean Dirksen intended to cease his efforts. In fact, he redoubled them. On January 19, 1966, Senator Dirksen formed a Committee for Government of the People (CGP). His aim was to utilize the CGP for the purpose of promoting a national constitutional convention to be called by resolutions passed by two-thirds of the state legislatures. In this manner the Senate could be circumvented by taking his case directly to state legislatures. This plebiscite approach to constitutional issues followed what became known to many political observers as the "Dirksen Doctrine." It meant the people, through their elected legislators, were to be given an opportunity to make their wishes known on a vital issue in a more direct manner than communicating with Congress or passively accepting judicial decisions. Relative to reapportionment, this approach almost succeeded, but as the state tally neared the two-thirds number, it faltered and ultimately died.

Paralleling his losing struggle on the apportionment issue was Dirksen's eventual defeat on his prayer amendment. What critics termed a quixotic crusade was to Ev a serious endeavor to preserve a spiritual foundation for the nation. "I'm not going to let nine men say to 190 million people, including children, when and where they can utter their prayers," vowed Dirksen. "I can see no evil in children who want to say that God is good and to thank Him for their blessings."[15] To rectify the situation Ev proposed a constitutional amendment that read as follows: "Nothing contained in this Constitution shall prohibit the authority administering any school, school system, educational institution, or other public building supported in whole or in part through the expenditure of public funds from providing or from permitting the voluntary participation by students or others in prayer. Nothing contained in this article shall authorize any such authority to prescribe the form or content of any prayer."[16]

In the ensuing Senate debate, Dirksen defended with all his might the supposition that prayers recited by children in the public schools were of salutary influence because they contributed to the building of character. "Prayer is the roadmap to God," Ev contended. "It should become the greatest adventure of young minds." He argued at length: "How strange that we spend hundreds of millions every year to develop physical fitness and harden the muscles of American youth, but when it comes to hardening the spiritual muscles through the practice and rehearsal of prayer, it becomes enshrouded in quaint legalism and the jargon of church and state. . . . I say give Caesar what he requires, but give God a little also."[17]

In addition to his personal feelings on the need for prayer or some form of spiritual communion with God, Dirksen believed the religious heritage of the nation had to be preserved. Concerning the antiprayer rulings of the Supreme Court, Ev warned, "Let these decisions stand without clarification and in due course Christmas, Santa Claus, Christmas carols, and everything else which has been so deeply entrenched in American religious tradition will go by the board."[18] In another line of reasoning Dirksen asserted: "If the profound legalisms of the Courts are carried to a logical conclusion, and to be fully consistent, perhaps God should be removed from the Court crier's exhortation at the opening sessions of the U.S. Supreme Court when he says, 'God save this Honorable Court.' But God also appears in the oaths which Senators take. His name appears on our coinage. . . ."[19]

Senator Dirksen was in great physical pain when his prayer amendment resolution came up for a vote on the Senate floor. He had been in Walter Reed Hospital for a checkup, having suffered from a flaring ulcer and abdominal pains, where he fell accidently from the bed and broke his hip. It so happened that Ev was sitting on the edge of the bed when he dozed off for a moment. As he later explained to a friend, "I am distressed beyond words that fatigue could induce a person to fall asleep for an instant and result in a forward fall that could have so many implications, including a fractured hip. . . ."[20] With eleven metal pins and one silver screw in his hip, Dirksen hobbled onto the floor of the Senate to make one last plea. "This country," he declared, "belongs to the people, not to the courts."[21] He rejected the substitute resolution offered by Senator Birch E. Bayh (D-Ind.) which would permit "voluntary silent prayer and meditation."[22] This was one of the few times Ev eschewed compromise. When the vote was taken on Dirksen's original resolution, dubbed the "Amen amendment"[23] by its opponents, it received a positive vote of forty-nine to thirty-seven. This was nine short of the needed two-thirds votes.

Not one to give up easily on something so dear to his heart, Dirksen redrafted his prayer amendment in the hope of attracting more support. It now read: "Nothing contained in this Constitution shall abridge the right of persons lawfully assembled, in any public building which is supported in whole or in part through the expenditure of public funds, to participate in nondenominational prayer."[24] "For this nation," Ev maintained, "to permit that decision [*Engle v. Vitale* (1962)] to stand endangers and does dishonor to our religious heritage."[25] Dirksen, like the Harvard sociologist Pitirim Sorokin (author of *The Crisis of Our Age* [1942]), feared American society would transform its cultural system from the "ideational" (one based on traditional religious beliefs) to the "sensate" (totally secular with a relativistic moral system).[26]

Much to his dismay, Dirksen's prayer amendment went down to defeat again by an even larger margin. Some twenty-five years have passed since the antiprayer ruling of the Court was made. Many other attempts at amending the U.S. Constitution have failed during this time. In April of 1979 Senator Jesse Helms (R-N.C.) introduced a bill to limit the appellate jurisdiction of the Supreme Court so that it could not render decisions involving voluntary prayer. In May 1982, President Ronald Reagan endorsed a constitutional prayer amendment. Neither approach has yet provided an avenue for Ev to win a posthumous victory in an area that was of such concern to him.

In addition to his fight for the prayer amendment and against the one person-one vote reapportionment, Senator Dirksen's name will always be linked to the major civil rights legislation of the twentieth century. During his tenure as minority leader, Dirksen did much to advance the cause of civil rights. His floor leadership in 1964 was largely responsible for breaking the filibuster of the southern Democrats, thus permitting passage of the Civil Rights Act of that year. In March of 1965 President Johnson called upon

Senator Dirksen for assistance in getting another civil rights measure enacted into law. Ev responded to the call and threw all his energies into securing passage of what ultimately emerged as the Voting Rights Act of 1965. The basic intent of the measure was to eliminate discriminatory impediments related to voting. This included provisions to outlaw the use of literacy tests and poll taxes. Dirksen tailored the language carefully to delimit the ban on poll taxes to those states actually using it to deny or abridge the right to vote rather than make it an all-inclusive abolition. By this precise banning of poll taxes, he hoped to avoid needlessly alienating states' rights conservatives from non-southern states.

Senate liberals, such as Paul Douglas (D-Ill.) and Edward M. Kennedy (D-Mass.), claimed Dirksen was watering down the bill too much, but President Johnson understood what Ev was doing. LBJ instructed Attorney General Nicholas Katzenbach and Majority Leader Mike Mansfield, who already agreed with Ev, to cooperate with Dirksen in order to ensure a successful cloture vote. Getting a law passed by the Senate was not a simple matter of legislative legerdemain; rather, it was a complex procedure of putting together a bill that eventually had sufficient support to bypass a filibuster.

Despite the personal discomfort associated with a series of illnesses, Dirksen set about to fashion a civil rights bill that would attract the widest possible support. He had to disarm and satisfy GOP conservatives from the Midwest and Far West or else they would not support him on the cloture vote. Ev was hospitalized by a case of intestinal influenza in February and again in March. He was forced to enter Walter Reed once more in May due to severe abdominal pains. President Johnson was extremely concerned about Ev's health problems. Thinking that perhaps Dirksen had stomach cancer, LBJ had special reports sent to him regarding the physical condition of the ailing minority leader. The president and his wife sent many flowers, get-well cards, pictures, and gifts to Ev, who both held in high personal esteem. When Dirksen literally got out of his sickbed to start work on the civil rights measure, LBJ wrote his old friend, "I want to tell you once more it means much to me to know you are up and at 'em again."[27]

Leaving the hospital after only a brief period of rest and con-valescence, Dirksen returned enthusiastically to his Senate duties. This was an oft-repeated pattern. Once back in his office he would smoke constantly, drink coffee incessantly, and imbibe bourbon and water periodically to ward off fatigue. If his stomach caused him too much trouble he would shift to Sanka, take antacids, and try to cut his smoking. The pressures of office no doubt contributed to tension-producing stomach problems that varied from bleeding ulcers to painful abdominal cramps. The doctors repeatedly warned Ev he needed more rest, but this medical advice went unheeded most of the time. The price of leadership was that it took its toll on Ev's aging body. In spite of recurrent bouts of illness, Dirksen was an unflagging worker and one not prone to complain about his physical infirmities.

Slowly but surely Senator Dirksen put together a civil rights bill that would be acceptable to most liberals, moderates, and non-southern conservatives. He notified Mike Mansfield on May 21 that the time had come to file a petition of cloture. By a vote of seventy to thirty the twenty-four-day filibuster was broken. Ev delivered twenty-three Republican votes. Without these the ex-tended debate carried on by southern Democrats could not have been stopped. Once the delaying tactics were terminated, the Voting Rights Act of 1965 was passed by a vote of seventy-seven to nineteen. Dirksen was joined by twenty-nine other Republicans in voting for its passage. Even before the measure actually was enacted LBJ gratefully acknowledged Ev's efforts in a letter to former President Eisenhower. Johnson wrote to Eisenhower, "The contribution of Everett Dirksen and others to the voting rights issue was immeasurably helpful to the national interest and unity."[28]

In 1966, President Lyndon Johnson submitted new civil rights legislation to Congress. Included in this legislative package were provisions that would provide for open housing; forbid discrim-ination in the selection of juries; provide for stricter enforcement of desegregation in schools and public facilities; enable broader enforcement powers for the Equal Employment Opportunity Committee; and make it a federal offense for any person or group of people to use threats or actual force in preventing any indi-vidual from exercising his or her constitutional rights. Personally,

Senator Dirksen was for all of these measures, but as minority leader Ev was fully aware that many white homeowners and those renting out one or two units were strongly opposed to open housing. In addition, the inflammatory rhetoric and violence of black power groups had caused a white backlash. This fear, whether justified or not, manifested itself in a demand for law and order lest white neighborhoods be forceably ghettoized only to be accompanied by more crime in the streets and ultimate transformation into slums.

President Johnson spent ninety minutes trying to persuade Dirksen to endorse the entire civil rights measure. Despite his pro-civil rights reputation, Ev refused to give his support to the open-housing provision, knowing full well he would catch considerable flak from liberals and leaders of black organizations. Yet he did not want to denounce his own constituents as racists and therefore refused to muster the necessary votes to end the usual southern filibuster.[29] When LBJ sent the attorney general to see if he could change Ev's mind, Dirksen once more explained his predicament to Nicholas Katzenbach. The latter reported the following back to the president: "Senator Dirksen is opposed to the Housing Title but not to the rest of the bill. However, he is committed to Senator Hruska not to move the jury titles at this time—so there is not much left. He told me that even if he would change his position it would not be possible for him to secure the votes necessary for cloture, and this may in fact be true."[30]

A House-passed civil rights bill nevertheless was placed on the Senate calendar for debate on September 6. Once debate commenced on the measure, the southern Democrats started their usual filibuster. Dirksen had informed Mike Mansfield that as minority leader he could not deliver enough GOP votes to invoke cloture. Mansfield, under pressure from LBJ, nevertheless tried twice to stop the filibuster. Both attempts failed. The first vote for cloture on September 14 was fifty-four to forty-two with only twelve Republicans supporting an end to debate. Another vote, fifty-two to forty-one, was taken on September 19. This time just ten Republicans favored ending the filibuster. Soon thereafter President Johnson withdrew the civil rights bill from Senate consideration.

No one could deny that Senator Dirksen was an indefatigable battler for civil rights, but he was always aware of what was politically feasible. His assessment of public opinion proved to be correct in the midterm elections held in the fall of 1966. In his home state of Illinois Senator Paul Douglas lost his seat to GOP challenger Charles H. Percy. While there were more reasons than one for Douglas's defeat, one factor was a white backlash in Cook County. This caused many urban Democrats to vote for the Republican candidate. In the Senate the number of Democrats fell from sixty-seven to sixty-four, while the Republican ranks increased from thirty-three to thirty-six. Among the newcomers to the upper chamber was Ev's son-in-law, Howard Baker. The latter, running as a Republican, won the Senate seat from Tennessee by defeating Governor Frank Clement (who had previously beaten incumbent Ross Bass in the Democratic primary). Unknown to Dirksen at the time, of course, was the fact that one day in the future Senator Baker would be the GOP minority leader, a presidential aspirant, and majority leader in the administration of President Ronald Reagan.

Because of Dirksen's actions in the 1965 civil rights bill debate, he was on the receiving end of much criticism from black leaders, and at times his office was picketed. What his detractors did not take into consideration was the simple fact that Ev could not get too far ahead of public opinion lest he dissipate his power to lead. Dirksen once admitted in a civil rights debate, "No one will embarrass the Minority Leader by charging him with having changed his mind or reversed his position on occasion. One cannot have been in this man's town for twenty-eight years . . . without developing a pretty tough skin and recognizing the verities of political life." He went on to make his point with a clever Dirksenism. "I remember the old ditty: 'The king of France with 20,000 men went up the hill and then came down again'; I have marched up the hill many times; I have marched down. God willing, if I am alive long enough, I suppose I will march up the hill again and march back down again. But when I reach the bottom of the hill, I will still be looking at the summit to see where I rightfully belong."[31]

It was not until the 1968 session of the Senate that Dirksen sensed a positive change in public opinion and a salutary shift in attitude among his fellow GOP senators. Even before Ramsey Clark, the new attorney general, and President Lyndon Johnson worked out the details of an administration civil rights bill, Senator Dirksen began thinking about a compromise version of his own making. Johnson's civil rights proposals were in essence a repeat of those placed before the Senate in 1966 and 1967. The southern Democrat filibuster could not be broken in 1966, and the threat of another dilatory talkathon in 1967 killed any hope for action that year. The opportunity for Ev to take the initiative came in February of 1968 when the House-passed measure providing federal protection for civil rights workers came before the upper chamber. Senators Edward Brooke (R-Mass.), a black, and Walter Mondale (D-Minn.) attached an open-housing amendment to the House version of this bill. Southern Democrats immediately began a filibuster to prevent a vote from being taken. Majority Leader Mansfield, thinking civil rights legislation was doomed anyway, filed a quick cloture motion in a perfunctory manner. Dirksen maintained his previous stance by voting against cloture in a tally that lost be only seven votes. Further indications that a more fluid situation existed came when Mansfield's motion to kill the Brooke-Mondale measure, in order to clear the Senate calendar, lost by a fifty-eight to thirty-four vote.

It was clear to Everett Dirksen that if an acceptable compromise were hammered out relative to open housing, the door could be opened for passage of the entire civil rights package. Dirksen knew he could depend upon the eastern liberals within the GOP, such as Javits, Case, and Brooke, but he needed to win over the midwestern conservatives to invoke cloture. If Ev could get the administration, through Attorney General Ramsey Clark, to tone down the provisions on the open housing section he, as minority leader, could openly announce his support for it. His switch would then become a bellwether for moderates, like Howard Baker, and conservatives, such as Jack Miller of Iowa, to join the civil rights bandwagon. President Johnson was receptive to the idea of compromise, having been reminded by legislative aide Larry Temple that "without Senator Dirksen there can be no cloture."[32]

Putting to use his crafty skills of settling differences between warring factions, Senator Dirksen set about to contrive a compromise that would win the day. The focus of his attention was to tone down the legal scope of the prohibitions against discrimination in the sale and rental of housing or apartment units by exempting private, single-family dwellings. Once this concession was made by administration forces, Ev announced publicly he was withdrawing his opposition to open housing. Anti-civil rights southerners were stunned by Dirksen's sudden about-face. "I do not apologize for my conduct," asserted Ev. "One would be a strange creature indeed in this world of mutation if in the face of reality he did not change his mind."[33] Black leaders and liberal pundits now sang praises for Ev's statesmanship, not really knowing what adroit machinations such leadership entailed.

In and out of the hospital with tension-induced illnesses, Senator Dirksen nevertheless undertook to sell the civil rights package to his right-wing colleagues. The bargaining process was an arduous chore. Ev confided to Mike Mansfield, who was also busy lining up Democrats, "It's easier to line up votes on your side of the aisle. I have to deal with some real sons of bitches."[34] Outsiders had no idea what was involved in corralling votes to end debate. "You remember I had to crawl on my hands and knees to some of my colleagues and beg them for a cloture vote," Ev shrugged while talking to a reporter. "I guess I'll have to do some more crawling and begging."[35]

Smoking chain-style despite frequent coughing spells, Dirksen toiled endlessly. He arrived early at his office and was one of the last to leave the Senate. His phone rang constantly. Ev was ever on the move. He would meet Mansfield to compare notes, huddle with a colleague, and then be off to a conference. All of this activity would take place interspersed amid participation in debate or attendance at regular committee meetings. It is no wonder that Ev's fatigue-racked frame often looked as if it would collapse. Dirksen's deep-lined face appeared ravaged by toil and time, yet he refused to stop punishing his body with a pace that would have killed many who were not as tough.

After a Herculean endeavor in finding votes, on March 1 Dirksen agreed with Mansfield that they should try for cloture. The cloture motion received a favorable vote of fifty-nine to thirty-five but failed to achieve the necessary two-thirds of those present and voting. Ev delivered the votes of twenty-one Republicans. He was disappointed that Mansfield could not get more Democrats to join in the attempt to end the filibuster. With renewed effort Dirksen made the rounds again, trying to add a few more GOP names to his head count in favor of ending debate. LBJ also got on the phone to seek converts among Democrats. On March 4 another attempt was made to invoke cloture. This time Mansfield and Dirksen succeeded by getting a vote of sixty-five to thirty-two, which constituted the slimmest margin of victory possible. Without the twenty-three GOP votes cast for this motion the filibuster could not have been broken.

The final impetus to enact the Civil Rights Act of 1968 came on April 4 when the Reverend Dr. Martin Luther King, Jr., was assassinated. Passage came quickly thereafter, and the Civil Rights Act was signed into law by President Johnson on April 11. LBJ sent a note to Dirksen, who by now was totally exhausted after his marathon ordeal, thanking him for his role in getting this legislation passed. "A month ago it seemed highly unlikely that the Senate would adopt a landmark civil rights bill in this session," Johnson conceded. The president then went on to commend old reliable Ev: "You should be proud of what you did for your fellow citizens."[36]

For his important role in the civil rights fight, Ev received both paeans of praise and severe panning. Liberal-left journalists realized there would have been no legislation without Dirksen's magic hand, yet some resented what they regarded as his interminable delay in coming out for an end to discrimination in housing. Being the quintessence of practicality, Ev evoked fewer cheers from that liberal segment of the press than if he had been an impotent idealist. This was so despite the fact he made it possible to have an effective open-housing law on the federal statute books. Dirksen always believed, as the Good Book said (to which Ev often referred as that "Ancient Parchment"), that there is a time and season for all things. Some political pundits dubbed him the "Prairie Statesman" or "King of the Senate," while others used less flattering epithets such as: "The Grand Old Chameleon," "Mr. Flip Flop," or the "Pitchman from Pekin."[37]

Amid this controversy, television commentator Howard K. Smith understood the basic truth when he summarized his TV documentary entitled "Everett Dirksen's Washington" with this keen observation: "Well, in the Kennedy and Johnson administrations, the rule of success has been—clear it with Dirksen."[38]

Senator Dirksen once had a reputation as a militant anticommunist crusader, but under the influence of President Eisenhower he had moderated his stance. While he was no longer considered a hard-liner, communism as totalitarian ideology was still repugnant to him. He sometimes felt that civil libertarians underestimated its threat as a meance to true democracy. One of the perpetual points of tension between the hawkish, conservative, Old Guard faction and the dovish, liberal wing of the GOP was the issue of communism. The right-wingers were in deadly earnest about containing the spread of communism at home and abroad. The Republican left wing, on the contrary, tended to view the militant anticommunism of the right as constituting an outdated and quixotic crusade against an illusory Red Scare. Everett Dirksen had the opportunity to reinforce his standing with those senators on the right when the question came up as to whether or not the existence of the Subversive Activities Control Board (SACB) should be continued. The SACB was a pet agency of the Old Guard. It had become a symbol of right-wing resistance to communist subversion within the United States. When the SACB came under fire in 1967, Dirksen made his conservative colleagues happy by doing battle for its continuance in the face of great odds.

Created by Congress in 1950, the SACB was set up for the purpose of "disclosing to the American people Communist-action, Communist-front, and Communist-infiltrated organizations."[39] The board was designed to serve in the capacity of a quasi court to hear and decide cases brought before it by the U.S. attorney general. It neither initiated nor conducted independent investigations but depended upon data supplied by the Department of Justice. The SACB was composed of five permanent members with a staff of nine. It received an annual appropriation of $300,000. This would have totaled an overall expenditure in excess of $5 million since its creation but for the fact that the sum of $849,000 was returned unspent.

The problem of whether to continue the life of the SACB probably would not have arisen in 1967 had it not been for President Johnson's appointment of Simon F. McHugh, Jr., to the board. Filling a vacancy on the SACB normally would not have caught the public's attention, but this appointee attracted considerable notice because of his youth and apparent lack of qualifications. Young McHugh was twenty-nine years of age, had no legal training, and yet was to receive a yearly salary of $26,000 to serve on the quasi-judicial SACB. Further scrutiny of McHugh's past revealed he was recently married to one of the president's former White House secretaries, and this appointment had all the trappings of a wedding present. Further controversy erupted when Senator William Proxmire (D-Wis.) claimed the SACB had had no assignments for the last thirty months. Proxmire not only wanted to embarrass President Johnson by rejecting the McHugh nomination but advocated killing the SACB outright by depriving it of any funds.

To those, like Proxmire, who wanted to abolish the SACB as an economy move, Dirksen stated publicly: "I'm frank to say they're not going to contrive [*sic*] it without a fight. . . . There is a tendency to believe that communism is not a dangerous threat. In my considered judgment it is a greater danger than it has ever been."[40] Ev argued that the U.S. Supreme Court was to blame for making the SACB so impotent because it had "handed down a few decisions that made it almost impossible for the Board to operate."[41] The law requiring communist or communist-affiliated organizations to register with the attorney general's office was declared unconstitutional by the Warren Court on the basis that it violated the Fifth Amendment by forcing self-incrimina-tion. Without registration, the Department of Justice had no subversive list or names of organizations to turn over to the SACB. In 1966 the attorney general had filed a petition for it to conduct hearings relative to the conduct of the radically oriented W. E. B. DuBois Clubs of America. The SACB was helpless when leaders of the organization in question made use of the Supreme Court's ruling and refused to offer any testimony. In 1967 the SACB could do nothing to make the public aware of the nature of the W. E. B. DuBois Clubs or any other group that ran counter to American democratic traditions by advocating revolution.

In defending the need to preserve the SACB, Senator Dirksen could only suggest that "we bring them in line with the court decisions and simply say, 'Go ahead with your work.' "[42] In addition to staving off deep cuts or total elimination of appropriations for the SACB, Dirksen had to downplay the allegation that LBJ was merely providing a sinecure for the husband of a former secretary. Speaking of the nominee for the SACB vacancy, Ev reasoned, "The fact that he married one of the President's former secretaries should not be a deciding factor in a matter of this kind." Resorting to Dirksenian levity, the minority leader rose to the occasion by making light of the situation. "Love is one of those great, all-consuming powers that knows no rules, no evidence; nothing." He inveighed in mock seriousness, "Love goes in where angels would not even tread."[43] This type of facetious rhetoric was high theater but quite irrelevant. With help from Mike Mansfield the nomination of McHugh was confirmed, and SACB's appropriation for fiscal 1968 received approval. Ev let it be known to Mike Manatos, the president's legislative liaison assigned to work closely with Dirksen, that he expected Attorney General Clark to start making use of the SACB. Manatos reported to Johnson in April of 1968 that Dirksen "indicates he caught 'hell and damnation' for his advocacy of new life for the Board, that he did so on the assurance of the Department of Justice that there were about one hundred cases which could be referred to the Board, and that the Attorney General has completely ignored the Board since." The Manatos memorandum concluded with the statement, "Dirksen feels he will be terribly embarrassed unless something is done to give the Board new life."[44] The bottom line of the message was in effect telling LBJ to lean on Ramsey Clark if the SACB were to survive another year. While technically the life of the SACB was extended (it would last only a few more years), the agency already had become moribund in terms of being an effective instrument to fight communism.

In general, Senator Dirksen proposed constructive amendments to modify the various Great Society proposals dealing with education, consumer protection, environmental concerns, urban problems, aid to the aged, and antipoverty programs. The Democrats had the votes to enact them, and therefore Ev sought to make them more manageable and at least partially funded. It was for this reason he opposed attaching Medicare to Social Security, knowing that this attachment would eventually bankrupt the system unless the personal monetary contribution (deducted from wages) was dramatically increased. Members of Congress were eager to increase medical benefits but were loathe to raise the amount individuals had to pay into Social Security. Although an increase in taxes is never popular in an election year, Dirksen helped President Johnson maneuver through the Surcharge-Excise Tax bill. Ev supported the $4 billion tax measure after LBJ pledged to reduce expenditures by the same amount.

The personnel make-up of the Supreme Court was important to Dirksen in terms of how the high Court would render decisions affecting political issues. On June 26, 1968, it was announced by President Johnson that Chief Justice Earl Warren would retire from the Supreme Court as soon as his replacement was confirmed by the Senate. Simultaneously the president nominated Justice Abe Fortas to succeed Warren as Chief Justice and Judge Homer Thornberry to replace Fortas as an associate justice. Prior to this announcement, LBJ, via Mike Manatos, had asked Senator Dirksen for his recommendations. Ev's first choice for the Warren vacancy was Treasury Secretary Henry H. Fowler. He cautioned against nominating Judge Thornberry of the Fifth Circuit Court of Appeals, although he was well qualified, because the former Democratic member of Congress had been a close personal friend of the president. It would, warned Dirksen, subject Johnson to the charge of cronyism.[45]

Disregarding Dirksen's counsel, the president nominated two of his close friends to the Supreme Court and thus left himself wide open to explicit charges of cronyism. Ev knew both nominees and considered them able jurists. Fortas, who would have been the first Jewish Chief Justice, was a liberal. Judge Thornberry, an ex-member of the U.S. House of Representatives from Texas, had been on the federal bench for five years and was considered a judicial moderate. While Dirksen would have preferred two other nominees, he considered them both amply qualified. Ev viewed the dual selections as constituting a reasonable attempt to balance one appointment against the other in terms of the liberal-conservative-moderate makeup of the upper chamber. In spite of Ev's endorsement of LBJ's Court appointees, Senator Robert F. Griffin (R-Mich.) and eighteen other Republicans came out against confirmation. Griffin's initial objections were twofold. First, he felt the nominations were crude examples of cronyism and, secondly, the Michigan senator believed these to be lame duck appointments that should be delayed until after the presidential election. Griffin, who also received help from some southern Democrats, let it be known he planned to conduct a filibuster to prevent a vote on the confirmation of Abe Fortas.

Within the Republican party, Senator Dirksen worked to win converts away from Griffin's group. Ev felt party opposition to Fortas's nomination might open the GOP to allegations of anti-Semitism. By early July Dirksen assured Mike Manatos and Marvin Watson, who represented the White House, that Fortas would eventually be approved.[46] When Ev told a press conference there would be no "organized filibuster" by the GOP, one reporter whom he did not know asked him, "What did the President promise you to support the nominations?" Dirksen replied indignantly, "That's, that's crass. It's an . . . outrage. I don't even know who the hell you are." Turning his back to the offensive newspaperman, Ev declared emphatically, "Why, my life would have been impoverished if I lived like that. I can't understand somebody who doesn't take me straight."[47] The question about a political quid pro quo was prompted by a previous newspaper story claiming Dirksen took his pro-confirmation stand to LBJ for having the Justice Department file seven cases with the SACB in order to prevent it from expiring after the first of January.

There is no doubt that Lyndon Johnson favored Everett Dirksen with patronage whenever he could. Robert D. Morgan, senior partner in the Peoria law firm of Davis, Morgan, and Wetherell (to which Ev belonged), was appointed by President Johnson to the federal bench. The state of Illinois also was given a much-sought-after atom-smasher to be built at Weston for $375 million. But anyone who believed that Ev and LBJ sat down and figured out secret deals whereby patronage goodies were traded for a supportive stand did not understand how the minds of these two pros operated. Certainly Johnson liked to reward Dirksen for his help whenever possible, and Ev was not bashful in letting the president know his recommendations for certain appointive positions. Whereas Dirksen's support could not be bought on any specific issue, Ev and LBJ did establish a friendly rapport conducive to the give and take of politics, and to the political swapping for which both were famous. Both men were shrewd bargainers and masters of practical politics.

During the hearings on the Fortas nomination, information came to light that the associate justice had accepted payment of $15,000 to conduct a seminar at the Law School of American University. It was also revealed that Justice Fortas had served as an advisor to President Johnson both on domestic and foreign affairs while a member of the high court. Despite these revelations Senator Dirksen voted with the eleven to six majority of the Judiciary Committee to recommend confirmation. Ev was politically wise not to make the Fortas confirmation a party matter. Each Republican would be allowed to vote his conscience. Dirksen was not convinced Fortas should be disqualified for his behavior, but he was politically astute enough not to become a martyr for the indiscretions of Fortas.

When Senator Griffin started a filibuster, and was quickly joined by a sizable group of Republicans and southern Democrats, Everett Dirksen refused to sign a cloture petition. The effort by Mike Mansfield on September 27 to invoke cloture was dealt a death blow when Ev joined twenty-three Republicans voting nay. Although the motion drew a majority vote of forty-five to forty-three, it was far from the two-thirds roll call tally needed to end the filibuster. Dirksen explained that he had given Fortas a vote in committee but could not do so on the cloture vote. Ev pointed to the Democrats and told reporters it was "essentially their problem."[48]

On October 10 President Johnson faced reality and withdrew the nominations of both Fortas and Thornberry. On the same day LBJ received a letter from Nobel Yates Dowell, a Democratic attorney from Mt. Vernon, Illinois, recommending that Everett

Dirksen be named Chief Justice. The political motivation for the suggestion was evident when the writer explained: "It would give us an acceptable Chief Justice nomination, and incidentally would elect our party candidate to the U.S. Senate, as it will be too late for the Republicans to place a candidate."[49] Since Ev was the GOP candidate, it certainly would have enhanced the chances of the Democratic challenger. A political ploy of this type was out of the question, however, and was given no serious consideration by Lyndon Johnson. Johnson realized he would not be able to secure Senate approval of any more nominees prior to the fall election. Consequently, it was his successor, Richard Nixon, who would fill the two vacancies on the Supreme Court.

A responsible minority leader frequently walks a political tightrope. His job calls for vocal opposition to the incumbent administration even while rendering support when the nation's vital interests are involved. In no area is this more crucial than in the realm of foreign policy. Partisanship, Dirksen believed, should stop at the water's edge. He therefore doggedly supported President Johnson's war policy even when it proved to be a failure.

Basically Everett Dirksen was in agreement with LBJ on the issue of Vietnam. Although the label "Cold War Warrior" has become a term of approbrium by revisionist historians, during most of Dirksen's tenure in the Senate the term was regarded as an appellation of honor and courage. During his last years he not only witnessed the heated dissension taking place in the nation but participated in the same struggle between hawks and doves that occurred in that most august chamber called the U.S. Senate. Although America's role in the Cold War relative to Vietnam was being reappraised and redefined, Dirksen pretty much defended the status quo. It was Ev's most controversial stance and, possibly, his greatest missed opportunity on the stage of history.

NOTES

1. Minutes, Republican Joint Congressional Leadership Conference, Mar. 9, 1966, RCLF-EMDC.

2. Text of speech in *Executive Club News* (Apr. 30, 1965), reprint in IF-EMDC.

3. Chicago *Tribune*, Sept. 27, 1966, C-EMDC.

4. "The Republican Future," *U.S. News and World Report* (May 3, 1965), reprint in IF-EMDC.

5. Paul O'Neil, "Grand Old King of the Senate," *Life* (Mar. 28, 1965), reprint in IF-EMDC.

6. Statement in minutes, Republican Joint Congressional Leadership Conference, June 1, 1966, RCLF-EMDC.

7. Alexander M. Bickel, *The Supreme Court and the Idea of Progress* (New York: Harper and Row, 1970), p. 12.

8. Text of regents' prayer in WP-EMDC.

9. Stanley J. Kutler, ed., *The Supreme Court and the Constitution* (New York: W. W. Norton, 1977), p. 594.

10. Text of S. 3069, Aug. 3, 1964, in LF-EMDC.

11. Text of S. J. 2, July 7, 1965, in WP-EMDC.

12. "Congress: Blackmail and Blackjack," *Newsweek* (Sept. 20, 1965), reprint in IF-EMDC.

13. "When 'One Person, One Vote' Came Up," *U.S. News and World Report* (Aug. 16, 1965), reprint in IF-EMDC.

14. *Congressional Record*, Aug. 11, 1965, reprint in LF-EMDC.

15. "The Greater Evil," Washington *Post*, Jan. 21, 1966, reprint in WP-EMDC.

16. John Richmond, "Dirksen's Prayer Amendment," *The Catholic Press*, Mar. 31, 1966, reprint in WP-EMDC.

17. "Dirksen Warns That Congress Must Face Court's Prayer Decree," *Baptist Bible Tribune*, Apr. 15, 1966, reprint in WP-EMDC.

18. *Congressional Record*, Sept. 19, 1966, reprint in WP-EMDC.

19. Press Release, Mar. 22, 1966, WP-EMDC.

20. EMD to Walter Trohan, May 16, 1966, papers of Walter Trohan, HCHL.

21. "Dirksen Angrily Bars Prayer Compromise," Washington *Post*, Sept. 20, 1966, WP-EMDC.

22. Ibid.

23. "Amen Amendment," *Time* (Sept. 30, 1966), reprint in IF-EMDC.

24. S. J. Res. 1, Jan. 11, 1967, text in WP-EMDC.

25. Press Release, Jan. 11, 1967, WP-EMDC.

26. Pitirim A. Sorokin, *The Crisis of Our Age: The Social and Cultural Outlook* (New York: E. P. Dutton, 1942), pp. 19-20.

27. LBJ to EMD, Mar. 6, 1965, Executive File, LBJL.

28. LBJ to DDE, Mar. 16, 1965, Executive File, LBJL.

29. "Open Housing," Washington *Post,* July 21, 1966, reprint in WP-EMDC.

30. Memorandum, Nicholas B. Katzenbach to LBJ, Sept. 9, 1966, Executive File, LBJL.

31. *Congressional Record*, Aug. 9, 1960, reprint in LF-EMDC.

32. Memorandum, Larry Temple to LBJ, Feb. 23, 1968, Executive File, LBJL.

33. "Ev's Mutation," *Time* (Mar. 8, 1968), reprint in IF-EMDC.

34. Paper, *Promise and the Performance*, p. 263.

35. "A Switch in Time," *Newsweek* (Mar. 11, 1968), reprint in IF-EMDC.

36. LBJ to EMD, Mar. 13, 1968, Executive File, LBJL.

37. Lloyd Shearer, "The Wizard of Ooze-72-And Still Oozing," *Parade* (Apr. 17, 1968), reprint in IF-EMDC.

38. "Everett Dirksen's Washington" (ABC-TV), Jan. 22, 1968, script in R&R-EMDC. The kinescope of this and many other television appearances of Senator Dirksen are preserved in the EMDC.

39. Statement of John W. Mahan, Chairperson of the Subversive Activities Control Board, July 28, 1967, text in WP-EMDC.

40. "Of This and That," radio and TV script for "Your Senator Speaks," July 24, 1967, in R&R-EMDC.

41. "The First Session of 90th Congress Becomes History," radio and TV script for "Your Senator Speaks," Dec. 11, 1967, R&R-EMDC.

42. *Congressional Record*, Oct. 10, 1967, reprint in WP-EMDC.

43. *Congressional Record*, July 24, 1967, reprint in LF-EMDC.

44. Memorandum, Mike Manatos to LBJ, Apr. 30, 1968, Executive File, LBJL.

45. Memorandum, Mike Manatos to LBJ, June 25, 1968, Executive File, LBJL.

46. Memorandum, Mike Manatos to LBJ, July 9, 1968, Executive File, LBJL.

47. "Summary of UPI News," July 29, 1968, For the President's Night Reading, LBJL.

48. "Summary of AP News," Sept. 27, 1968, For the President's Night Reading, LBJL.

49. Nobel Yates Dowell to LBJ, Oct. 10, 1968, Executive File, LBJL.

10

Two Cold War Warriors and the War in Vietnam

THE LANDSLIDE VICTORY won by Lyndon Johnson in the presidential election of 1964 gradually turned into a political nightmare for the proud Texan as the U.S. involvement in Vietnam deepened. Hundreds of thousands of American troops seemed bogged down in the perpetual quagmire of a jungle war that took a huge toll in lives and military hardware. Soon funds earmarked for Great Society programs were being siphoned away for a war that kept escalating in size and scope, yet little significant dissent was heard from 1964 to 1966. Liberals within the Democratic party were generally still supporting the war, as were the media, intelligentsia, clergy, labor leaders, and broad masses. Basically most Americans, as did Everett M. Dirksen, agreed with the president that as leader of the Free World, the United States should defend the idealistic principle of self-determination at whatever price.

Behind the Iron Curtain there existed, as the aftermath of the second World War, a group of Eastern European satellites that were victims of Soviet imperialism. In enunciating the containment policy, Harry S. Truman vowed to check communist aggression and in 1950 expanded this policy to Asia by seeking to protect the territorial integrity of the Republic of South Korea. John Foster Dulles and Dwight D. Eisenhower created the Central Treaty Organization (CENTO) and the Southeast Asia Treaty Organization (SEATO) to protect the right of self-determination for certain Middle East and Asian countries. Later John F. Kennedy took steps to defend South Vietnam militarily. Within this frame of reference Lyndon B. Johnson escalated U.S. involvement in this area, believing his action was morally justifiable as an expression of America's commitment to defend freedom everywhere in the world. This penchant for globalism, defending self-determination for all the Free World, was not militarily realistic and should have been curtailed. Typical, perhaps, of American idealism was LBJ's unselfish devotion to an abstract idea. Its attempted consummation was initiated without clear consideration of the power realities, distances, difficulties, and costs involved.

Congressional leaders, by and large, found it easier to deal with concrete domestic issues rather than involve themselves in the day-to-day matters of implementing foreign policy. When it came to domestic affairs, Everett Dirksen, in his capacity as minority leader, found it desirable to maintain a certain ductility relative to his own position. This permitted him sufficient flexibility to accommodate and deal with the ideological spread within the Republican party. In the realm of international affairs, however, Dirksen had less room to maneuver. He perceived his role as minority leader to be one of rendering support to President Johnson on all military aspects of the prosecution of the war in Vietnam. This position evolved first from Ev's sincere commitment to the principle of self-determination; second from his intense desire to see communist expansion checked; and finally from a conviction that once foreign policy was established the minority party should back the president in a show of bipartisan solidarity. In the sense that the GOP had far more hawks within its ranks than doves, Dirksen's task was made easier. As the Vietnamese conflict worsened, however, it became possible for Republicans to take the lead in criticizing the war and offering alternatives for its termination. This sentiment grew within the Republican party as the antiwar movement increased in tempo. Dirksen, however, holding the same idealistic views as Lyndon Johnson, could not seize this opportunity. The minority leader not only kept his own party's criticism muted but repeatedly chastised dovish Democrats, such as George McGovern of South Dakota, for unleashing attacks on LBJ.

Despite his idealism relative to the principle of self-determination and his opposition to communism, Dirksen did not automatically champion U.S. intervention in Vietnam when that area was brought within the parameter of America's containment policy. In 1954, when the French needed help at Dien Bien Phu, Dirksen vocally opposed American involvement in Indochina, and this was the same policy adopted by Eisenhower. Ev raised his eyebrows when John F. Kennedy sent a contingent of troops to Vietnam, and in 1964 wondered whether it would not be best if Lyndon Johnson candidly told the American people what his intentions actually were relative to broadening the war. Yet subsequently, in each case, Ev gave his support to the president as commander-in-chief. Thus when presidential decisions were made involving intervention in South Vietnam, Dirksen blindly followed presidents when they formulated foreign policy. He thus forfeited an opportunity to play a constructive opposition role.

Senator Dirksen believed that it was impossible for a nation to fight a war with a cacophony of divisive voices all claiming to speak for the nation. It was imperative for the nation to display "a united front to the entire world," according to Dirksen's mode of thinking, or one would be giving aid and comfort to the nation's enemies. Ev voted for the Gulf of Tonkin Resolution and in doing so gave LBJ great latitude in carrying out its intent. As minority leader, Ev articulated the GOP position as follows: "When it comes to foreign policy, we recognize, of course, that the President is the conductor of the foreign policy of the country."[1]

Following this line of logic, Dirksen also defended Lyndon Johnson's 1965 military intervention in the Dominican Republic. On April 28 the president announced he was sending 405 U.S. Marines to the Dominican Republic ostensibly to protect American lives and property. LBJ had received information from the U.S. ambassador in Santo Domingo that there was a distinct possibility a communist-dominated faction might win the civil war then going on in this Central American country. When Johnson conferred with leaders of Congress, including Dirksen, some Democrats such as J. William Fulbright of Arkansas, chairman of the Senate Foreign Relations Committee, disapproved of the president's action. Ev upheld LBJ's response in Latin America by placing the Republicans uncritically in support of the president. Dirksen declared: "We're behind you one hundred percent. We cannot stand to have another communist government in the Caribbean."[2] The latter, of course, was a reference to the communist regime of Fidel Castro in Cuba. JFK's greatest failure, in Dirksen's judgment, was the failure of the young and inexperienced president to bring about the ouster of the Cuban dictator when the opportunity presented itself. By not doing so, the Soviet Union was given the opportunity to establish a military alliance, with bases, from which to jeopardize the future security of the United States.

In backing Johnson's Vietnam policy, Dirksen believed that America's motive was simple and clear: "All we want is for the communists to stop their aggression and let the South Vietnamese choose their own form of government."[3] What he did not understand was the relationship between an ideal end and a practical means. Once committed in actuality to the defense of self-determination, Ev considered the ensuing battle as a moral crusade for the preservation of freedom. What he failed to perceive was the inability of the United States to be able to accomplish it militarily. Despite the difficulty of fighting a limited land war in the jungles of Vietnam, Ev rationalized continuation of the war by arguing in favor of the domino theory. Ev contended: "We cannot retreat from our position in Vietnam. If Vietnam went down the drain, it could conceivably cost us all of Southeast Asia."[4]

Since there was never any doubt in Dirksen's mind about the moral rectitude of defending South Vietnam's right of self-determination, he could not understand criticism based upon any other viewpoint. The brutal effects of the war, the lack of military success, the divisiveness, the loss of life, and the high cost all eluded him. Thus he never applied his usual constructive approach, that is, of building a party consensus. The Republican party had the golden opportunity of reviewing and reevaluating American policy, and of refashioning it along more successful lines. There was a consistency about Dirksen's foreign policy views in that his earlier isolationism and later internationalism were motivated by the same idealistic impulse. Each attempted to eliminate the ambiguities and complexities of international relations, one by escaping and the other by crusading. In either case, evil ostensibly was to be either avoided or eradicated—thus attempting to achieve the illusory goal of a perfect world.

Senator Dirksen did have private misgivings about some aspects of the way President Johnson handled the Vietnam War. First of all Ev wondered whether the administration could in practical terms fight a war against poverty in the United States and simultaneously wage an effective war in Vietnam. Dirksen also doubted the wisdom of the manner in which LBJ was enlarging American participation in the Vietnam War without leveling candidly with the public as to just exactly what was involved relative to men and matériel. During 1965 the air force stepped up its bombing of targets within North Vietnam and the number of American troops in South Vietnam was increased from 20,000 to 190,000. By midsummer the draft call was raised to 35,000 per month. The national budget for fiscal 1965-66 was $94.4 billion, of which $49 billion was earmarked for military spending. The deficit would total almost $2.3 billion. Dirksen began seriously to question in public whether Lyndon Johnson could have "a Great Society with all these authorized expenditures and push up that administration budget, and run a war at the same time."[5] Perhaps the biggest error in Dirksen's career was in not taking a firmer stand on this point. Dirksen was essentially correct in his appraisal and could have had a very positive effect if only he had chosen to do so.

Ultimately, however, once the Johnson administration committed itself to a war policy, Senator Dirksen forever remained loyal. He was an indomitable hawk. It may have represented patriotic idealism writ large, but Ev's stand nevertheless was then irreversible. When such doves as Frank Church (D-Idaho) began to suggest a negotiated settlement, Dirksen was not reticent in reprimanding them. Ev scolded his dovish colleagues in the Senate, "In all seriousness, there are some fundamentals that have been sidestepped in all this impassioned pleading for us to default on our promise to South Vietnam."[6] In opposing a negotiated settlement as tantamount to appeasement, Senator Dirksen stood his ground. "I say to my distinguished colleagues who are advocating negotiations: Before you try to entice free men back into the Red bear trap of negotiation, tell the aggressors to show some evidence of good faith."[7]

Everett Dirksen could never be persuaded that any termination of the Vietnam War except total victory might be in the best interest of the United States. Speaking as part of the generation that experienced Munich and the appeasement of Hitler, Dirksen encouraged the Senate to remain steadfast: "The most basic of these deeply held principles is that no nation has the right to change the international map by external violence. On that principle rests the difference between order and anarchy in a dangerous and feverish world. It is for that principle that our men are fighting and dying right now in the jungles of Vietnam."[8]

The hawkish Everett Dirksen was ever quick to respond to dovish-inspired verbal criticism of the president, whether leveled by a Democrat or Republican. Ev once lamented, "When a President is assailed after doing what he deems best for the country and in the national interest only to be charged in some quarters for being responsible for the bloodletting and for planning even greater casualties and destruction, what does it do to the spirit?"[9] In one heated verbal exchange with George McGovern (D-S.D.), a leading dove, Ev decried the defeatist and deprecatory statements made by the South Dakotan "in this chamber which echoes with the courageous words of brave men now gone." In a rancorous tone McGovern replied, "There are still brave men in the Senate. It doesn't require any particular bravery to stand on the floor of the Senate and urge our boys to fight harder . . . it won't be U.S. Senators who die. It will be American soldiers who are too young to qualify for the Senate."[10] The sad truth is that no real dialogue emerged from these angry exchanges. Real debate should have taken place and Dirksen was partially responsible for the absence of thorough and extended discussion.

Dirksen almost single-handedly kept Republicans from raising the Vietnam issue. He continually restrained House minority leader Gerald R. Ford (R-Mich.) when the latter wanted to raise the issue. Following a meeting of the Republican Joint Congressional Leadership Conference, the Michigan congressman told newspeople, "We question the logic of committing U.S. ground forces on a large scale to fight the war in Southeast Asia."[11] It was Ford's contention that North Vietnam should be beaten into total submission by a tight naval blockade and by relentless and unlimited use of strategic bombing. Ford's own war experience against Japan in the Pacific during World War II, as a gunnery officer on the carrier *U.S.S. Monterey,* convinced him that the massive use of American ground troops was a mistake when America possessed such superior sea and air power. In a subsequent meeting of the same group, Senator Dirksen pointedly took issue with Ford's statement. Ev publicly disagreed with Ford and stressed the need for maintaining a truly bipartisan foreign policy in order to further "national security ahead of partisan advantage" and to "avoid furnishing grist for the propaganda mills of an enemy."[12] Here again the Republican minority may have had the opportunity to shorten the war; once more Dirksen prevented it.

On still another occasion, during the "Ev and Jerry Show," Senator Dirksen publicly registered his disapproval over another remark made by Representative Ford. The GOP House minority leader leveled a critical blast at President Johnson for his "shocking mismanagement"[13] of the war in Vietnam. Ev immediately corrected his Republican colleague by indicating that while there may have been some "misjudgment" on the part of the president, that did not mean LBJ was guilty of mismanaging the war. Dirksen went on to lecture Ford: "I just don't deliver a hard judgment like that unless I have some hard facts. I just wouldn't do it." Ev completed his admonition by telling the man who himself would be president one day in the future, "You don't demean the chief magistrate of your country at a time when a war is on."[14] In deference to Dirksen, the Republicans lost another chance to influence the conduct of the war by giving LBJ unrestrained freedom to do what he wanted.

As a patriot of the old school, Dirksen could not understand nor appreciate the integrity of antiwar protestors. Mingling pride with indignation, Ev utilized the pages of a nationally distributed magazine to defend old-fashioned and unquestioning patriotism. He wrote: "It is something more than mere attachment to an entity which includes territory, social structures, and some form of government. It embraces also a deep devotion to the principles and purposes, to the traditions and achievements, to the hopes and dreams of his country. It is the spirit—primeval, moving, meaningful. It is deeply possessive of the basic and best instincts of man."[15]

The violent upheaval during the LBJ presidency was a tortuous experience for Everett Dirksen. The minority leader's commitment to civility, the democratic process, and free speech made it hard for Dirksen to sympathize in particular with radical demonstrators who flaunted the law, shouted down speakers with whom they disagreed, or advocated overthrowing the American system of government. "Dissent we encourage and approve," he vowed. "Violence in any form and for whatever purpose, we condemn, now and hereafter."[16]

The eruption of New Left radicalism and the rise of their counterculture baffled Senator Dirksen. To Ev such things as God, home, church, education, and law and order constituted the very essence of the American way of life.[17] For militant revolutionaries to advocate the casting aside of middle class morality and to scoff at all authority appeared to Dirksen as the harbinger of total anarchy. Ev decried the "surrender of authority" by college officials to members of the Students for a Democratic Society, whom Dirksen called "militant and often armed groups of insurgents."[18]

The only weapons which Senator Dirksen had available to fight against the swelling tide of what seemed to be revolutionary violence were words and laws—the tools of a legislator. Since Ev thought legitimate protest had on too many occasions exceeded legal bounds, he sponsored legislation to punish those who desecrated the American flag and to increase protection for the besieged Capitol. Still stunned by the fact that educated students could become radicals and revolutionaries, he called for the creation by the federal government of a National Law Foundation. Somehow, Ev felt, a way had to be found to instill a respect for law and order in young people or democracy itself might be doomed. Dirksen was steadfast in his insistence that the United States was a nation of laws and that no individual or group stood above the law.

In the reasoned judgment of Everett Dirksen, "no person has a right to act against the public safety, anywhere, any time." To him it was imperative that "the protection of life must be primary and total." Ev rejected the revolutionary doctrine which justified breaking the law, even killing, when such action forwarded political objectives. "Punishment of those who break the law," Dirksen insisted, "must be swift and decisive—no matter who they may be."[19] He came to the conclusion that "mob anarchy and a riotous display of force have reached a point in the cities that could almost be called a war."[20]

Adversity seemed to draw Dirksen and Johnson closer together. At a testimonial for Ev, held only a few months before the president removed himself as a candidate for reelection, LBJ praised the minority leader in the following words: "He is a great American. He is a great human being. He is one of my dearest friends."[21] In turn Ev reacted to LBJ's withdrawal of his presidential candidacy by making the consoling statement: "There can be no thought that Lyndon Johnson is confessing personal defeat or quitting in the face of the mounting problems at home and overseas. This is an impossible thought."[22] Despite it being an election year, Dirksen sympathized with Johnson right up to the end. He personally liked the proud Texan and felt sorry for the many woes that befell LBJ. He tried to lighten his load. Once Ev, on the spur of the moment, phoned the President and asked him to come on over to the Senate for a drink and some conversation. Dirksen also invited Mike Mansfield and some other LBJ intimates for some talk and relaxation. Johnson surprised them all when he came over with two of his beagle hounds. This got a big laugh all around. Later Dirksen reported the event on his regular television program for Illinois constituents by saying, "It was like coming home for him. He was escaping loneliness for a little while."[23]

An important question also faced Everett Dirksen in 1968. Would he, himself, run for a fourth term in the U.S. Senate? Ev was seventy-two years of age and had frequently been in and out of the hospital with various ailments. He suffered from emphysema, to the extent that he took regular medication and needed to inhale oxygen from a tank in his office; had recurrent abdominal attacks; was bothered constantly by ulcer flareups; still had a slight limp from his healed broken hip; and was racked by coughing spells—no doubt caused from excessive smoking. Ev's wife Louella urged him to retire. She suggested they move away from Washington, D.C., to live in their winter home (which was named "Contentment")[24] located in De Bary, Florida. Louella felt her husband's life might be prolonged if Ev were removed from the tension-filled environment in the capital.

Senator Dirksen did give considerable thought to getting away from the anxieties associated with public service, but on February 17 Ev announced publicly his intention to seek reelection. "The easy road would be to walk away and let the fire burn," declared Dirksen. "But to retreat from an unfinished war or from unresolved and baffling problems would be alien to every conviction which I cherish."[25] The white-haired septuagenerian thus set the stage, although unknown to him at the time, for his last political campaign. Voters in Illinois would have one more opportunity to applaud or oppose the record of their battle-scarred veteran of many political wars.

NOTES

1. "The President and the Republican Minority," statement by Everett M. Dirksen on radio and TV, Apr. 13, 1964, script in R&R-EMDC.

2. Rowland Evans, Jr. and Robert D. Novak, *Lyndon B. Johnson: The Exercise of Power* (New York: The New American Library, 1968), p. 541.

3. Lloyd Shearer, "The Wizard of Ooze-72-And Still Oozing," *Parade* (Apr. 17, 1968), reprint in IF-EMDC.

4. "Meet the Press" (NBC-Radio and TV), Feb. 2, 1964, script in R&R-EMDC.

5. "Issues and Answers" (ABC-Radio and TV), Jan. 9, 1966, script in R&R-EMDC.

6. *Congressional Digest* (Apr., 1965), reprint in IF-EMDC.

7. Remarks by Everett M. Dirksen, Minority Leader, Feb. 18, 1965, text in R&R-EMDC.

8. *Congressional Record,* May 24, 1967, reprint in WP-EMDC.

9. William J. Eaton, "Critics Broke LBJ's Spirit," Chicago *Daily News,* Apr. 1, 1968, C-EMDC.

10. Robert Sam Anson, *McGovern: A Biography* (New York: Holt, Rinehart and Winston, 1972), p. 160.

11. Press Conference, July 1, 1965, transcript in RCLF-EMDC.

12. Minutes, Republican Joint Congressional Leadership Conference, July 29, 1965, RCLF-EMDC.

13. "Dirksen Disagrees with Ford," *U.S. News and World Report* (May 2, 1966), reprint in IF-EMDC.

14. Jerald F. Terhorst, *Gerald Ford and the Future of the Presidency* (New York: Joseph Opaku Books, 1974), p. 100. See also Gerald R. Ford, *A Time to Heal: The Autobiography of Gerald R. Ford* (New York: Harper and Row, 1979), p. 83.

15. EMD, "Let's Not Make Patriotism a Dirty Word," *Pageant* (May 16, 1968), reprint in R&R-EMDC.

16. EMD, "The State of the Congress," Dec. 7, 1967, text in R&R-EMDC.

17. Press Release, Aug. 3, 1967, text in R&R-EMDC.

18. Press Release, May 1, 1969, text in R&R-EMDC.

19. Press Release, Aug. 3, 1967, text in LF-EMDC.

20. Tom Littlewood, "Ev Calls Riot Talk Sign LBJ Fails," Chicago *Sun-Times,* Feb. 24, 1968, C-EMDC.

21. "An LBJ Tribute to Dirksen," *U.S. News and World Report* (Dec. 11, 1967), reprint in IF-EMDC.

22. EMD, "A Senator's Notebook," Apr. 3, 1968, text in R&R-EMDC.

23. "Just Me and the Dogs," May 21, 1968, script in R&R-EMDC.

24. LD, *Mr. Marigold,* p. 223.

25. Press Release, Feb. 17, 1968, text in R&R-EMDC.

11

The Last Hurrah: Dirksen's Final Campaign

THERE WERE A FEW within the ranks of the GOP who thought Senator Everett Dirksen was too old to run for reelection in 1968. Stalwart Bourke B. Hickenlooper (R-Ia.), who was the same age as Ev, was retiring. The Iowan felt Dirksen should make a grand exit as minority leader at this time rather than wait until the new breed of young Turks deposed him. Hugh Scott of Pennsylvania, a liberal Republican, was eager to fill Ev's shoes, and others in this wing of the party likewise hoped for Ev's replacement as their chief spokesperson. In the House, sixty-eight-year-old Charles Halleck, of "Ev and Charlie Show" fame, who had already lost his leadership post, decided to retire. He likewise advised Dirksen to step down before being pushed out.

When it became known that Dirksen was slated to be the chairperson of the Platform Committee at the national convention, the Republican Governors' Association passed a resolution calling for the appointment of fifty-year-old Governor Raymond P. Shafer of Pennsylvania as co-chairperson. Ev simply refused to accept retirement or even acknowledge the rumors that he was over the hill either physically or mentally. "Age is a state of mind, and heart, and will," declared Dirksen. "Age is no factor."[1]

Over and above what appeared to be negative aspects of winning reelection, there were some important plus factors in Dirksen's favor. As a politico, for instance, Ev possessed a unique charisma that set him far above most professional politicians. Also advantageous was Dirksen's high visibility and almost bigger-than-life stature in the upper chamber. It made him one of the best-known political figures in contemporary America. Tourists viewed him as a national monument. Dirksen's office was inundated with mail and requests for personal appearances. Cartoonists had a perpetual field day caricaturing Dirksen, all of which added to the luster of his image as a lovable character. In his old age, with a truly august and venerable appearance, Ev looked the way a senator should look. In the minds of most GOP voters Ev was the contemporary "Mr. Republican."[2] He attracted the votes of many independents, and all but hard-core Democrats usually split their ticket to cast a vote for the senior senator from Illinois.

Everett Dirksen had an uncanny way of grabbing the spotlight, but doing it in such a way as not to make it obvious. A good example of the way he could garner publicity was through his good-natured crusade to have the yellow marigold designated the national flower emblem. Commencing in 1961, initially as a personal favor to David Burpee[3] (president of W. Atlee Burpee Company, a well-known nursery famous for its flower seeds and bulbs), Dirksen sponsored resolutions periodically until his death to have the marigold (*Tagetes erecta*) named the national flower. It was Ev's oratory that elevated the debate over the merits of the marigold into a media event that caught the public's attention. Sometimes Dirksen would come up with a botanical ditty, such as the words from William Wordsworth's poem, "The Daffodils," that went like this: "Ten thousand saw I at a glance / Tossing their heads in sprightly dance."[4]

Sponsoring the marigold allowed Senator Dirksen to give full sway to his showmanship while permitting him to engage in some good-natured fun. Sometimes when the Senate was bogged down or its members suffering from fatigue, with tempers flaring, Ev would rise and give one of his patented marigold speeches. The galleries would fill, good humor would be restored, and his resolution would be buried as it always was. The marigold became closely associated with Dirksen's name even though he loved many other flowers just as much as this particular one. Senator Margaret Chase Smith (R-Me.), who in mock debate had always championed the rose, paid tribute to Dirksen's memory the day the Illinois senator died by laying a single golden-colored marigold on top of the now empty minority leader's desk. It was a sentimental gesture deeply appreciated by the entire Senate. That august body observed the gesture in reverent silence. Louella carried on the campaign for making the marigold the national flower emblem after Ev's death, but her campaign proved unsuccessful. Dirksen's hometown of Pekin continues to observe its annual fall "Marigold Festival," which attracts huge crowds to view the beautiful array of marigolds. In honor of his patron in the Senate, David Burpee developed a special marigold with a five-inch bloom which was named appropriately the "Senator Dirksen."

Perhaps the greatest contributing factor to Everett Dirksen's celebrity status late in his life was the fact that he became a showbiz star. This phenomenon came about after Ev recorded an LP album with Capitol Records called "Gallant Men, Stories of the American Adventure." Dirksen's recitations (using only the spoken word with a background of music) hardly seemed the vehicle to stardom. Yet he made a hit with his rich, resonant voice reciting sonorous prose renditions of such patriotic readings as the "Gettysburg Address," "Pledge of Allegiance to the Flag," and the "Star-Spangled Banner." Also recited were such historical narratives as "The Story of the Battle for Independence," "The Story of Gettysburg," and "The Story of the Statue of Liberty." This long-playing recording became a best seller and skyrocketed on the charts. It eventually won for Ev a gold record for selling over 500,000 copies to top such established stars as Elvis Presley, Dean Martin, and Bob Dylan. Dirksen's performance was deemed so good he was awarded a Grammy in 1967 by the National Academy of Arts and Sciences. Ev's motivation for making the record was to sustain the traditional American values in face of the challenge from a counterculture which had disdain for them.

There seemed to be only one real obstacle to Ev's reelection in 1968 and that was the state of his health. After returning from Pasadena, California, where he served as the grand marshal of the Tournament of Roses Parade, Dirksen came down with the flu. After battling it a few days he was forced to enter Walter Reed. Soon he was up and about again. In February Ev announced for reelection and in March he was in the hospital once more. This time he had reinjured his hip (but did not fracture it) after slipping while trying to change a light bulb in a fixture above the dining room table. This was the same hip that had needed spikes to hold it together while mending. Fragile, yet seemingly indestructible, Ev and his wife went to their winter home in Florida to allow the senator to rest and relax while recovering fully from his fall. It was not an auspicious start for an old war-horse whose aged body bore the scars of many political battles. But, strange as it may seem, the general public viewed Everett Dirksen as they did John Wayne or Bing Crosby. They were legends in their own time, sort of national institutions who were regarded as immortal—or so it seemed.

The befuddled situation among Democrats in 1968 also aided Ev's reelection cause. Mayor Richard J. Daley, the undisputed boss of Chicago's Democratic machine, slated William G. Clark to oppose Dirksen. Clark was the Illinois state attorney general. He was a competent candidate but was not well known in the state. Why was Clark chosen in the first place? Mayor Daley, a hawkish supporter of the Vietnam War, put thumbs down on state treasurer Adlai E. Stevenson III. The latter was the son of the Democratic presidential nominee in 1952 and 1956 and UN ambassador, and consequently commanded considerable attention by virtue of his lineage. Young Stevenson was a dove on the war issue and this motivated Daley to bypass the junior Stevenson even though he would have been the strongest Democratic challenger. (After Dirksen's death Stevenson did win the Senate seat over Ev's immediate GOP successor.) Ironically, during the course of the 1968 campaign, Clark also shifted to a strong anti-Vietnam War position.

William Clark was really not in the same political league as Senator Dirksen. Despite attempts by Mayor Daley to get Clark some free national publicity at the Democratic National Convention[5] in order to counter Ev's role as chairperson of the GOP Platform Committee, nothing could camouflage the fact that the Illinois Democrat was a political nonentity. He was pitted against a senatorial statesman still being touted by some as presidential timber. Ev no longer harbored White House aspirations and took himself out of the 1968 presidential race very early by quipping, "That boat left the dock a long time ago."[6]

From 1964 onward Dirksen had concentrated on preventing Barry Goldwater from once more becoming the Republican presidential nominee by working to eliminate John Birchers from the GOP and preventing Goldwaterites from securing top posts in the party machinery. Ev, for instance, helped George Murphy of California get the nod over pro-Goldwater Peter H. Dominick of Colorado as head of the Republican Senatorial Campaign Committee. Dirksen worked in Illinois for the nomination of Richard M. Nixon. Ev considered Nixon a good party loyalist; "Kosher,"[7] as he put it. Dirksen was aware, furthermore, that in the 1966 mid-term elections 66 percent of the GOP candidates running with Nixon's support, including Ev's son-in-law Howard Baker, won, while only 44 percent of the Republicans running without Nixon's help managed to triumph over Democratic opponents. Senator Charles Percy wanted the favorite son designation from Illinois, but Ev eventually headed his state's delegation with fifty pledged to Nixon. The other eight, including Percy, were for Nelson Rockefeller.

In trying to unseat Dirksen, William Clark was hard pressed to find a winning issue. Ignoring the fact that Lyndon Johnson occupied the White House and the Democrats controlled Congress for the last four years, Clark nevertheless sought to exploit the Vietnam issue by posturing as a dove. Moreover, because he was forty-three years old, Clark stressed his youth in contrast to Dirksen's advanced years. The Democratic challenger, following the tactic of previous contestants for Ev's Senate seat, hauled out the hackneyed charges that Dirksen was a tool of the special interests and a "bar to social change."[8] When all else failed to attract the attention of voters, Clark resorted to futile rhetorical blasts. In one such none-too-imaginative verbal broadside Clark called Ev a "political faker, a moral fraud, and a revolving-door Senator."[9]

Everett Dirksen's strategy was simple enough. He ignored Clark. It was not until fall that Ev even returned to Illinois for serious campaigning. Once on the campaign trail Dirksen kept on the high road. He talked about what was good in America; denounced lawlessness; and called for an honorable peace in Vietnam based on "progressive de-Americanization of the war."[10] The latter phrase was taken from the Republican platform, of which Ev was the primary author, and referred to what later became popularly known as Vietnamization of the war. Louella and those close to Senator Dirksen worried more about his health than about his opponent. It was obvious to insiders that the senator was suffering from severe fatigue—at times to the point of exhaustion. On some occasions rallies were cut short to conserve his strength. In a few instances, when his stomach was bothering him, Ev would rely too much upon antacids and alcohol to dull the pain. Downing bourbon on an empty stomach left him a bit tipsy once or twice. It was amazing, nevertheless, how with a few hours' rest Dirksen could regain his energy.

When the election returns were counted Dirksen had outpolled Clark by a vote of 2,181,218 to 1,936,484. In winning by a margin of 53 percent Ev carried 99 out of the 102 counties in Illinois. Cook County, conspicuously missing from Dirksen's tally column, remained the stronghold of the Democrats.

Whereas Dirksen concentrated most of his campaigning in Illinois on his own reelection, he did play a key role in the 1968 Republican National Convention held at Miami Beach, Florida. Ev served as chairperson of the 102-member Platform Committee. It would be his objective to reconcile not only the traditional conflict of liberals and conservatives, but of doves versus hawks. As it turned out, predictably, the biggest dispute was over the Vietnam plank. Doves, such as Jacob Javits, wanted to go so far as to specify that the National Liberation Front should participate in the peace negotiations then taking place in Paris, France. On the other hand hawks, such as Barry Goldwater, wanted a stern statement to the effect that nothing short of total victory for the U.S. and South Vietnam would be acceptable. It was Dirksen who skillfully fashioned a compromise plank. Pledged was a "program for peace in Vietnam" not at "any price," but "based on the principle of self-determination, our national interests, and the cause of long-range world peace." This was to be attained by "a strategy permitting a progressive de-Americanization of the war.

. . ." A promise was also made to continue the Paris negotiations "as long as they offer any reasonable prospect for a just peace."[11]

In a partisan tone, and with the presidency up for grabs, Senator Dirksen's speech at the GOP National Convention contained the harshest criticism he ever hurled at the Johnson administration. For a political pro, it was the time and setting for a display of one-sided partisanship. When Ev moved to the rostrum, after being introduced to the vast throng in attendance, he received a prolonged ovation. Hamming it up to sustain the crowd's good humor, Ev quipped, "I accept the nomination."[12]

By way of introducing the platform Dirksen launched into an attack on the Democratic administration. "You hear here at home that we have a sick society," he asserted. "Well, my friends, only radicals who traffic in trouble and only extremists who are intolerant of moderation, and only the cerebrating pessimists who are bemused by a mote in America's eyes say it. No, fellow citizens, we're not sick. We're not even indisposed. We're mismanaged." His castigation of LBJ then culminated in a jarring crescendo. Summarizing all the criticisms leveled at the Johnson administration for its alleged failures, Ev charged:

> How cynical, how mocking that political slogan, the "Great Society." Never has an undeclared war embroiled America so long, never was the casualty toll greater and never the outcome so remote. Never have we been so overextended around the world; never has our prestige been so low, our alliances so weakened; our image so impaired. Never has an Administration so disregarded the limits of our resources or patience or willingness—indeed our inability—to police and sustain a bellicose and insatiable world.[13]

Although Richard Nixon had the GOP nomination for the presidency sewed up, stop-Nixon movements periodically arose in fruitless attempts to head off the inevitable. For instance, there were rumors prior to the convention that Everett Dirksen and Governor Ronald Reagan of California were going to enter the fray as a presidential team—Ev heading the ticket and Reagan as the vice-presidential nominee. Governor Reagan was to nominate Dirksen and, in turn, be selected as Ev's running mate when and if the latter got the nod. Whatever move was afoot to promote one or another of these two candidates was quashed when Dirksen announced publicly "it is in the bag"[14] for Nixon. Reagan also made it known that statements indicating his desire for the vice-presidency were "categorically untrue."[15]

Once former Vice-President Nixon was nominated for the presidency, Dirksen pushed his son-in-law, Senator Howard Baker of Tennessee, for second place on the ticket. Richard Nixon made the final decision, however, and picked Governor Spiro T. Agnew of Maryland. Dirksen was not exactly overjoyed with Nixon's choice. During the ensuing campaign when Agnew charged that Senator Hubert H. Humphrey, the Democratic presidential nominee, was "squishy soft" on communism, Ev took the Maryland governor to task. Dirksen defended Humphrey by saying, "I'm not aware of any evidence."[16] Agnew later retracted the allegation by modifying his statement.

Of Richard Nixon, with whom Dirksen never had been close, Ev noted in his syndicated column: "Mr. Nixon played a good game. He was not lured into any dark corners. He had it figured out in advance."[17] It was Dirksen's contention from the outset that the Democrats could not keep the White House unless the GOP candidate made some error. Humphrey, as the surrogate for LBJ, made a good run at it but dissension within the Democratic party handicapped him from the start. In Illinois, Dirksen—at the head of the state ticket—helped Nixon. The latter drew 47.1 percent of the vote to Humphrey's 44.2 percent (with third party candidate George Wallace polling 8.5 percent).

The aftermath of the 1968 election for Everett Dirksen was one of restrained elation. He had renewed his mandate with Illinois voters. Seven other GOP candidates won seats formerly held by Democrats, so the 91st Congress would have a total of forty-three Republicans in the Senate. Upon returning to Washington, D.C., Ev dropped in on LBJ for a friendly chat. Several days later the president sent Dirksen a picture of the get-together with the inscription, "To Ev My Best LBJ."[18] Mike Manatos also congratulated Senator Dirksen on his reelection and added the comment: "As one who has watched you perform at close range, I subscribe to the good judgment of the voters of your state."[19]

Senator Dirksen was reelected minority leader as soon as the

Senate reconvened for business. With verve and enthusiasm, Ev looked forward to serving the incoming Republican president. With the Democrats still in control of Congress Dirksen also had a chance to break the record for holding the office of Senate minority leader longer than any other Republican. Perhaps it was an ill omen when illness quickly felled Ev soon after his return to work. From the White House, LBJ sent a pep-talk type of note to Dirksen telling him he was needed back in harness: "We need you there and want you well so that you can continue to give us all the strength of your leadership and goodness."[20]

One of the first defeats Dirksen suffered after his own reelection was in the selection of a GOP whip in the Senate. Thomas Kuchel, the previous whip, had lost his bid for renomination in the Republican primary to Dr. Max Rafferty, an ultraconservative superintendent of public schools (Rafferty subsequently lost the general election to Democrat Alan Cranston). This necessitated an election for party whip, and Dirksen backed his close friend Roman Hruska of Nebraska for the post. Ev believed it was time to groom a successor. He felt the Nebraskan was the ideal person to succeed him. The latter represented Middle America, had learned to become more flexible, and repeatedly helped Dirksen round up conservative votes on controversial measures. Ev did his usual politicking and thought he had the job sewed up for Hruska. Dirksen was severely jolted when Hugh Scott of Pennsylvania, representing the liberal faction, defeated Hruska by a vote of twenty-three to twenty.

This was one of the first indications of Ev's ebbing power on the Hill, and it would not be the last. Now that a Republican occupied 1600 Pennsylvania Avenue, for instance, the "Ev and Jerry Show" became a casualty of circumstances. It was canceled. President Richard Nixon, not Dirksen, would now be the chief spokesperson for the GOP. While Ev was given the honor of being chairperson of the Joint Inaugural Committee and was given a prominent place by Nixon in the proceedings, the limelight was on the president—not on the minority leader. Senator Dirksen was aware he would have to make adjustments; he was, however, a bit disturbed when Nixon surrounded himself with a bevy of aides, a kind of palace guard, who seemed inclined to isolate the president from members of Congress. Ev had found it easier to phone or see LBJ personally than to get through to Nixon. Had Dirksen lived through Nixon's first term, one wonders if the Watergate scandal would have occurred. Many of the secret machinations could not have been promulgated with a powerful figure like Dirksen looking over the president's shoulder. In his syndicated column Senator Dirksen gave President Nixon some excellent advice. It was that the new GOP executive name his administration the "Responsible Society."[21]

For one so dedicated to his leadership duties in the Senate, Everett Dirksen had few pleasures aside from politics. Ev enjoyed playing with his grandchildren, Cynthia and Derek, but above all else he relished the time spent in his beautiful garden. Working there was a form of relaxation for Dirksen; it constituted for him a type of spiritual experience. In being close to the soil Ev combined communing with nature with his religious prayer-meditation. In describing his personal relation with God Dirksen explained: "I talk to Him about my aspirations every day. Most people call it prayer. I have thought of it as conversation with Him." Ev disclosed, "I have felt God's presence in my life for as long as I can remember." In advising others to cultivate a garden Dirksen counseled everyone to "work in the soil, where one can see the whole miracle of creation."[22]

It was obvious that in terms of his own religious beliefs Dirksen placed less emphasis upon doctrines or dogma and much more importance on the intimate and personal relationship between human beings and their Creator. While not being highly introspective or one with a philosophic bent of mind, Ev nonetheless did ponder what life was all about. In a metaphysical sense Dirksen defined history as follows:

> [It] is but the enfoldment of a divine pattern. If not this, it can only be a materialistic drift. If there be a creative hand behind this universe, there must be a creative hand in its unfoldment and direction. Everything in it—sun, moon, stars, planets, their distances, the calibration so that people will neither freeze nor scorch to death, the procession of the seasons, man's subsistence—all rise to testify to the amazing adjustment in the universe to preserve

life. And surely the creative force would not provide it all in such meticulous detail and then ignore its ultimate destiny.[23]

President-elect Nixon was invited to Senator Dirksen's annual birthday gala in January of 1969. Though the relationship between Ev and Nixon was professionally cordial, it was not intimate. Richard Nixon paid deference to Dirksen and promised those in attendance that next year's party would be in the White House. Little did the gathering know that by the next year Everett Dirksen would be dead and that about the same time four years hence events would be in motion to remove Richard Nixon from the White House. Lyndon Johnson, now a lame duck president, also sent Ev his last birthday message: "I want to add my voice to your legion of friends and admirers in saying, Happy Birthday—and many more of them. Lady Bird joins me in wishing you much health and happiness in the coming year."[24]

Before exiting Washington, D.C., LBJ penned a sentimental last farewell to Everett Dirksen. The president wrote: "The time of my departure grows near, but I leave with a sense of pride in the quality of friends I have made over the years. I am indeed proud to call you 'my friend'—a good friend, a steadfast friend, a loyal friend. You have helped lighten the load that I have carried as President and you have enriched my life. Thank you, from the bottom of my heart."[25] Mike Manatos also prepared to depart from the capital. He too sent Ev a note indicating his own feelings. "I take this opportunity to tell you that I very much cherish the association we have enjoyed."[26]

In terms of dealing with Richard M. Nixon as president, Senator Dirksen, as minority leader, soon found his relationship with the chief executive far different than it had been with previous occupants of the Oval Office. Eisenhower, JFK, and LBJ all courted him and made themselves readily available to him. Now Dirksen had to go through presidential aides, a zealous Praetorian Guard, as it were, before reaching Nixon. In the pre-Nixon presidency, Ev was a major figure among those making GOP policy. Dirksen also played a principal role in dispensing the patronage doled out by Democratic presidents. Now he was consulted infrequently or even ignored in these areas. Despite these slights, Ev defended the new administration from criticism. "On the basis of the first sixty days," asserted Dirksen, "I cannot guarantee that this administration will be a success but I can say it is well begun."[27] Reacting to Democratic charges that Nixon was too slow in presenting his proposals to Congress, Dirksen declared, "High store is placed not on how fast the programs can be speeded to action, but how soundly conceived and organized these programs will be."[28]

Ev's first clash with the Nixon administration came over high-level appointments made by the president. Dirksen had been spoiled by LBJ, who made it a practice to clear major appointments with the minority leader and even permitted him to make recommendations. Lyndon Johnson once complained in feigned anger to Ev, "Dammit, Everett, if I am not careful you'll have a marker on every appointment to every agency in town."[29] When President Nixon sent the name of Dr. John H. Knowles to the Senate for confirmation as assistant secretary for health and scientific affairs within the Department of Health, Education, and Welfare, Dirksen blocked it. Since the Knowles nomination was backed by HEW Secretary Robert H. Finch, it became a contest between a member of Nixon's cabinet and the minority leader.

Dirksen did not like what he believed was Dr. Knowles's social welfare approach to medicine. The latter was also opposed by the American Medical Association (AMA), an organization with which Ev was in basic agreement in regard to limiting federal involvement in health insurance plans. Upon being asked by reporters what he would do if the Knowles appointment received Senate confirmation, Ev replied: "When Napoleon sent Marshall Ney to Russia, he told him he would have plenty of time to discuss with him how he conquered that country and no time to discuss how he lost the battle. And I have no time to dicuss Dr. Knowles."[30] After it became apparent that Ev had the votes to block the appointment, President Nixon intervened to withdraw the nomination. Dirksen not only won this round in the Potomac skirmish for power but established his presence as a minority leader the president would have to deal with.

Whether the president liked it or not, Everett Dirksen did exert his authority on other occasions when he deemed it necessary. The ouster of Clifford L. Alexander, chairman of the Equal Em-

ployment Opportunity Commission (EEOC), was such an occasion. Ev promised to "get somebody fired" because of complaints to him by businessmen of alleged harassment by Alexander
or other EEOC officials.[31] Shortly thereafter, Ronald L. Ziegler,
White House press secretary, announced that Alexander would
not be reappointed as head of the EEOC. Dirksen also led the
fight against the retention of William J. Driver as director of the
Veterans Administration (VA). Driver supposedly allowed VA
employees to engage in campaign activities while on duty and to
use government-owned automobiles for this purpose. Ev likewise
sidetracked the appointment of Franklin Long of Cornell University to be director of the National Science Foundation upon
learning that the prospective appointee had apparently been a
backer of both Eugene McCarthy and Robert F. Kennedy. Since
he was not consulted in advance, Dirksen had no compunction
in blocking appointments he did not agree with even if it meant
bucking the administration.

Those who doubted Dirksen's integrity always pointed to Ev's
long-standing opposition to legislation making it mandatory for
members of Congress to disclose their financial interests. They
claimed that such a stance proved Dirksen had something to hide.
Ev had over and over maintained, "My life is an open book."[32]
On the Senate floor he contended, "Whenever you require every
citizen to disclose, then I'm ready to do the same thing."[33] Ev
eventually changed his position and voted for passage of the
Standards of Conduct Act of 1968. The public wanted some type
of ethics measure following the exposures of alleged malfeasance
on the part of Justice Abe Fortas; Robert "Bobby" Baker, secretary
to the Senate Democrats; and Senator Thomas Dodd (D-Conn.).
Revelations indicating that Fortas accepted fees while sitting on
the bench forced his resignation. Baker ostensibly used his position to engage in dubious financial dealings. Finally, Senator
Dodd was censured by his colleagues for improper use of campaign contributions. Dirksen voted for Dodd's censure and for
an ethics law that would forestall repetition of such practices. To
Ev, any conduct on the part of a senator that besmirched the
reputation of the upper chamber by personal corruption was in
and of itself unpardonable.

When, in accordance with the law, financial disclosures were made by Senators for the first time in 1968, Dirksen was among sixty-one who reported additional income from speeches and writing. Ev's income, outside of his Senate salary, amounted to $18,158.[34] Most of the moneys received were honorariums for speeches and fees for writing articles, including a syndicated column. About one-fifth came from television or other professional performances. Investigative reporters wanting to get something on Dirksen scrutinized his financial statement with great care. While a few honest mistakes were found, one attributing a $1,000 honorarium to First Federal Savings and Loan Company of Chicago when Ev actually received no fee at all, no deliberate discrepancies were uncovered. Likewise, close examination of Dirksen's connection with the law firm of Davis, Morgan, and Witherell "failed to show any link . . . between the known clients of the Peoria firm and Dirksen's efforts in behalf of companies before federal regulatory bodies."[35] Five days later *Newsweek* reported the findings of its intensive investigation into Dirksen's finances and it too vindicated him from allegations of personal venality or conflict of interest.

At the time of Everett Dirksen's death, there were those who still waited to uncover evidence of cupidity and dishonesty by virtue of what would be discovered in the estate. The total value of Ev's estate was $302,235, according to documents filed with the Tazewell County Circuit Court. About half of this amount, $150,000, was the appraised value of Dirksen's personal papers and memorabilia. These papers, consisting of over 1.2 million pages filling eleven large shipping crates, are now housed in the Everett McKinley Dirksen Congressional Leadership Research Center located in Pekin. Among this vast collection were correspondence, texts of speeches, scripts of television interviews and appearances, newspaper clippings, some fifty films and TV kinescopes, books, pictures, and other memorabilia. Of the total estate, some $20,000 was in the form of future royalty rights from his records, an advance on a proposed taped radio program to have been called "Decisive Moments," and a book manuscript under contract from Hawthorn Books entitled, "So You Want to be a Senator." Stocks, bonds, and a savings account totaled $34,088.

Payment of life insurance policies ran to $65,713. Before entering the hospital, Dirksen transferred most of his property to his wife. The homes in Virginia and Florida were valued at $105,000. A $53,379 campaign account was later given to the Dirksen Center to provide additional research facilities for scholars and students of government. The federal inheritance taxes came to $14,520 and state taxes totaled $361.12.[36]

In the twilight of his long political career, and despite the ravages of time, the seventy-three-year-old Dirksen loved the give and take of debate, the sound of the quorum bell, participation in parliamentary maneuvering, and the excitement of close roll calls. His last legislative endeavors were mixtures of victory and defeat. Ev did much to save President Nixon's proposal for a safeguard antiballistic-missile system. Opposition to the ABM was strong among the more liberal, dovish Republicans and Democrats. Marshaling twenty-nine Republican votes, Ev helped defeat an amendment by Margaret Chase Smith (R-Me.) which would have provided funds only for research but would have prevented the deployment of ABMs. The measure lost by a tie vote of fifty to fifty with Vice-President Agnew using his prerogative to cast an additional vote against it. Another amendment to stop ABM distribution, sponsored by John Sherman Cooper (R-Ky.) and Philip A. Hart (D-Mich.), was beaten by a fifty-one to forty-nine vote. It was Dirksen who saved the ABM for Nixon even though the final vote, fifty-eight to nine, was taken after Dirksen's death.[37]

When the first session of the 91st Congress met, Dirksen had personal measures he was very much interested in advancing. As was expected, he dropped his prayer amendment in the legislative hopper as well as co-sponsoring a bill forbidding interstate transportation of obscene and salacious materials. In regard to the sale of pornographic books and magazines to minors, Dirksen argued for local control. He contended, "I know of no other good way and besides, it makes good sense, in our free society, that a jury of our peers in a community should have something to say about the moral standards which shall prevail for the youngsters of that community."[38] Dirksen, with Roman Hruska (R-Neb.), also introduced a bill to tighten federal control and increase penalties for the transportation and sale of narcotics, depressants, stimulants, and hallucinogenic drugs. Ev reasoned, "I think everybody knows the danger that besets our society today in connection with abuses in the drug field."[39]

Other legislation bearing Ev's stamp were the following measures: first, a proposed amendment to the Civil Rights Act of 1965 that would have authorized the establishment of a National Voting Advisory Commission "to study further the matter of discrimination and corrupt practices."[40] Second, Dirksen joined with Senator Wallace F. Bennett (R-Utah) in introducing S. 1384, the "Federal Employees 'Freedom of Choice' Bill," that would protect right-to-work activity on the part of government employees by statute rather than executive order.[41] Third, after a fire destroyed a house only 200 feet from Abraham Lincoln's Springfield home, Governor Richard B. Ogilvie and others prevailed upon Dirksen to sponsor legislation to place the Lincoln shrine under the protection of the National Park Service. Ev introduced S. 2256 in the Senate, while Representative Paul Findley (R-Ill.) proposed a corollary measure in the House, to "authorize the Secretary of Interior to establish the Lincoln Home Area National Historical Site."[42] And finally, for the last time, although Ev did not know it, he once more called for the marigold to be designated the national floral emblem of the United States. "I grow thousands of them every year for my own delight and the delight of my neighbors . . . ," Dirksen reminded his colleagues. "When it comes to beauty, I can think of nothing greater or more inspiring than a field of blooming marigolds tossing their heads in the sunshine and giving a glow to the entire landscape."[43]

When S. 192 for the study and investigation of campus disorders came up for debate, Dirksen was for it. He decried the irresponsibility of those college officials who allowed anti-Vietnam protestors virtually to take over college campuses. "What we have witnessed by college officials is surrender of authority to militant and often armed groups of insurgents who often have been led by individuals who were not students of the university." Lawlessness and lack of civility were intolerable to Ev. Remembering how hard it was for him to even attend college, it made him feel that "millions of parents, who at some considerable sacrifice have been able to send their sons and daughters to college, resent this unlawful interference with the students' education."[44]

One compromise Senator Dirksen worked out with Mike Mansfield was almost ruined by the uninvited interference of Vice-President Agnew and Treasury Secretary Kennedy. As minority leader, Ev prevailed upon Majority Leader Mansfield to agree to a six-month extension of the 10 percent income tax surcharge. This in itself had been difficult to obtain, since at first Mansfield agreed to a three-month, then a five-month, and finally a six-month extension—but no more. Any year-long extension was to await passage of an omnibus tax-reform bill, which would be forthcoming before the end of the session. But Vice-President Agnew and Secretary of the Treasury Kennedy wanted a one-year extension and nothing else. These two convinced enough Senate Republicans to eschew compromise, so the one-year extension was defeated forty-one to fifty-nine. Then it was up to Ev to save the day. He and Mansfield prepared a substitute motion, extending the surcharge six months, as they had previously agreed, which was adopted by a fifty-one to forty-eight vote.

Everett Dirksen's last legislative battle was in the cause of fiscal responsibility. Ev supported the pending student loan bill, which provided long-term loans to college students. But Jacob Javits and other liberals—Democrats and Republicans alike—decided to add $275 million to the emergency appropriation before the upper chamber recessed. Congress had agreed to put a $192.9 billion lid on spending, and the addition of $275 million would result in expenditures going above the self-imposed limit. Dirksen scolded his colleagues: "What makes me even unhappier is that, first of all, we placed a ceiling upon expenditures to be made by the Executive, and then we undertake to kick off that ceiling which we imposed in the first place. It was done legislatively."[45] President Nixon backed Dirksen by threatening to impound the funds, but the Senate nevertheless rejected Ev's motion to delete the extra money by a vote of fifty-six to thirty-eight.

No one in the Senate suspected, including Ev himself, that Dirksen was laboring under a severe affliction. The minority leader was so used to having chronic bronchitis and breathing difficulties that these chest infirmities were not considered critical.

Even the extreme fatigue suffered by Ev caused him no undue alarm. So it was that on August 9, three days before speaking against adding funds to the student loan appropriation bill, Senator Dirksen went to Walter Reed Hospital for a routine physical examination. An x-ray of the chest revealed a dark spot on the right lung. Still not knowing that he had lung cancer, Ev was scheduled to return for more extensive tests on August 14. It was ironic that Senator Dirksen lost the last legislative battle in which he was engaged. Even more fateful were the last words he ever spoke in a Senate debate. In his breathy voice Ev said, "My time has expired."[46]

NOTES

1. "Age Won't Bar Race: Dirksen," Chicago *Tribune,* Jan. 30, 1968, C-EMDC.

2. This title was first bestowed upon Senator Robert A. Taft of Ohio.

3. David Burpee to EMD, Dec. 19, 1960, and EMD to David Burpee, Jan. 4, 1961, LF-EMDC.

4. *Congressional Record*, Jan. 8, 1965, reprint in LF-EMDC.

5. Memorandum, John B. Criswell (Treasurer, Democratic National Committee) to James R. Jones, June 18, 1968, LBJL.

6. Stephen Ness and David S. Broder, *The Republican Establishment: The Present and Future of the G.O.P.* (New York: Harper and Row, 1967), p. 21.

7. William Safire, *Before the Fall: An Inside View of the Pre-Watergate White House* (Garden City, N.Y.: Doubleday, 1975), p. 47.

8. "Clark Calls Dirksen Bar to Social Change," Chicago *Tribune,* Apr. 30, 1968, C-EMDC.

9. Charles Nicodemus, "Clark Calls Dirksen a Fraud," Chicago *Daily News,* Apr. 30, 1968, C-EMDC.

10. "Republican Platform — 1968," in *National Party Conventions, 1831-1972* (Washington, D.C.: Congressional Quarterly, 1976), p. 108.

11. Ibid.

12. Lewis Chester, Godfrey Hodgson, and Bruce Page, *An American Melodrama, The Presidential Campaign of 1968* (New York: The Viking Press, 1969), p. 467.

13. EMD, "A Republic—If You Can Keep It," delivered before the Republican National Convention, Aug. 8, 1968, text in IF-EMDC.

14. "Issues and Answers" (ABC-TV), Aug. 4, 1968, script in R&R-EMDC.

15. Telegram, Ronald Reagan to EMD, Aug. 7, 1968, Republican National Committee Papers, DDEL.

16. Robert W. Peterson, *Agnew: The Coining of a Household Word* (New York: Facts on File, Inc., 1972), p. 16.

17. EMD, "A Senator's Notebook," Nov. 11, 1968, R&R-EMDC.

18. Mike Manatos to EMD with enclosed picture, Nov. 18, 1968, LBJL.

19. Mike Manatos to EMD, Nov. 19, 1968, LBJL.

20. LBJ to EMD, Nov. 23, 1968, LBJL.

21. EMD, "A Senator's Notebook," Mar. 20, 1969, R&R-EMDC.

22. EMD, "Man Is Not Alone," *Guideposts* (Oct., 1969), reprint in R&R-EMDC.

23. "The Leader," *Time* (Sept. 14, 1962), reprint in R&R-EMDC.

24. LBJ to EMD, Jan. 4, 1969, Executive File, LBJL.

25. LBJ to EMD, Jan. 17, 1969, Executive File, LBJL.

26. Mike Manatos to EMD, Dec. 31, 1968, Executive File, LBJL.

27. "The First Sixty Days," Press Release, Mar. 20, 1969, R&R-EMDC.

28. EMD, " A Senator's Notebook," Apr. 16, 1969, R&R-EMDC.

29. Valenti, *Human President,* p. 184.

30. Rowland Evans, Jr., and Robert D. Novak, *Nixon in the White House: The Frustration of Power* (New York: Random House, 1971), p. 63.

31. Chicago *Daily News,* May 14 and 16, 1969, C-EMDC.

32. Chicago *Daily News,* Sept. 8, 1969, IF-EMDC.

33. *Congressional Record,* Sept. 12, 1969, reprint in IF-EMDC.

34. Chicago *Tribune,* May 7, 1969, C-EMDC.

35. Chicago *Daily News,* July 11, 1969, C-EMDC.

36. Dick Streckfuss, " 'Ev' Dirksen's Estate Rich in Memorabilia," Bloomington (Ill.) *Daily Pantagraph,* Mar. 6, 1971.

37. Charles Peters, and Timothy J. Adams, eds., *Inside the System* (New York: Praeger, 1970), pp. 161-66.

38. *Congressional Record,* July 16, 1969, reprint in LF-EMDC.

39. Ibid.

40. *Congressional Record,* June 30, 1969, reprint in LF-EMDC.

41. Text of S. 1384, Mar. 7, 1969, LF-EMDC.

42. Text of S. 2256, May 27, 1969, LF-EMDC.

43. *Congressional Record*, Feb. 4, 1969, reprint in LF-EMDC.
44. *Congressional Record*, May 1, 1969, reprint in LF-EMDC.
45. *Congressional Record*, Aug. 12, 1969, reprint in LF-EMDC.
46. Ibid.

12

One Last Fight
and the Final Trip Home

ON TUESDAY, AUGUST 12, 1969, Senator Dirksen as usual had a busy day in the Senate. It included participating in debate on the floor, attending a committee meeting, and taking care of appointments in his office. Despite the outward appearance of normality, Senate aides were aware that Ev looked visibly tired as he carried out his duties. His breathing was more labored than usual and frequent coughing spasms racked his body, causing him to convulse. As he walked down the corridor, his limp, stemming from the broken hip, seemed more noticeable. Even though his shoe had been built up to compensate for this, when Ev was near exhaustion the leg tended to drag slightly. In a matter-of-fact way Dirksen informed Glee Gomien, his longtime secretary, that he would not be in his office the next day. He told her in private about the spot on his lung and the need for further examination to ascertain what should be done. At this point Mrs. Gomien was apprehensive but not unduly upset, since the senator had been in the hospital so many times before; therefore, this visit did not seem of a critical nature at the time.

At Walter Reed Hospital, more chest x-rays were taken of Senator Dirksen. He also was subjected to many other tests. The spot on the upper lobe of Ev's right lung had actually grown larger since the previous set of x-rays taken just a few days before. The tumor had undoubtedly enlarged, but the doctors could not diagnose accurately whether the growth was malignant or benign. What had to be decided was whether to use just radiation as a treatment or to remove the tumor via surgery. Factors militating against an operation were his advanced age, seventy-three; emphysema; hardening of the arteries; and an enlarged heart that frequently beat at an irregular pace.

It was a difficult decision that faced Dirksen. The doctors at Walter Reed, all specialists, were strongly of the opinion Ev's lung tumor was malignant. At the rate this cancerous growth was enlarging, if not removed it would mean an early death despite any treatment by radiation or chemotherapy. Surgery seemed the only sure way of preserving Dirksen's life for any length of time. On the positive side were Ev's fantastic recuperative powers. He had always been able to bounce back from all serious illnesses in such a short time as to amaze attending physicians. Returning briefly to his Virginia home, Heart's Desire, Dirksen dicussed the situation with Louella. He also spent many hours praying over it. Ev knew instant death on the operating table was a distinct possibility, but he also knew that an agonizing death from cancer was inevitable if he did nothing. Dirksen did not want to die, but he did not fear death. His greatest fear was over the fact he might become totally incapacitated and not be able to continue serving in the Senate. With a serenity characteristic of one who trusted in divine providence Ev calmly informed Colonel Alan R. Hopeman of Walter Reed that he would consent to immediate surgery. The date set for Dirksen's operation was Tuesday, September 2.

Before checking in at Walter Reed on August 29, Senator Dirksen spent his time completing unfinished business. He specifically wanted to finish a memoir-type manuscript entitled, "So You Want to be a Senator." Ev also worked to complete articles for his syndicated column so that it would run uninterrupted while he was convalescing. Always the realist in this type of situation, Dirksen made contingency plans for his death or for the possibility he would emerge from the operating table with permanently impaired mental facilities. He had most of his property legally transferred to Louella and signed necessary papers in case he would be an invalid for a long period of time. To his wife he gave a presigned resignation from the Senate if events turned out that either physical or mental disability made such a move necessary. He loved the Senate, and it was still on his mind.

When Everett Dirksen, accompanied by Louella, set off for Walter Reed, he took his bulging briefcase with him. Typical of Ev, he could not really get away from his work—not even in a hospital. Dr. Hopeman wanted his patient to rest completely and do nothing, but Dirksen's work habits were so ingrained it was impossible for him to remain totally idle for very long. He continued to work on the minority leader's report dealing with both the achievements and unfinished business of the 91st Congress. Among the items Dirksen listed under "what they have not done" were appropriations, electoral reform, crime, foreign aid, East-West trade, legislative reorganization, urban renewal, housing, voting rights, law and order, and a "responsible approach to budget ceiling." Enumerated as praiseworthy were the following: "has done no irreparable harm"; "resisted radical group demands"; "kept attuned to the people"; and "reaffirmed devotion to sound principles." The notation was also made: "Transition from a radical and ultra-liberal view to a more moderate and conservative view takes time."[1]

Senator Dirksen's operation was scheduled for 8:45 a.m. on the morning of September 2. Dr. Hopeman headed a team of surgeons who performed a three-hour operation on Everett Dirksen. A tumor, less than an inch in diameter, which tests showed to be malignant, was removed from the upper lobe of the right lung. To be positive that all cancerous tissue was eliminated, one-third of the lung was removed. The doctors were sure it had not spread any further. The operation, then, in terms of its immediate objectives, was a total success.

Recovery seemed extraordinarily rapid considering the extent of the major surgery. Dirksen was kept in an intensive care room with a breathing tube in his nostril and another plastic tube in his chest for drainage purposes. His heart was being monitored and nurses kept him under observation constantly. Louella was at Ev's bedside all the time. By Thursday, September 4, Joy and Howard Baker dropped in for a visit. Senator Baker noted that his father-in-law was "bright, cheerful, and alert."[2] With his vital signs all returning to normal it appeared as if once again Ev's miraculous recuperative powers would bring him through this ordeal. It seemed Dirksen would soon be taken off the critical list.

Early Saturday morning, September 6, Everett Dirksen became very restless. In moving about he inadvertently pulled the drainage tube from his chest. Using local anesthesia, doctors replaced the tube. By afternoon Ev was sitting up in bed. He ate lunch and chatted with Louella. Senator Dirksen joked with his doctor and tried to get him to remove the ban on both smoking and drinking. Being a chain smoker, Ev craved a cigarette. Moreover, he would have appreciated a sip of Jack Daniels, his favorite bourbon. Despite the personal discomfiture suffered by Dirksen, the prognosis for recovery seemed bright and all looked well when the Senator dozed off to sleep that night.

Sunday, September 7, was the tragic day of disaster. Senator Dirksen awoke early that morning feeling fine. He ate breakfast and talked with Louella. While eating lunch at noon Ev was already making plans to get back to some kind of a work schedule. Suddenly, at about 2:52 p.m., according to the hospital report, Everett Dirksen "sustained a sudden cardiac and respiratory arrest." For two hours physicians worked frantically to get his heart started again. All of their efforts were to no avail. In the cold, clinical language of the medical profession, "all resuscitory efforts were unsuccessful."[3] At 4:52 p.m., with Louella and Joy at his bedside, Senator Dirksen was pronounced dead. The valiant heart of a gallant man had finally succumbed to the ravages of time and illness. The medical personnel who were present, many of whom had watched Ev recover from other serious bouts with illness, found it hard to believe that Everett Dirksen was actually dead.

On Monday, September 8, the U.S. Senate paid tribute to the departed Dirksen. That day's session was opened by the Senate chaplain, the Reverend Dr. Edward L. R. Elson, with a special prayer. His supplication read, in part, as follows: "We thank Thee for Thy servant and our comrade, Everett McKinley Dirksen, who has fought a good fight, kept the faith, finished his course, and is at rest with Thee. . . . May the integrity of his manhood, the radiance of his character, his gentle but subtle humor, and his sense of the divine in all things remain as an abiding legacy for all generations. May his golden voice, now silenced on this side, be lifted with the everlasting choirs invisible on the other side of the great divide."[4]

Following the chaplain's prayer two resolutions were presented to the Senate. Hugh Scott, GOP whip and acting minority leader, speaking for himself and Mike Mansfield, the Democratic majority leader, asked for immediate consideration of Senate Resolution 253. Vice-President Spiro T. Agnew announced subsequently, "Without objection, the resolution is considered and unanimously agreed to." It read in part: "Resolved, that the Senate has heard with profound sorrow and deep regret the announcement of the death of the Hon. Everett McKinley Dirksen, late a Senator from the State of Illinois."[5] Another portion of the resolution called for the president of the Senate to appoint a committee to attend the funeral. A second resolution, number 254, was also approved without objection. It invited members of the House of Representatives, the president, the chief justice and justices of the Supreme Court, the diplomatic corps, and other high government officials to attend the memorial service in the Rotunda of the Capitol on Tuesday, September 9, 1969, at 12 o'clock noon. The Senate then adjourned in memory of the departed minority leader.

The body of Everett M. Dirksen lay in state in the Capitol Rotunda for twenty-four hours. It was fitting that the walnut casket rested upon the same catafalque which bore the coffin of Abraham Lincoln over one hundred years before. All around were great banks of golden marigolds, red and white carnations, red roses, and green ferns. An honor guard composed of five members of the armed forces stood at attention while thousands of mourners passed by the bier. Dirksen was only the fifth member of the Senate to be so honored. The other four were Henry Clay of Kentucky (1852); Charles Sumner of Massachusetts (1874); John Logan of Illinois (1886); and Robert A. Taft of Ohio (1953).

Present at the memorial service on September 9 were all the important dignitaries in Washington. Members of the U.S. Senate were in attendance en masse. After placing a floral tribute at the foot of the catafalque, President Richard M. Nixon delivered a fitting eulogy. Focusing on the theme that Dirksen had been a practitioner of the "old politics," the president described Ev as a "politician in the finest sense of that much-abused word." Nixon praised Dirksen for being willing to compromise and not wanting to make permanent enemies out of political adversaries. Although he used words for weapons, the president observed, Dirksen's word was his bond. "A politician in the Dirksen tradition knows both the name of the game and the rules of the game," asserted Nixon. "And he seeks his ends through time-honored democratic means." For this reason, maintained Nixon, "while he never became President, his impact and influence on the nation was greater than that of most Presidents in our history." Alluding to Ev's status as a living legend during the latter years of his lifetime, the president said, "Only a privileged few live to hear the favorable verdict of history on their careers."[6]

Giving the response on behalf of the family, Senator Howard H. Baker spoke briefly. Putting aside his own personal grief, he described his deceased colleague and father-in-law as one who "sought to follow many of the precepts of the Lincoln legacy." Baker explained, "Both men understood with singular clarity that a great and diverse people do not speak with a single voice and that adherence to rigid ideology leaves little room for compromise and response to change." He talked of Dirksen's deep religious faith, the hardship of his youth, his wit, and his lack of egotism. "He was of the people," Baker declared. In concluding his remarks, the senator from Tennessee said simply: "He was an idealist, but he was a realist as well, and in the end he chose calmly to risk his life, electing uncertain surgery in order to gain the opportunity to live and serve further; and he lost. But in losing he fixed with permanence the image of a noble man of the people."[7]

The funeral service for Everett Dirksen took place on September 10 at the National Presbyterian Church in Washington, D.C. After its conclusion, the body was flown to Pekin on Air Force One. This was Ev's final trip home. On September 11 a graveside service was held at the Glendale Memorial Gardens before final interment. In delivering the burial rites Chaplain Elson intoned: "The last march is ended; a mighty man of God has answered his last roll call. His battles are all fought, his victories all won; and he lies down to rest awaiting the final bugle call."[8]

The cemetery in which Everett Dirksen was laid to rest was a part of the flat prairie of central Illinois. Located just east of Pekin, it was a new burial ground adjacent to Milo Miller's dairy farm. Ev's old friends and neighbors were sure he would have liked the location of his grave. He had loved Pekin. Dirksen once told a New York City journalist, "It is a pretty place to be from, and to go back to."[9] Now Ev was back home again in the heart of Illinois.

In his memoirs, *With No Apologies* (1979), Senator Barry M. Goldwater testified to the greatness of the man who first urged him to enter politics. He described the departed minority leader as a "political giant" who was "always humble, reasonable, and more concerned with the future prosperity of the nation than he was in the personal fortunes of Ev Dirksen." Goldwater further extolled Dirksen as one who possessed a "deep and fundamental understanding of the character of American politics and the American electorate." This permitted the Illinoisan, in Goldwater's judgment, to serve as a "bridge from the past to the present." The one-time GOP presidential nominee also regarded Ev as his "wise counselor, my most constructive critic." The Arizonan was sure Dirksen was a "great American" whose "record of service to the American Republic entitles him to the respect and gratitude of every degree of citizen."[10]

It was during the decade from 1959 to 1969 that Everett M. Dirksen earned the designation of senatorial statesman. Using the words of Walt Rostow, formerly LBJ's special assistant for national security affairs, "Within Dirksen was an instinct and desire to throw his weight behind the great measures that shaped American policy—at home and abroad—when he felt the time was ripe and the stage was set to perform as the reconciling patriot."[11] Dirksen was a "giant as a legislator," attested Gerald R. Ford. "He left an indelible imprint on many major laws that will live in the statute books for many, many years."[12] President Dwight D. Eisenhower once remarked about Ev, "He might have been able to work wonders with majority support."[13]

But the fact remained that Dirksen was perpetually the minority leader although, as such, he still worked legislative wonders. While leading the loyal opposition, or his "troops" as he called them, Ev outdistanced in effectiveness all of his predecessors in the twentieth century, including the following GOP minority leaders: Jacob H. Gallinger of New Hampshire (1911-18), Charles McNary of Oregon (1933-44), Wallace White of Maine (1944-47), Kenneth Wherry of Nebraska (1949-51), H. Styles Bridges of New Hampshire (1952), Robert A. Taft of Ohio (1953), and William Knowland of California (1955-58).

In practicing the art of minority statecraft Everett Dirksen achieved a level of greatness denied many who are perpetually cast in the role as party spokesman for the loyal opposition. While not on the same level as a Henry Clay who, as a founder of the Whig party and its presidential nominee many times, opposed the Jacksonian Democrats, or a John C. Calhoun, who pleaded for a lost cause, Dirksen nevertheless secured a safe niche in congressional history as a master practitioner of minority politics within the confines of the U.S. Senate. With parliamentary skill, civility, calm persuasiveness, and effective oratory, Dirksen proudly carried the banner of conservative Republicanism in an era of liberal welfarism and deficit spending. Forseeing the future problems that would result from unbalanced budgets and a growing national debt, he strove to further more concern for fiscal responsibility while accepting the concept of positive government. He was often a voice crying in the wilderness, but one compelled by duty, as he saw it, to seek the long range welfare of the nation.

Although born in a small town and reflecting the value system of his early environment, Dirksen matured into a national leader cognizant of the needs of others beside his local constituency. Describing Dirksen as a political leader who acted with a "consciousness of the scrutiny of history," Senator Charles Mathias (R-Md.) eulogized him by saying: "He was a product of the country . . . called the Heartland. More than a geographical area, it is a region of the national consciousness. When it changed, Dirksen moved, and history—in cumulative majesty—shifted. . . . But until he moved, change stood in precarious suspension and looked back over its shoulder, nervously, at the senior Senator from Illinois, through whose bloodstream the current of our history seemed mysteriously to flow."[14]

After the death of Everett Dirksen, his minority leader position passed on to another, just as Ev had obtained it after the passing of Kenneth Wherry. Hugh Scott of Pennsylvania, the whip, won the post in 1969. When Scott retired in 1976, Senator Howard Baker, Dirksen's son-in-law, was successful in winning the office of minority leader. With his father-in-law as a prototype, Baker patterned his successful minority leadership on the Dirksen model. In 1981 Baker attained that which eluded Dirksen, namely, the post of majority leader. In 1984 Baker resigned from the Senate to once more make a future try at the presidency. The latter was an office Dirksen, too, had once aspired to attain.

After Everett died, Louella Dirksen found a void in her life that was hard to fill. She had completely subordinated her personal activities to those of Ev for so long, it took her some time to formulate an independent life. That had been done voluntarily for she found her happiness linked to Ev's work. Mrs. Dirksen now accepted appointments to committees dedicated to public service, became a member of the board of directors of the First National Bank of De Bary, Florida, and led a continued but unsuccessful campaign to get the marigold adopted as the national floral emblem of the United States. In 1964, after the townspeople of Pekin agreed on the construction of a combination public library and Everett McKinley Dirksen Library, Louella spent much time soliciting private contributions to supplement those raised by a public bond issue. Shuttling between De Bary and the nation's capital, while interspersing frequent visits to Pekin (never missing a marigold festival in her old hometown), Louella lived a busy and fulfilling life.

On July 16, 1979, ten years after her husband's death, Louella Dirksen died of cancer at the Sibley Memorial Hospital in Washington, D.C. She was eighty years old. After a funeral service in the nation's capital, her body was returned to Pekin. There she was buried beside her beloved husband, to whom her life had been dedicated. Her memoir, *The Honorable Mr. Marigold,* is in reality an old-fashioned love story about their married life. It remains her final tribute to a man to whom she was a devoted wife and political helpmeet.

Based on the plans drawn up by Major J. Norman Shade of Pekin and John E. Velde, Jr., chairman of the library board, a $450,000 bond issue was passed and $2 million was collected from private sources to construct the Everett McKinley Dirksen Library.[15] The latter, as a permanent memorial, was to house Dirksen's papers and contain exhibits of memorabilia related to Ev's House and Senate career. In 1968 it was decided to enlarge the Dirksen portion of the library and rename it the Everett McKinley Dirksen Congressional Leadership Research Center. With its construction completed in 1975, the Dirksen Center was dedicated on August 19 by President Gerald R. Ford, a one-time member of the "Ev and Jerry Show." John Casserly, one of the president's speech-writers, indicated facetiously he would like to prepare the remarks Ford would utter that day. "I want to write that one," quipped Casserly. "We'll put on an Ev and Abe Lincoln Show."[16] Everett Dirksen would have admired both the humor and the linkage to the Prairie Statesman whom he had idolized since his boyhood days in Illinois.

The vast archival holdings of the Everett McKinley Dirksen Congressional Research Center permits scholarly research not only on Dirksen's long political career but on problems relating to Congress. The younger generation, through photographs and collections of video and audio recordings, may see and hear Everett Dirksen as he was when he stalked the halls of Congress. The center's endowment fund finances scholarships, sponsors seminars, and presents annually the Everett McKinley Dirksen Award for Distinguished Reporting of Congress at Capitol Hill. Students of government may examine the millions of papers and documents relating to the momentous issues of the 1940s, 1950s, and 1960s. Because of the center's existence, the Dirksen model as the archetypical minority leader may offset the trend of rising ideological confrontation and single-issue politics engendered by special groups not concerned with the nation's overall welfare. A study of Dirksen's contributions and mistakes might also moderate the American tendency to swing from ostrich-like isolationism to starry-eyed globalism.

In front of the Everett McKinley Dirksen Congressional Leadership Research Center there is a huge, bigger-than-life-sized bronze bust of Senator Dirksen. Sculptured by Carl Tolpo of Dundee, Illinois, it is a visual tribute worthy of Ev's memory. The Dirksen Center itself, however, remains the living monument. Here are preserved his papers for students of government to study. Future leaders of the nation's legislative branch would do well to examine carefully all facets of the career of this superb politician whose congressional leadership and statesman-like stature contributed so much to the strength and vitality of the two-party system. Certainly the American people will be well served in the future if his exemplary experience as a longtime member of Congress is distilled to yield its practical wisdom and many insights into the lawmaking process. In doing so, the lasting influence of Senator Dirksen reminds us all that whereas a minority must ultimately yield to the majority will, dramatic changes can be made more acceptable by adherence to the principle of compromise. This Dirksenian lesson, if perpetuated, will help assure the preservation of democracy itself in a world where true self government is a rare and perishable commodity.

NOTES

1. Briefcase Contents, WP-EMDC.
2. "Dirksen Dead in Capitol at 73," New York *Times,* Sept. 8, 1969, IF-EMDC.
3. Ibid.
4. *Everett McKinley Dirksen Late a Senator from Illinois, Memorial Addresses Delivered in Congress* (Washington, D.C.: Government Printing Office, 1970), p. 1, hereafter cited as *Everett McKinley Dirksen.*
5. Ibid.
6. Eulogy Given By the President, Sept. 9, 1969, in *Everett McKinley Dirksen*, pp. 11-13.
7. Response by Senator Howard H. Baker, Sept. 9, 1969, in *Everett McKinley Dirksen*, pp. 13-14.
8. Committal Statement by Chaplain Elson, Sept. 11, 1969, in *Everett McKinley Dirksen*, p. 25.

9. Richard B. Stolley, "A Pretty Good Place to be from, and Go Back to," *Life* (Sept. 19, 1969), in *Everett McKinley Dirksen*, p. 270.

10. Goldwater, *With No Apologies,* pp. 225-26.

11. W. W. Rostow, *The Diffusion of Power: An Essay in Recent History* (New York: Macmillan, 1972), p. 339.

12. Eulogy by Gerald R. Ford, in *Everett McKinley Dirksen*, p. 167.

13. Dwight David Eisenhower, *The White House Years: Waging Peace, 1956-1961* (Garden City, N.Y.: Doubleday, 1965), p. 385.

14. Eulogy by Charles Mathias, in *Everett McKinley Dirksen*, p. 127.

15. Pekin Daily *Times,* Jan. 10, 1964, C-EMDC.

16. John J. Casserly, *The Ford White House: The Diary of a Speech-writer* (Boulder, Colo.: Associate University Press, 1977), p. 135.

Selected Bibliography

MANUSCRIPT COLLECTIONS

Anderson College (Anderson, Indiana). Papers of Charles E. Wilson.
Chicago Historical Society. Papers of Paul H. Douglas.
Church of Jesus Christ of Latter-day Saints, Archives (Salt Lake City, Utah). Papers of Ezra Taft Benson.
Dartmouth College (Hanover, New Hampshire). Papers of Sherman Adams.
Dwight D. Eisenhower Library (Abilene, Kansas)
    Ann Whitman File
    Diary of Dwight D. Eisenhower
    Diary of James Hagerty
    Papers of Ezra Taft Benson
    Papers of Leonard Hall
    Ralph Flanders Oral History
    Republican Congressional Leadership File
    Republican National Convention Papers
    White House Calendar
Everett McKinley Dirksen Congressional Leadership Research Center (Pekin, Illinois)
    Everett McKinley Dirksen Collection:
        Briefcase Contents
        Chicago Office File
        Clippings
        Glee Gomien File
        Information File
        Joint Republican Congressional Leadership File
        Legislative File
        Memorabilia Collection

Public Works File
Remarks and Releases
Working Papers
Franklin D. Roosevelt Library (Hyde Park, New York)
Official File
Harry S. Truman Library (Independence, Missouri)
Official File
Herbert C. Hoover Library (West Branch, Iowa)
Papers of Bourke B. Hickenlooper
Papers of Robert E. Wood
Papers of Walter Trohan
Post-Presidential Papers of Herbert C. Hoover
Illinois State Historical Society (Springfield, Illinois)
Papers of Scott W. Lucas
Indiana University (Bloomington, Indiana)
Records of the Willkie Clubs of America
John F. Kennedy Library (Boston, Massachusetts)
Kansas State Historical Society (Topeka, Kansas)
Papers of Alfred M. Landon
Papers of Clifford R. Hope
Papers of Frank Carlson
Library of Congress (Washington, D.C.)
Papers of Robert A. Taft
Lyndon B. Johnson Library (Austin, Texas)
Confidential File
Congressional File
Diary Index Cards
Executive File
Files of White House Aides
General File
News Release
Oral History Interviews of Everett M. Dirksen
Minnesota State Historical Society (St. Paul, Minnesota)
Papers of Hubert H. Humphrey
Princeton University (Princeton, New Jersey)
John Foster Dulles Oral History Project
Papers of John Foster Dulles
Sam Rayburn Library (Bonham, Texas)
Papers of Sam Rayburn
Stonehill College (North Easton, Massachusetts)
Papers of Joseph W. Martin, Jr.

University of Illinois (Urbana, Illinois)
    Papers of Charles B. Shuman
University of Iowa (Iowa City, Iowa)
    Iowa Authors' Collection
    Progressive Party Papers
University of Kentucky (Lexington, Kentucky)
    Papers of Alben W. Barkley
University of Oklahoma (Norman, Oklahoma)
    Papers of Robert S. Kerr
Western Reserve Historical Society (Cleveland, Ohio)
    Papers of George M. Humphrey
Wisconsin State Historical Society (Madison, Wisconsin)
    Papers of the Americans for Democratic Action
Yale University (New Haven, Connecticut)
    Walter Lippmann Collection

ORAL HISTORY MEMOIRS, INTERVIEWS, AND CORRESPONDENCE

Sherman Adams, Leslie J. Arends, Russell Campbell, Louella C. Dirksen, Thomas Reed Dirksen, Arthur Ehrlicher, Gerald R. Ford, Barry M. Goldwater, William D. Jansen, Frank Jibbens, Margaret Juchems, William Kumpf, Martin B. Lohman, Roy Preston, Harry E. Rainville, George E. Reedy, Norman Shade, and Carl Von Boeckman.

PUBLIC PAPERS AND COLLECTED WORKS

Everett McKinley Dirksen, Memorial Addresses Delivered in Congress. Washington, D.C.: Government Printing Office, 1970.
Johnson Presidential Press Conferences. New York: Earl M. Coleman Enterprises, Inc., 1978. 2 vols.
Nixon Presidential Press Conferences. New York: Earl M. Coleman Enterprises, Inc., 1978.
Public Papers of the Presidents of the United States Dwight D. Eisenhower Containing the Public Messages, Speeches, and Statements of the President January 20, 1953 to January 20, 1961. Washington, D.C.: Government Printing Office, 1961. 8 vols.

BOOKS

Aaron, Jan. *Gerald R. Ford: President of Destiny.* New York: Fleet Press, 1975.

Adams, Sherman. *Firsthand Report: The Story of the Eisenhower Administration.* New York: Harper and Brothers, 1961.

Adler, Selig. *The Isolationist Impulse, Its Twentieth Century Reaction.* New York: Collier Books, 1961.

Anson, Robert Sam. *McGovern: A Biography.* New York: Holt, Rinehart and Winston, 1972.

Baker, Ross K. *Friend and Foe in the U.S. Senate.* New York: Free Press, 1980.

Baldwin, Louis. *Hon. Politician: Mike Mansfield of Montana.* Missoula, Mont.: Mountain Press, 1979.

Bauer, Fred, ed. *Ev, The Man and His Words.* Old Tappan, N.J.: Hewitt House, 1969.

Beyer, Barry K. *Thomas E. Dewey, 1937-1974: A Study in Political Leadership.* New York: Garland, 1978.

Casserly, John J. *The Ford White House: The Diary of a Speechwriter.* Boulder Colo.: Associate University Press, 1977.

Chester, Lewis, Godfrey Hodgson and Bruce Page. *An American Melodrama, The Presidential Campaign of 1968.* New York: Viking Press, 1969.

Christian, George. *The President Steps Down: A Personal Memoir of the Transfer of Power.* New York: Macmillan, 1970.

Cohn, Roy. *McCarthy.* New York: New American Library, 1968.

Cosmon, Bernard and Robert J. Huckshorn. *Republican Politics, The 1964 Campaign and Its Aftermath for the Party.* New York: Praeger, 1968.

Cutler, John Henry, *Ed Brooke: Biography of a Senator.* Indianapolis: Bobbs-Merrill, 1972.

De Tolendano, Ralph. *RFK: The Man Who Would Be President.* New York: G. P. Putnam's Sons, 1967.

Detzer, David. *The Brink: Cuban Missile Crisis, 1962.* New York: Thomas Y. Crowell, 1972.

Dirksen, Everett M. and Herbert V. Prochnow, *Quotation Finder.* New York: Harper and Row, 1971.

Dirksen, Louella with Norma Lee Browning. *The Honorable Mr. Marigold, My Life with Everett Dirksen.* Garden City, N.Y.: Doubleday, 1972.

Divine, Robert A. *Second Chance: The Triumph of Internationalism in America During World War II.* New York: Atheneum, 1967.

Douglas, Paul H. *In the Fullness of Time: The Memoirs of Paul H. Douglas.* New York: Harcourt Brace Jovanovich, 1972.

Edwards, Jerome E. *The Foreign Policy of Col. McCormick's Tribune, 1920-1941.* Reno: University of Nevada Press, 1971.

Eisenhower, Dwight D. *Mandate for Change, 1953-1956.* New York: New American Library, 1963.

———. *The White House Years.* Garden City, N.Y.: Doubleday, 1965. 2 vols.

Eisenhower, John S. D. *Strictly Personal.* Garden City, N.Y.: Doubleday, 1974.

Evans, Rowland, Jr. and Robert D. Novak. *Lyndon B. Johnson: The Exercise of Power.* New York: New American Library, 1968.

———. *Nixon in the White House: The Frustration of Power.* New York: Random House, 1971.

Flanders, Ralph. *Senator from Vermont.* Boston: Little, Brown and Company, 1961.

Ford, Gerald R. *A Time to Heal: The Autobiography of Gerald R. Ford.* New York: Harper and Row, 1979.

Franklin, Jay. *Republicans on the Potomac.* New York: McBride, 1953.

Fried, Richard M. *Men Against McCarthy.* New York: Columbia University Press, 1976.

Gerson, Louis L. *John Foster Dulles.* New York: Cooper Square, 1967.

Goldman, Eric F. *The Tragedy of Lyndon Johnson.* New York: Alfred A. Knopf, 1969.

Goldwater, Barry M. *With No Apologies, The Personal and Political Memoirs of United States Senator Barry M. Goldwater.* New York: William Morrow, 1979.

Gorman, Joseph Bruce. *Kefauver: A Political Biography.* New York: Oxford University Press, 1971.

Graham, Otis L., Jr. *Toward a Planned Society: From Roosevelt to Nixon.* London: Oxford University Press, 1976.

Griffith, Robert. *The Politics of Fear: Joseph R. McCarthy and the Senate.* Lexington: University of Kentucky Press, 1970.

Griffith, Winthrop. *Humphrey, A Candid Biography.* New York: William Morrow, 1965.

Gruening, Ernest. *Many Battles: The Autobiography of Ernest Gruening.* New York: Liverright, 1973.

Hartley, Robert. *Charles H. Percy: A Political Perspective.* Chicago: Rand McNally, 1975.

Hatfield, Mark O. *Not Quite So Simple.* New York: Harper and Row, 1968.

Hess, Stephen and David S. Broder. *The Republican Establishment:*

The Present and Future of the GOP. New York: Harper and Row, 1967.

Howard, Robert P. *Illinois: A History of the Prairie State.* Grand Rapids, Mich.: William B. Eerdmans, 1972.

Hughes, Emmet John. *The Ordeal of Power: A Political Memoir of the Eisenhower Years.* New York: Atheneum, 1963.

Humphrey, Hubert H. *The Education of a Public Man: My Life and Politics.* Garden City, N.Y.: Doubleday, 1976.

Javits, Jacob K. *Order of Battle: A Republican's Call to Reason.* New York: Atheneum, 1964.

Johnson, Lady Bird. *Lady Bird Johnson: A White House Diary.* New York: Holt, Rinehart and Winston, 1970.

Johnson, Lyndon Baines. *The Vantage Point: Perspectives of the Presidency, 1963-1969.* New York: Holt, Rinehart and Winston, 1971.

Jonas, Manfred. *Isolationism in America, 1935-1941.* Ithaca, N.Y.: Cornell University Press, 1966.

Jones, Charles O. *The Minority Party in Congress.* Boston: Little, Brown, 1970.

Jones, Rochelle and Peter Woll. *The Private World of Congress.* New York: Free Press, 1979.

Katcher, Leo. *Earl Warren: A Political Biography.* New York: McGraw-Hill, 1967.

Kearns, Doris. *Lyndon Johnson and the American Dream.* New York: Harper and Row, 1976.

Kessel, John H. *The Goldwater Coalition, Republican Strategies in 1964.* Indianapolis: Bobbs-Merrill, 1968.

Kimball, Penn. *Bobby Kennedy and the New Politics.* Englewood Cliffs, N.J.: Prentice-Hall, 1968.

Larson, Arthur. *Eisenhower: The President Nobody Knew.* New York: Popular Library, 1968.

Lasky, Victor, *J.F.K.: The Man and the Myth.* New York: Macmillan, 1963.

Latham, Earl. *The Communist Controversy in Washington, From the New Deal to McCarthy.* Cambridge, Mass.: Harvard University Press, 1966.

Lippman, Theo. Jr. *Senator Ted Kennedy.* New York: W. W. Norton, 1976.

Lodge, Henry Cabot. *As It Was: An Inside View of Politics and Power in the '50s and '60s.* New York: W. W. Norton, 1976.

McDowell, Edwin. *Barry Goldwater: Portrait of an Arizonan.* Chicago: Henry Regnery, 1964.

MacNeil, Neil. *Dirksen: Portrait of a Public Man*. New York: World Publishing, 1970.

Martin, John Bartlow. *Adlai Stevenson of Illinois: The Life of Adlai E. Stevenson*. Garden City, N.Y.: Doubleday, 1976.

Martin, Joseph, as told to Robert J. Donovan. *Joe Martin, My First Fifty Years in Politics*. New York: McGraw-Hill, 1960.

Mathews, Donald R. *U.S. Senators and Their World*. New York: Random House, 1960.

Mayer, George H. *The Republican Party, 1854-1966*. New York: Oxford University Press, 1967.

Mazo, Earl. *Richard Nixon: A Political and Personal Portrait*. New York: Harper and Brothers, 1959.

Meyer, Frank S., ed. *What Is Conservatism?* New York: Holt, Rinehart and Winston, 1964.

Miller, William "Fishbait," as told to Francis Spatz Leighton. *Fishbait: The Memoirs of the Congressional Doorkeeper*. New York: Warner Brooks, 1979.

Miller, William J. *Henry Cabot Lodge, A Biography*. New York: James H. Heineman, Inc., 1967.

Mooney, Booth. *The Politicians: 1945-1960*. Philadelphia: J. B. Lippincott, 1970.

Moos, Malcolm. *The Republicans: A History of Their Party*. New York: Random House, 1956.

Morgan, Anne Hodges. *Robert S. Kerr: The Senate Years*. Norman: University of Oklahoma Press, 1977.

Murphy, George. *Say—Didn't You Used to Be George Murphy?* London: Bartholomew House, 1970.

Ness, Stephen and David S. Broder. *The Republican Establishment: The Present and Future of the G.O.P.* New York: Harper and Row, 1967.

Nixon, Richard M. *RN: The Memoirs of Richard Nixon*. New York: Grosset and Dunlap, 1978.

O'Brien, Lawrence F. *No Final Victories: A Life in Politics—From John F. Kennedy to Watergate*. Garden City, N.Y.: Doubleday, 1974.

O'Connor, Len. *Clout: Mayor Daley and His City*. Chicago: Henry Regnery, 1975.

O'Neill, William L. *Coming Apart: An Informal History of America in the 1960s*. Chicago: Quadrangle Books, 1971.

Paper, Lewis J. *The Promise and the Performance: The Leadership of John F. Kennedy*. New York: Crown, 1975.

Parmet, Herbert S. *Eisenhower and the American Crusades.* New York: Macmillan, 1972.

Patterson, James T. *Mr. Republican: A Biography of Robert A. Taft.* Boston: Houghton Mifflin, 1972.

Peabody, Robert L. *Leadership in Congress: Stability, Succession and Change.* Boston: Little, Brown, 1976.

Pekin Sesquicentennial, A History. Pekin, Ill.: Pekin Chamber of Commerce, 1974.

Penny, Annettee Culler. *Dirksen: The Golden Voice of the Senate.* Washington, D.C.: Acropolis Books, 1968.

Peters, Charles and Timothy J. Adams, eds. *Inside the System.* New York: Praeger, 1970.

Peterson, Robert W. *Agnew: The Coining of a Household Word.* New York: Facts on File, 1972.

Porter, David L. *The Seventy-sixth Congress and World War II, 1939-1940.* Columbia: University of Missouri Press, 1979.

Porter, Kirk H. and Donald Bruce Johnson. *National Party Platforms, 1940-1960.* Urbana: University of Illinois Press, 1961.

Quirk, Lawrence J. *Robert Francis Kennedy: The Man and the Politician.* Los Angeles: Holloway, 1968.

Reedy, George E. *The Presidency in Flux.* New York: Columbia University Press, 1973.

———. *The Twilight of the Presidency.* New York: World Publishing, 1970.

Reichard, Gary W. *The Reaffirmation of Republicanism, Eisenhower and the Eighty-third Congress.* Knoxville: University of Tennessee Press, 1975.

Rieselbach, Leroy N. *Congressional Politics.* New York: McGraw-Hill, 1973.

Ripley, Randall B. *Power in the Senate.* New York: St. Martin's Press, 1969.

Robinson, James A. *Congress and Foreign Policy-Making: A Study in Legislative Influence and Initiative.* Homewood, Ill.: Dorsey Press, 1962.

Ross, Douglass. *Robert F. Kennedy: Apostle of Change.* New York: Trident Press, 1960.

Rovere, Richard H. *Senator Joe McCarthy.* New York: World Publishing, 1966.

Royko, Mike. *Boss: Richard J. Daley of Chicago.* New York: E. P. Dutton, 1971.

Safire, William. *Before the Fall: An Inside View of the Pre-Watergate White House*. Garden City, N.Y.: Doubleday, 1975.

Scheele, Henry Z. *Charlie Halleck: A Political Biography*. New York: Exposition Press, 1966.

Schlesinger, Arthur M., Jr. *The Imperial Presidency*. New York: Popular Library, 1974.

Schoenebaum, Eleanor W., ed. *Political Profiles: The Eisenhower Years*. New York: Facts on File, 1977.

Shadegg, Stephen. *Clare Booth Luce, A Biography*. New York: Simon and Schuster, 1970.

Sidey, Hugh. *A Very Personal Presidency: Lyndon Johnson in the White House*. New York: Atheneum, 1968.

Smith, Margaret Chase. *Declaration of Conscience*. Garden City, N.Y.: Doubleday, 1972.

Sorenson, Theodore C. *Kennedy*. New York: Harper and Row, 1965.

Stein, Herbert. *The Fiscal Revolution in America*. Chicago: University of Chicago Press, 1969.

Steinberg, Alfred. *Sam Rayburn: A Biography*. New York: Hawthorn Books, 1975.

Straight, Michael. *Trial by Television*. Boston: Beacon Press, 1954.

Stromer, Marvin E. *The Making of a Political Leader: Kenneth S. Wherry and the United States Senate*. Lincoln: University of Nebraska Press, 1969.

Sundquist, James L. *Politics and Policy: The Eisenhower, Kennedy, and Johnson Years*. Washington, D.C.: Brookings Institution, 1968.

Terhorst, Jerald F. *Gerald Ford and the Future of the Presidency*. New York: Joseph Opaku Books, 1974.

Thomson, Charles A. H. and Frances M. Shattuck. *The 1956 Presidential Campaign*. Washington, D.C.: Brookings Institution, 1960.

Valenti, Jack. *A Very Human President*. New York: W. W. Norton, 1975.

Vestal, Bud. *Jerry Ford, Up Close: An Investigative Biography*. New York: Coward, McCann and Geoghegan, 1974.

Wenst, Lloyd. *Chicago Tribune: The Rise of a Great American Newspaper*. Chicago: Rand McNally, 1979.

Whitcover, Jules. *The Resurrection of Richard Nixon*. New York: G. P. Putnam's Sons, 1970.

———. *White Knight: The Rise of Spiro Agnew*. New York: Random House, 1972.

White, Theodore H. *The Making of the President, 1968*. New York: Simon and Schuster, 1970.

Wicker, Tom. *JFK and LBJ: The Influence of Personality Upon Politics.*
New York: William Morrow, 1968.

Index

seats in 1968, 217; still controls Congress in 1968, 218; Bobby Baker scandal, 224; liberals support student loan fund, 226; Jacksonians referred to, 237
Democrats. *See* Democratic party
Deutch, Eberhardt: Dirksen-Bricker amendment, 103
Dewey, Thomas E.: Governor of New York, 34; Dewey-Bricker ticket, 39-40; 1944 presidential nomination, 40-41; Dirksen aided 1948 campaign, 53; Eisenhower supporter, 76-79; Dirksen's "down the path of defeat" speech, 79; helps pick Nixon as vice-president, 81
Dewey-Bricker ticket. *See* Dewey, Thomas E.
Dien Bien Phu: French defeat in Indochina War, 201
Dirksen, Antje Conrady: Dirksen's mother, 2
Dirksen, Benjamin Harrison: Dirksen's brother, 2; not drafted in World War I, 10
Dirksen, Danice Joy: birth of, 16; helps in 1950 campaign, 55; votes for first time, 63; takes vacation, 64; marries Howard Baker, Jr., 69; visits Dirksen at Walter Reed, 232
Dirksen, Everett McKinley: birth, 3; Beantown gang, 4; nickname of Lute, 4; Pekin High School, 53-56; small town of Pekin, 7; participation in theater, 7-8; job on Minneapolis *Tribune,* 8; joins ROTC, 9; attendance at University of Minnesota, 9-10; enlists in Army in 1917, 11-12; creation of Dirksen Brothers Bakers, 12; acting with Pekin Players, 13; meets Louella Carver, 14; joins American Legion, 14; wedding, 15; elected finance commissioner, 16; birth of daughter, 16; 1930 congressional campaign, 17-19; 1932 congressional campaign, 18-24; New Deal Hundred Days, 26-30; supports isolationism, 31-33; support of FDR's interventionist policies in 1941, 33-34; chairman of Republican National Congressional Committee (1938-46), 34-35; *Fortune Magazine* feature story, 35-36; supports Mackinac Charter, 36;

organizations Dirksen belonged to, 37; Draft Dirksen for President petition, 37; opposes court packing plan, 38; proposes Midwest-West alliance with Governor Warren, 39-40; supports Dewey in 1944, 40-41; world tour, 42; writes book entitled *Communism in Action,* 43; supports Vandenberg's bipartisan foreign policy, 43-44; selective support of Truman's domestic policies, 45-46; blindness and resignation from House in 1948, 46-49; return of eyesight, 53; joins Peoria law firm, 54; Senate campaign against Scott Lucas, 57-66; allies with Taft, 67; supports Taft presidential candidacy, 68; political alliance with McCarthy, 69-72; supports Taft over Eisenhower, 74-82; Congressional junket to Asia, 84; serves on McCarthy's committee, 85-88; opposes McCarthy's censure, 89-91; Committee of One Thousand Republicans, 91; becomes a follower of Eisenhower, 92-93; floor leader for Eisenhower, 98-101; opposes Bricker amendment, 103; supports Modern Republicanism, 104-5; 1956 senatorial campaign against Stengal, 105-8; elected assistant minority leader, 112-13; elected minority leader, 114-15; builds Virginia home called "Heart's Desire," 117; Civil Rights Act of 1960, 118-19; good rapport with LBJ, 120; leadership qualities praised, 121-22; voting record, 122-23; vice-presidential hopeful in 1960, 123; 1960 presidential election; 127-30; creates Republican Joint Congressional Leadership Conference in 1961, 131-32; "Ev and Charlie Show" begins, 132; critical of JFK, 133; supports JFK's foreign policies, 134-39; his statecraft governed by Burkean formula, 140; opposes Yates for Senate, 141-44; Kennedy assassination, 145-46; friendship for LBJ, 150-52; ailments, 153; pragmatic political philosophy, 154; Civil Rights Act of 1964, 155-60; supports Goldwater for president, 160-61; Goldwater rejects civil rights plank, 162; Dirksen Doc-

Note on the Authors

EDWARD L. AND FREDERICK H. SCHAPSMEIER have long been interested in American political history. They earned bachelor's degrees from Concordia Teachers College in 1949, master's degrees from the University of Nebraska-Omaha in 1952, and doctoral degrees from the University of Southern California, Frederick in 1964 and Edward in 1965. Since then, they have published extensively on American and midwestern history. Among their collaborative efforts are *Henry A. Wallace of Iowa: The Agrarian Years, 1910-1940* (1968) and *Prophet in Politics: Henry A. Wallace and the War Years, 1940-1965* (1968). Edward is currently Distinguished Professor of History at Illinois State University in Normal, and Frederick is John McN. Rosebush University Professor at the University of Wisconsin-Oshkosh.